Messiah or Antichrist?

Messiah or Antichrist?

A Study of the Messianic Myth
in the Work of Zola

Anthony John Evenhuis

Newark: University of Delaware Press
London: Associated University Presses

© 1998 by Associated University Presses, Inc.

All rights reserved. Authorization to photocopy items for internal or personal use, or the internal or personal use of specific clients, is granted by the copyright owner, provided that a base fee of $10.00, plus eight cents per page, per copy is paid directly to the Copyright Clearance Center, 222 Rosewood Drive, Danvers, Massachusetts 01923. [0-87413-634-2/98 $10.00+8¢ pp, pc.]

Associated University Presses
440 Forsgate Drive
Cranbury, NJ 08512

Associated University Presses
16 Barter Street
London WC1A 2AH, England

Associated University Presses
P.O. Box 338, Port Credit
Mississauga, Ontario
Canada L5G 4L8

The paper used in this publication meets the requirements of the American National Standard for Permanence of Paper for Printed Library Materials Z39.48-1984.

Library of Congress Cataloging-in-Publication Data

Evenhuis, Anthony John, 1937–
   Messiah or antichrist? : a study of the messianic myth in the work of Zola / Anthony John Evenhuis.
   p. cm.
   Includes bibliographical references and index.
   ISBN 0-87413-634-2 (alk. paper)
   1. Zola, Emile, 1840–1902—Criticism and interpretation.
2. Messianism in literature. I. Title.
PQ2538.E92   1998
843'.8—dc21   97-35062
                                                                                                             CIP

PRINTED IN THE UNITED STATES OF AMERICA

Contents

1. The Judeo-Christian Messianic Tradition — 9
2. The Genesis of the Messianic Myth — 19
3. From Messianic Dreams to Messiah Complex — 28
4. False and Flawed Messiahs — 47
5. The Messianic Merry-Go-Round — 66
6. The Great Apostasy — 85
7. Messianic Myth in Crisis — 123
8. From Death and Disaster to Messianic Hope — 166
9. The Impossible Quest — 209
10. Toward a Humanist Messiah — 231
Conclusion — 264

Notes — 270
Bibliography — 277
Index — 282

Messiah or Antichrist?

1
The Judeo-Christian Messianic Tradition

IF JUNG AND HIS DISCIPLES ARE RIGHT, MESSIANIC HOPES AND ASPIRAtions are as old as the human race: they are part of our mythical worldview; they may be triggered off by any crisis situation that threatens us with fear, insecurity, or despair.

Not unique to the Hebrew culture, belief in a coming Savior or Deliverer was found among other Semitic groups who are said to have passed it on to the Zoroastrians. However, since Zola's work shows no evidence of the author's familiarity with the wider Semitic or Persian cosmogonies, this introduction will limit itself to a survey of the biblical tradition on which Zola was brought up and that seems to have colored much of his writing. Roger Ripoll, in the opening pages of his authoritative thesis, discerns in the whole of Zola's work "l'exaltation d'un messianisme progressiste"[1] (the glorification of a "progressist" form of messiahship—All translations are by Anthony and Edith Evenhuis). While the general notion of Messiah is well-known and some work has been done on identifying messianic figures in a given Zola novel,[2] modern readers need a more systematic overview of the subject if they are not to miss many messianic scenarios and allusions in his novels.

An early awareness of the irremediable folly of man, a traumatic encounter with the sordid side of sexuality, coupled with (or leading to) his loss of religious faith, will tend to turn Zola's messianic myth inside out: for a long time, he will see a world exploited and led astray by false messiahs or threatened with destruction by a nihilistic Antichrist. Nevertheless, after the death of his mother and his own conversion to the joys of sexuality with Jeanne Rozerot, the positive messianic myth will return with a vengeance: Apocalypse will yield to Utopia.

The term Messiah (Hebrew *mashiah*) is simply the equivalent of the Greek Christos or "anointed one." In its more general sense, it is used in the Hebrew Scriptures for any individual who has been anointed to be a priest, prophet, or king. In this sense, King David repeatedly applies it to himself, for instance, in Ps. 18:30, where he thanks the Lord for showing mercy to his "mashiah, to David and his seed for ever."[3]

The same David refuses to eliminate his predecessor, Saul, because he acknowledges him as the Lord's *mashiah* who was not to be touched. In fact, the psalmist refers to the whole wandering Exodus crowd as "anointed ones," when he quotes the divine injunction that they were not to be interfered with (anti-Semitics beware!):

> He suffered no man to do them wrong: yea, he reproved
> kings for their sakes;
> Saying, Touch not my anointed [plural], and do my prophets
> no harm.
>
> (Ps. 105:14–15)

(The Israelites of the Old Testament were exhorted to see themselves collectively as God's prophets—his representatives or spokespersons among the Gentile nations.)

In the light of the very wide applicability of the term, then, Christian or Jewish commentators should not be too shocked that Zola consciously presents the hero of *Germinal* in the guise of a latter-day messiah (more correctly, a false or mistaken messiah) or that, on the last pages of his *Rougon-Macquart* cycle, he proposes Clotilde's newborn child as a possible messiah of the future. Admittedly, religiously based misgivings are more understandable when Zola, in his *Quatre evangiles* [Four Gospels], enters into competition with the authors of Scripture and endows later heroes like Mathieu and Luc with aspirations, experiences, and achievements that are frankly messianic.

In most instances, Zola's use of the messianic motif derives from a biblical tradition that is much more exclusive. The very use of terms such as *Savior, Redeemer*, or *Messiah* implies, of course, that there is a critical or undesirable situation to be delivered from. And so, quite apart from the Jungian coping mechanism just referred to, it makes sense that the messianic theme in Scripture should emerge especially at times when individuals or groups are in dire trouble—a phenomenon that Zola latches onto when he has Etienne preach his utopian gospel to the oppressed and starving miners.

In the more exclusive sense of the word, the Messiah is a Savior, Redeemer, or Healer who will ultimately crush the Evil One; deliver his people from darkness, sin, and death; set the world to rights; and bring in a millennial kingdom of justice, truth, and peace, when the earth will be filled with the glory of God "as the waters cover the sea" (Hab. 2:14).

In the early stages, the Old Testament messianic tradition predates any historical prophets, priests, and kings and goes right back to the Genesis account of the Fall. Even before Eve has learned her punishment for eating from the forbidden tree, she hears the Lord God tell the serpent that, one day, her seed will crush its head (Gen. 3:15). Accordingly, she rejoices at the birth of her firstborn son, since he could be the promised Deliverer: "I have received a man from the Lord!" (Gen. 4:1)—but only to realize later the extent of her mistake. Far from being the awaited Messiah, Cain, as his brother's murderer, as a shedder of innocent blood, is the archetypal "man of sin," a prefiguration of Antichrist. It is to be noted, then, that messianic hopes and disillusionments go back to the earliest memories of time: false messiahs are not a recent development.

Slowly the expectation of a promised Savior takes shape. Aging, childless Abraham, a stranger in a strange land, is told repeatedly that in him, and in his seed, "all the nations of the earth shall be blessed" (Gen. 22:18)—an early indication of the universal relevance of Messiah (a detail the Hebrews tended to lose sight of). The promise is repeated to Abraham's son Isaac and then to the fugitive Jacob, when he thinks Esau is after his blood. Having become the father of twelve sons and having been renamed Israel, that patriarch prophesies on his deathbed that the scepter will not depart from his son, Judah, "nor a law-giver from between his feet until Shiloh [the peaceful one] shall come; and unto him shall the gathering of the people be" (Gen. 49:10). The promised Messiah, then, will be a judge, a bringer of peace, and a restorer of national unity.

The Book of Job, believed to be the oldest part of the Bible, records the messianic hopes of yet another patriarch—wretched Job, the victim of Satan's spite, as he sits in the ashes of affliction and loss, bereft of all of his children, betrayed by wife and friends, utterly bewildered by the dealings of his Maker. The composer Handel, in his oratorio, *The Messiah*, has given worldwide currency to Job's moving confession of faith: "I know that my redeemer liveth, and that he shall stand at the latter day upon the earth." Even though worms destroy not only his skin, but his whole body, Job goes on, "yet in my flesh shall I see God" (Job

19: 25–26). Note this early intimation that the Messiah, here seen in relation to the individual, is divine and that he is a latter-day deliverer from death (an allusion to faith in a resurrection).

Aging Moses, the original Deliverer of Israel, the archetypal lawgiver, brings his rebellious people to the very border of the Promised Land and then is told that he can take them no further (flawed by disobedience, he cannot be a prototype of the Messiah). Yet, at that moment of frustration and apparent failure, he looks beyond his immediate successor, Joshua, and prophesies that, one day, God will raise up from among his people another prophet, a man like Moses, whom they are to listen to or face the consequences (cf. Deut. 18:18, 19).

David, the first king to come from the tribe of Judah and, in many ways such an ideal prototype of the Messiah that the latter is often referred to as the "son of David," or as "my servant David," echoes Moses' warning. Early in the Book of Psalms, he paints a scenario of nations and rulers plotting "against the Lord and his anointed," but then quotes Jehovah acknowledging the rejected Messiah as his son and promising him the nations for his inheritance: "Yet have I set my king upon my holy hill of Zion. . . . Thou art my Son. . . . Thou shalt break them (the nations) with a rod of iron. . . ." (Ps. 2:6, 7, 9). The same David who proclaims that the future Messiah will be a universal king, forestalls, in his own experience, the paradox of his suffering and abandonment: "My God, my God, why hast thou forsaken me . . . all my bones are out of joint . . . they pierced my hands and my feet . . . they part my garments among them. . . ." (Ps. 22:1, 14, 16, 17) but ends his psalm on a note of triumph: "I will declare thy name (the name of God) unto my bretheren" (verse 22). Merging his own death with that of the Messiah, David writes in Ps. 16: ". . . my flesh shall also rest in hope. For thou wilt not leave my soul in Sheol [the grave or the underworld]; neither wilt thou suffer thy holy one to see corruption" (Ps. 16:9–10). Writing an ode to a future king, who is obviously not his son, Solomon, David makes no bones about his divinity: "Thy throne, O God, is for ever and ever" (Ps. 45:6) and again at the opening of Ps. 110: "The Lord said unto my Lord, Sit thou at my right hand, until I make thine enemies thy footstool."

The Hebrew prophets abound in messianic passages. By the time of Isaiah, who wrote in the troubled days before the Babylonian captivity, faith in the divinity of the future Messiah is well established. Most readers will recognize the words, put to music by Handel, which are quoted from Is. 9:6: "For unto us a child is born, unto us a son is given: and the government shall be upon his shoulders; and his name shall be called Wonderful, Counseller, the mighty God, the everlasting Father, the Prince of Peace." Yet that same prophet, sharing the paradoxical double vision that intrigued David, devotes his moving fifty-third chapter to the sorrows of the suffering servant—his trials and death that lead up to glorification. In this chapter, Isaiah is the first to declare that the rejected man of sorrows is in fact bearing the sins of the whole of humanity: "But he was wounded for our transgressions . . . the Lord hath laid on him the iniquity of us all" (Isa. 53:5–6). Those who have heard, in their tender years, Isaiah's "kingdom" prophecy about the wolf dwelling with the lamb and the leopard lying down with the young goat (Isa. 11:6), are not likely to forget it, although most adults will be more familiar with Isaiah's earlier reference that has become inseparable from the world's aspirations for millennial peace: ". . . they shall beat their swords into ploughshares and their spears into pruninghooks; nation shall not lift up sword against nation, neither shall they learn war any more" (Isa. 2:4). Isaiah's idyll about Messiah's peaceful reign is confirmed by Ezekiel. This prophet-priest, held captive in Babylon, wrote the famous passage about the Shepherd-King who will regather the scattered sheep of Israel into their own land and rule over them in a land of enduring peace: "And David, my servant shall be king over them; and they all shall have one shepherd . . . my servant David shall be their king for ever" (Ezek. 37:24–25). Daniel, another captive prophet, had colorful dealings with at least three Babylonian kings. He lends cosmic proportions to the emerging picture of the Messiah. His vision of the stone "cut out without hands" (note the expression), which grinds to dust Nebuchadnezzar's gigantic dream-statue, representing successive world powers, is a memorable parable of Messiah's ultimate triumph (Daniel, chapter 2). In a later passage, Daniel is the first to evoke the Last Judgment: " . . . the judgment was set and the books were opened" (Ezek. 7:10) whereupon he introduces "one like the Son of man," coming with the clouds of heaven and taking his stand before the Ancient of Days (Jehovah) who then grants him eternal kingship:

And there was given him a dominion, and a glory, and a kingdom, that all people, nations and languages, should serve him; his dominion is an everlasting dominion, which shall not pass away, and his kingdom that which shall not be destroyed. (Dan. 7:13–14)

By way of a bridge to the New Testament vision of Messiah, it is useful to quote the later prophet Zecharaiah, who seems to have exercised his ministry as Jerusalem and the temple were about to be rebuilt (after the Babylonian disaster). Zecharaiah highlights the paradoxical humility of the messianic king as he comes riding into the capital ... on a donkey: "Rejoice greatly, O daughter of Zion, shout, O daughter of Jerusalem: behold, thy king cometh unto thee: he is just and having salvation, lowly, and riding upon an ass" (Zech. 9:9).

Given the original meaning of the term *messiah*, it is both fitting and convenient to sum up the Old Testament tradition under three headings:

1. As anointed prophet, he will act as God's spokesperson: he holds the future and must be listened to;
2. As high priest, he will bless his people, act as a mediator between God and man, and will bear their sins. In this capacity he becomes the Savior from evil, darkness, and death;
3. As king, he will be both the peaceable Shepherd-Ruler, who guides, feeds, protects, and unites his flock, and the mighty, divine lawgiver, judge, and ultimate Lord of all.

Although the New Testament focuses on *Christ* (already the Septuagint term for Messiah) from beginning to end, it is remarkable that it adds but little to the unfolding of his identity and role.

In the first chapter of Luke's gospel, the angel Gabriel tells Mary that she will conceive a son by the Holy Spirit, that this Jesus (Hebrew *Yeho-shua* = "Jehovah-Savior") will be called the Son of the Highest and that "the Lord God shall give unto him the throne of his father David" (Luke 1:32).

That messianic message is repeated to humble shepherds in the well-known words: "For unto you [= for your benefit] is born this day in the city of David a Savior who is Christ the Lord" (Luke 2:4). As a Gentile himself, Luke makes much of the three foreign magi, who have come looking for the king of the Jews, but finish up presenting their gifts to the most lowly born of babies.

The apostle John launches his gospel with the famous declaration that the Word is God and then has John the Baptist identify Jesus to Andrew and a companion. Andrew rushes off to tell his brother Peter: "We have found the Messiah" (John 1:41). Jesus may reveal himself to individuals such as the woman by the well and the man born blind, but he consistently takes the humble part, simply calling himself the Son of Man (from the Hebrew *ben Adam*). This lowly profile is part of the Old Testament scenario of the suffering servant, but it did not appeal to the Jews of the period who expected a heroic, conquering deliverer to rid them of Roman oppression. Admittedly, Jesus acts like a Messiah when he calls to repentance, announces that the kingdom of God is at hand, feeds the hungry, heals the sick, claims authority to forgive sins, and even raises the dead, but in one of his first public addresses (the Sermon on the Mount), he calls the poor blessed, says the humble and meek will inherit the earth, and calls on his listeners to love their enemies and pray for their persecutors! (Matt. 5). And even his closest disciples are taken aback when he tries to get through to them that he "must go unto Jerusalem, and suffer many things of the elders and chief priests and the scribes, and be killed, and be raised again on the third day" (Matt. 16:21). Messiah's death and Resurrection had not been among the clearest aspects of Old Testament predictions.

Actually, it is not until his trial that Jesus publicly and explicitly claims messiahship: Again the high priest asked him: " . . . Art thou the Christ, the Son of the Blessed? And Jesus said, I am: and ye shall see the Son of Man sitting at the right hand of power, and coming in the clouds of heaven" (Mark 14: 61–62)—an allusion to Daniel's messianic prophecy that results in an immediate verdict of blasphemy and that remains the essence of Jewish rejection of Jesus as the promised Messiah. Shortly after, Jesus, confronted for the first time with Roman authority, tells the puzzled governor that "now" his "kingdom is not of this world" (John 18:36).

Official rejection by the religious authorities results in the revelation of two new aspects of messiahship—headship of the church (unbelieving Israel is temporarily set aside as Messiah's heritage) and the proclamation of a return to earth "in glory," the so-called Second Coming, so that Messiah may complete his task.

When Jesus questions the disciples on public perceptions of his identity, Peter is the only one to come up with the messianic formula: "Thou art the Christ [the Messiah], the Son of the living God" (Matt. 16:16). Jesus then treats this answer as a special revelation from God and plays on the Greek meaning of Peter's name (*petros* = "stone, piece of rock"), by promising that, on this rock (*petra* = "rock, ledge, crag") he will build his church—an institution that will bring together into one body Jewish and Gentile believers, under the headship of Christ. The Messiah, then, is not just a timely deliverer of the Jews, but orders the establishment of a worldwide body: "All power is given unto me in heaven and in earth. Go ye therefore, and teach all nations. . . ." (Matt. 28: 18–19). In St. Paul's figurative language, the church becomes the bride, whose wedding to Christ is to be concluded in Heaven at the end of time.

For our purposes, there is no need to explore in detail the complex subject of the Second Coming. Suffice it to say that, according to New Testament doctrine, Christ will return to earth to receive his bride (= to take the church to be with himself), to be reconciled to Israel and save it from destruction (Armageddon), to resurrect and judge all men, and to set up his eternal kingdom (cf. Matt. chapters 24 and 25).

Practicing Jews, of course, are still awaiting Messiah's first coming. They do not share the Christian belief that the death and Resurrection of Messiah are foreshadowed in the Old Testament, although their own history would help them to concur with Jesus' warning about false prophets and false messiahs: "For there shall be false Christs and false prophets and shall show great signs and wonders" (Matt. 24:24). Leaving the Gospel presentation of Messiah, we could sum up the New Testament epistles by saying that they place great emphasis on the Resurrection of Christ and proclaim him as Son of God: those who repent, put their faith in Messiah, and accept his lordship will receive pardon from sin and the gift of eternal life.

The remainder of this introduction will be devoted to a study of Antichrist—a figure alluded to by one Old Testament prophet and elaborated on by some New Testament writers. He may be defined provisionally as one who sets himself up either in antagonism to, or in the place of, Christ (the Greek prefix *anti* means both "against" and "instead of"). Given Zola's preoccupation with Apocalypse and his presentation of a series of genuine and false messiahs, such a survey is clearly called for.

Before venturing into the mysterious Book of Revelation—where fools rush in and angels fear to tread—it is wise to find one's feet in the Old Testament Book of Daniel. In a series of graphic visions, that prophet evokes four beasts, or world empires (Daniel's own explanation), the fourth of which is described as "dreadful and terrible, and strong exceedingly . . . and it has seven heads and ten horns (kings)" (Dan. 7:7). Three of these horns are plucked out by a little horn that has the eyes of a man and a "mouth speaking great things against the most High" (Dan. 7:8).

In the next chapter, this blasphemous ruler seems to be identified with "a king of fierce countenance and understanding dark (occult) sentences"—a deceptive destroyer of many, including the Jews (Dan. 8:23). He will even presume to stand up against the "Prince of princes," but will be broken "without hands"—a phrase recalling the "stone cut out without hands" (Messiah) that pulverizes Nebuchadnezzar's dream-statue in Dan. 2.

In a final reference, the evil ruler is described as follows:

> . . . and he shall exalt himself . . . above every god, and he shall speak marvellous things against the God of gods. . . . Neither shall he regard the god of his fathers, nor the desire of women. . . . He shall enter also into the glorious land (Israel) . . . yet he shall come to his end. (Dan. 11:36, 37, 41, 45)

The evil figure that haunts various chapters of Daniel is not identified by name, but biblical scholars often link him with the person St. John calls "Antichrist," the latter-day figure, says John, who will not simply deny the incarnation of Christ, but who rejects both the Father and the Son: "He is Antichrist, that denieth both the Father and the Son" (1 John 2:22). St. Paul seems to have in mind the same figure when he refers to "that man of sin" and "the son of perdition." In any case his description of him certainly recalls the language of Daniel: " . . . Who opposeth and exalteth himself above all that is called God, or that is worshipped, so that he as God sitteth in the temple of God" (2 Thes. 2:3–4). Having digested this, we should be in a better position to do battle with the various monsters that roam the Book of Revelation. St. John successively describes one beast, one dragon, and then two further beasts, in terms very reminiscent of the prophet Daniel. The first beast is said to arise from the bottomless pit (hell) that makes it sound like the Devil (Rev. 11:7). The next creature to appear is a great, red dragon "with seven heads and ten horns." It unsuccessfully pursues a woman [humanity, Israel, or Mary] who is about to give birth to a child [Messiah]; it is defeated by the archangel Michael and cast down to earth. John himself identifies it as "that old serpent, called the devil and Satan, which deceiveth the whole world" (Rev. 12:9).

Next the apostle John describes a beast (empire) that arises from the sea (the nations). Empowered by the dragon, it also boasts seven heads (the seven hills of Rome, the early Christians thought) and ten horns, which links it both with Satan and the fourth beast in Dan. 7 (where it was interpreted as a world empire). But now some new details emerge: one of the horns recovers from a mortal wound, whereupon it is worshiped and opens its mouth in blasphemy against God (Rev. 13:5).

We now seem to be face-to-face once again with the evil ruler in Daniel's prophecy who speaks out against the God of gods and the Prince of princes (Jehovah and his Messiah)—none other, in fact, than Antichrist.

St. John completes his sequence with a beast that arises out of the earth. It has two horns, "like a lamb," but "it speaks like a dragon" (Rev. 13:11), that is, it looks like the Messiah, as described in Rev. 5, but it speaks like the Devil. Is this beast just another symbolic representation of Antichrist, or is it to be identified with the figure that John calls "the false prophet" (Antichrist's Goebbels, his minister for propaganda, so to speak)? In any case, it directs worship to the wounded beast and sets up a great, animated image for idolatrous purposes. After the battle of Armageddon, dragon, beast, and false prophet all finish up in the lake of fire (Rev. 20:10).

Zola would not want us to ignore the figure of Babylon, depicted as "a great whore," sitting on the back of the scarlet dragon. Described by St. John as a seductress and corruptress of nations, with her lust and the lure of her luxuries, she has been variously interpreted by scholars as a fallen, apostate, persecuting church (in contrast to the faithful, virgin-bride of Christ) or a subversive, materialistic, mercantile world power. Her spectacular downfall occupies the whole of Rev. 18. Though not strictly part of the messianic or the antimessianic myth, she is a key-figure in Zola's apocalyptic scenario and we shall need to consider her from time to time. Zola himself does not seem to have been able to make up his mind whether the great whore is simply perverted, obsessive sex, turned into a destructive idol (*Nana*), whether she is the licentious, spendthrift, corrupt Paris of the Second Empire (*L'Argent*), or the Rome of his *Trois villes* that is more interested in money, power and survival than in saving the poor and oppressed.

2
The Genesis of the Messianic Myth

THE BIBLICAL SCENARIOS EXAMINED IN THE INTRODUCTION CONFIRM the commonsense view that hope of a redeemer or messiah may come alike to an individual in crisis (guilty Eve, childless Abraham, fugitive Jacob, wretched Job, frustrated Moses) and to a nation in turmoil (Israel around the time of the Babylonian captivity).

Many would favor the Freudian theory that individuals or nations that have suffered in their self-esteem, through loss of status or a painful failure, sometimes "compensate" by indulging in heroic or messianic dreams. Honoré de Balzac, mediocre at school, unattractive to girls (for the time being!), neglected by his father, and cruelly treated by his mother, projects into his later novels his craving for fame and glory, as he features powerful leaders, spectacular criminals, or mystical giants of the spirit. Mauriac's fatherless young hero, Yves, in his *Le Mystère Frontenac*, yields to a similar longing in an amusing manner: one morning, despairing of a positive response to his poems from a publisher, he jumps onto the family table and shouts: "Je suis roi! Je suis roi!" [I am a king! I am a king!].

Of course the phenomenon is not limited to literary figures or heroes of fiction. Of late many historians have meditated on the frustrations of young Hitler, unable to enter the Vienna Art Academy, and on the national humiliation of Germany after the Treaty of Versailles. In the process, they have gained profound insights into the delusion of a whole nation—a disorientated people that focused a messianic dream upon its self-styled führer, only to find, in time, that it had unleashed a nightmare worthy of Antichrist himself.

Some may incline to the Jungian belief that the figure of messiah constitutes a primordial, innate archetype, a basic aspect of the way in which we perceive reality, a mythical blueprint essential to what it means to be human and capable of hope. In any case, whether spontaneous compensation or preexisting archetype, juvenile hero worship, or plain wishful thinking, the messianic dream is a common human attribute, a coping mechanism or spiritual resource to which Zola would not have been a stranger.

When seven-year-old Emile lost his engineer-father in 1847, he and his mother were soon faced with protracted financial problems and were forced into ever-more cramped living conditions: their social standing clearly suffered; they lost face. It is quite reasonable to assume that young Zola's deprivations would have inspired him with a dream of restoring the family fortunes. Indeed, this must have seemed possible when a relation's influence enabled Zola to pursue his baccalauréat in Paris. However, setbacks such as his repeated scholastic failure, severe illness and, initially the humblest of clerical employment, must have made him wonder: Could he be the family messiah or was he a failure?

Anyone may speculate, of course, but is there any objective evidence to suggest that our author was interested in rebuilding a reputation for himself and his family? Readers of his *Correspondance* will have been amused by the young writer's ambition, expressed with disarming frankness. The same readers may well have been bored later by his persistent efforts to have his father given due credit in Aix for designing and constructing the Tholonet dam. The present writer has just returned from an early-morning pilgrimage to the tomb Zola had raised in the Aix cimetière Saint-Pierre. In unusually large letters, the massive slab bears the inscription:

A
MON PERE
ET
A MA MERE
(TO MY FATHER AND TO MY MOTHER)

One suspects that Zola's vigorous campaign must have contributed to the wording of the leaflet-information that is offered to tourists: "François Zola, 1795—1847, Ingénieur, constructeur du barrage du Tholonet, Père d'Emile Zola" [Engineer, builder of the Tholonet dam, Father of Emile Zola].

It is not difficult to understand how poverty-stricken Zola developed a keen social conscience, a compassionate awareness of the struggles of the disadvantaged; witness his early story

"Soeur-des-Pauvres," [Sister of the Poor], included in his *Contes à Ninon* [Tales for Ninon] (1864). This deeply symbolic tale makes a good starting-point for a survey of our author's lifelong literary involvement in the messianic myth.

Still somewhat inexperienced as a writer, Zola barely manages to hide his cards. When he opens his tale with the evocation of a rich-born, but now indigent orphan-girl, who has a kind heart for the poor, the informed reader smiles at the simple sex-inversion and reads on for more insights into the youthful author's psyche. In the story, the girl is adopted by her harsh uncle and aunt. Following an act of kindness, she receives an old and worn sou from a lady who later turns out to have been the Virgin. The mother of Christ had distilled the coin from the tears offered her by the faithful poor. The narrator is conveying, in allegorical terms, that the sufferings of the deprived, received in a virginal heart (Zola's own), may become a source of blessing. Shortly, Zola's literary gift, partly born of his compassion, will start to have similar effects: the heroine soon discovers that the coin has magical qualities. In true messianic style, she will use it to feed the hungry and to be reconciled to her hard-hearted relations. When she redirects the gratitude of her followers to Jesus and Mary, it becomes clear that the author is still deeply religious.

This is no longer obvious in the very next tale—"Aventures du grand Sidoine et du petit Médéric" [Adventures of Big Sidoine and little Médéric]—in which Zola projects himself onto a robust giant and to a puny thinker:

> Ils avaient seize ans tous les deux, étaient nés le même jour, à la même minute.... Ils sont un même être en deux êtres différents. (pp. 103)[1]

> [They were both sixteen and had been born on the same day and at the same minute.... They are one and the same being in two different beings.]

we are informed by way of clue. Together the ill-assorted pair set out for Le Royaume des Heureux [the Kingdom of the Blessed].

Sidoine, a distant relative of Gargantua and Pantagruel, no doubt, is a potential messiah: before leaving the local scene, he shifts a mountain to redirect a river of life into a barren plain (shades of Zola's father and his Tholonet dam). However, when he fails to consult the greater wisdom and sensitivity of his tiny companion, strategically ensconced in his ear, he is inclined to drastic, nihilistic solutions. While he contemplates the Egyptian desert scene from the top of a pyramid, for instance, he becomes impatient when a blue and a green army below are reluctant to engage in battle. Sidoine simply obliterates the Greens and buries them in the sand. Offered the throne by the Blues, our irascible messiah initiates a reign of *almost* universal contentment. But he cannot sustain his messianic role. Eventually he is banished for having adjudicated a cow to be black *and* white, when the opposing factions wanted a black *or* white verdict. With such irrational and difficult subjects, Sidoine finds himself incapable of keeping up the millennium.

Accordingly, the unequal friends head east to resume their quest and, indeed, they find a happy realm where everything is in harmony. Its compassionate queen, Primevère (=Primrose), had been recognized at her birth as a messianic figure: "Un Messie était né" (p. 106) (A Messiah had been born). She has made her palace-grounds a sanctuary for underprivileged creatures, hoping naively to bring them all to unity, equality, and concord.

Once again, however, Zola runs the scenario of paradise lost. In this ideal kingdom, the refugees grow tired of their bland diet of sweetened milk (man is not made for a diet of nursery innocence). Each animal now proposes his own specialty as a universal food: the lion—red meat; the goat—grass; the silkworm—mulberry leaves, et cetera. When a young cat proposes milk, all the others become so enraged that they regress to the law of the jungle and mutually devour each other. Sidoine, like one side of Zola, perhaps, cannot cope with the inherent violence of nature. In his disgust, he reverts to his nihilistic solution of destroying the survivors with a terrible blow of his fist.

Médéric, his better half, will teach him that humans should not interfere with the necessary laws of nature (an insight that will come to Zola's Dr. Pascal, once he has found fulfillment in his love for his niece, Clotilde[2]): "Remarque l'absurde justice de ton coup de poing" (p. 189) [Note the absurd justice dealt out by your blow].

Messiah-queen, Primevère, too, mourns over her creatures that could not forget their cruel teeth and claws, but she finds consolation in the embraces of Médéric, transferring all her love and compassion to him. It is almost as though young Zola is telling us that whoever finds true love can dispense with the idealistic, messianic dreams of adolescence.

As for Sidoine, the flawed messiah, with his desire for conquest and his unthinking cruelty, he agrees to transfer his belligerent energies to cultivating the soil for bread and wine. The moral of the tale is clear: nihilism is not the answer, since it involves us in the destructive wrath of Antichrist, but messiahship too has its limits. We may feel called to redemptive missions, but reality is resistant and nature is cruel. On the last page of his story and, significantly, of the volume as a whole, the narrator is tempted with universal skepticism: "Je crois que l'homme n'est rien. Je doute de tout le reste. . . ." (p. 195) [I believe man is nothing. I have doubts about everything else. . . .] but he opts for the most positive solution he can envisage by recommending "la bêche et le baiser," [literally the spade and the kiss] work and love. Our young, idealistic author has already glimpsed the visions he will elaborate in *Fécondité* [Fertility; 1899] and in *Travail* [Work; 1901].[3]

Something has evidently happened to Zola between conceiving the unmitigated messianic dream of "Soeur-des-Pauvres" and enacting the more disillusioned pragmatism of Sidoine and Médéric. For a veiled confession of how the author came to lose faith in the traditional Christian Messiah, we need to go back in time and turn to the very early tale "Le Sang," [Blood] included in *Contes à Ninon*, [Tales for Ninon] but first published in *La Revue du mois* (Lille) in 1863.

This grim story juxtaposes the nightmares of four soldiers who have been in combat all day and who finally try to sleep in a field strewn with dead bodies. The first, Gneuss, has his "chanson joyeuse" (happy song) cut short by a mournful cry of agony (for Zola, too—other tales bear witness to the fact[4]—the terror of death has broken in upon the cheerful enthusiasm of youth). Thereupon, Zola inverts the well-known messianic parable in Ezek. 47 about an ever-growing stream (water to the ankles, to the knees, to the waist, water to swim in, a river that cannot be crossed) that brings fertility and healing to the nations. In contrast, Gneuss dreams about a trickle of blood that grows into a stream, a river, a torrent, and finally a rising lake that creeps up to his lips (Gneuss, alias Zola, is increasingly obsessed with man's inhumanity to man).

Next morning, Elberg, the second companion wakens Gneuss from his troubled sleep and shares with him his own dream. It opens on a vision of paradisiac freshness, representing the innocence of the world in its infancy (probably, in projection, Zola's own childhood as well). But then a somber, hateful individual betrays his tender, loving brother with a kiss before murdering him. (Zola has merged his version of the Cain and Abel story with the treachery of Judas.) We should note first of all that, at this stage, the author presents the Fall of man, not in sexual terms—Eve's forbidden fruit—but in terms of hatred, violence, and broken trust: Zola has not yet experienced his trauma with the fallen girl he tried to reclaim. On the conscious level, no doubt, he intends the Cain and Abel allusion to render man's fall into envy and violence. On a subconscious level, it may well mirror his own intimation that, deep within him, a dark and angry self is taking over from his innocent and poetic self and threatening to displace it. The end of the story (not yet covered) suggests that the reference to the Judas-kiss foreshadows that Zola is about to betray the Messiah he has worshiped so far and that he will do so with a show of respect and affection).

In Elberg's dream, when the earth drinks in the innocent blood of the slain brother, this inaugurates an era of fear, dispersion, and predation: "Le grand brigandage de la création commença. . . . Le monde se mordit la queue et se dévora éternellement" (p. 57) [Creation's great brigandage began . . . The earth bit its own tail and devoured itself forever]. The third soldier, Cléria, also relates a dream that portrays life as a bloody saga. His tale of human sacrifice, murder, suicide and kings or priests fomenting strife simply confirms Gneuss's initial vision. Cléria's nightmare, too, closes on an abysmal lake of blood that is set to overflow and destroy the world. Not only, then, has Zola lost the joyful song of his youth, his dream of the innocence of paradise, but he is already substituting a vision of Apocalypse: "La fin est proche", dit Gneus" (p. 60) ["The end is nigh," said Gneus]. The fourth companion spells out Zola's emerging notion of a failed messiah. In his dream, Flem climbs a barren, scorched hillside and witnesses the Crucifixion. Jesus weeps on the Cross with a resigned smile on his face. The conclusion Flem draws from this constitutes the crux of the whole story (the aforementioned Judas-kiss): "Voyant sa grandeur dans la mort, je disais: 'Cet homme n'est pas un roi'" (p. 61) [Seeing his greatness in death, I said: "This man is not a king."]. Flem's tribute to the crucified is two-edged, to say the least: Jesus may be unlike the kings in Elberg's dream who incite to war, but if he is not a king, he cannot be Messiah either.

So far Zola's rejection of the traditional Messiah is only suggested in ambiguous terms, but the picture soon loses its ambiguity. Flem introduces a "fauvette" (a warbler) that sings a song of sad disappointment. It had stained its feathers red in the blood of the world, but had then washed them clean again in a pure spring (Zola's romantic dream of escaping from encroaching guilt to the "innocence" of nature) and thought it had found refuge on the shoulders of this just man (a veiled symbol of Zola's adolescent recourse to religion as a way of preserving purity, added to his desire to identify himself with the suffering Christ, to be a little messiah born on the shoulders of the great Messiah). But alas, the blood of Jesus has dyed its feathers red again. That is to say that, to Zola's mind, the passion of Christ, far from solving the problem of human evil, is part of it, has compounded it. The agonized question the bird voices at this point is highly significant:

> "Où trouverai-je ton frère, ô Jésus! pour qu'il m'ouvre son vêtement de lin? Ah, pauvre maître, quel fils né de toi lavera mes plumes que tu rougis de ton sang?" (p. 61)

> ["Where shall I find your brother, oh Jesus, so that he may open his linen robe for me. Ah, poor Master, what son, born of you, will clean my feathers that you stained red with your blood?"]

Zola has given a considerable twist to the well-known fairy tale about the robin that received its redemptive spot from a drop of Jesus' blood. In the light of the world's violence and evil (a projection of his own guilt, Freudians would suggest), he has concluded that Jesus' death was in vain and that a new messiah is called for. The Nazarene may have been a good man and a just man, but the world is no better now than it was before his Crucifixion. The warbler's final words, for all their poetry, simply repeat that message: "Regarde, la terre est méchante comme hier. Jésus est mort et l'herbe n'a pas fleuri" (p. 62) [Look, the earth is as wicked as it was yesterday. Jesus has died and the grass has not flowered]—a view shared by Flem who, on his awakening, finds the earth as hostile, barren, and thorny as ever. Roger Ripoll is quite correct when he notes that the Crucifixion story, as related in "Le Sang," is a symbol of death and failed redemption.[5]

It should be stressed that, while Zola is disillusioned with a Christianity that does not seem to have redeemed the world, he has not given up the messianic myth altogether. This is borne out by the end of the story. The four companions bury their weapons in a deep hole and, while waiting for a brother or son of Jesus to appear, they head for a forgotten valley, known to Gneuss, where they may set their hands to the plough. The hidden valley is simply a more modest, toned-down symbol of Zola's quest for paradise lost, reminiscent of the maternal shelter afforded Lamartine in the "Vallon" (=valley) of his childhood.[6] The earlier allusion to a son or brother of Jesus leaves the door open for another messianic figure that may emerge to save the world.

It has been suggested in this chapter that Zola's messianic dream originated in his family's loss of status as well as in his personal failures and deprivations. Like so many troubled adolescents, he unconsciously looks for comfort and hope in dreams or tales featuring some form of succor or salvation (cf. the child from a broken home who aspires to be a social worker, a nurse, or a doctor). In the jargon of contemporary psychology, we might say that young Zola is inclined to indulge in a "self-nurturing" messianic dream.

In the course of analyzing three significant tales from Zola's *Contes à Ninon*, we have followed his gradual shift from messianic idealism to the sorrowful denial of the Christian Messiah and, eventually, to a possible renunciation of messiahship in general.

The heroine of the first tale, "Soeur-des-Pauvres," is a fully fledged messianic figure who is pure, devout, and efficacious. Defeating poverty and healing broken relationships, this virginal character incorporates the religious values of Zola's youth—a compassionate creed centered on Mary and Jesus, the pure Mother and her messianic Son.

The repetitive plot of "Le sang" makes it clear that what begins to wean Zola from Christianity and its Messiah is the problem of a violent world, given over to death. No longer able to identify with the Resurrection, he is left with a crucified Jesus whose death fails to bring in the promised kingdom.

By the time of writing "Aventures du grand Sidoine et du petit Médéric," Zola is bordering on universal doubt. He has realized that an ill-guided messiah like Sidoine is likely to stumble into unthinking cruelty and into the perilous dream of nihilism (the temptation to make a fresh start, at the price of some form of Apocalypse). Zola will feature various nihilists in his later novels—Savourine, in *Germinal*, is the most notorious—but never in a positive light. Even the most well-meaning and idealistic of saviors, like Queen Primevère, the person explicitly born to be a messiah, has to reckon with the inherent folly of man and the irremediable cruelty of nature.

And so Zola's faith in the messianic myth falters. Maybe, he thinks, the recipe of "la bêche et le baiser" (work and love), offers a more realistic way of investing life with meaning and worth. At the end of the story that concludes his volume, Zola tries to have it both ways: the messianic queen agrees to marry the wise and energetic champion of work and love. But are not potential messiah figures supposed to abstain from mortal love (cf. the Samson and Delilah story)? It will take Zola many years to resolve that quandary!

3
From Messianic Dreams to Messiah Complex

NORMALLY, ONE WOULD HAVE EXPECTED ZOLA'S INTEREST IN MESSIanic dreams to wane as he approached maturity and, especially, as his eyes opened to a violent, sinful world—a world that the Cross had not redeemed to his satisfaction. Yet, strangely, the author's loss of faith in Christ (his faith in God will survive for the time being) in no way reduces his fascination with messianic themes.

His first novel, *La Confession de Claude* [Claude's Confession] (1865), may feature a would-be messiah who fails provisionally, if not definitively, but both the second novel, *Le Voeu d'une morte* [A Mother's Dying Wish] (1866), and the third, *Les Mystères de Marseille* (1867), will star positive messiah figures. Admittedly, the fourth, *Thérèse Raquin* (1867), and the fifth, *Madeleine Férat* (1868), introduce heroines who pin their hopes on very dubious saviors, thus bringing us back to square one.

It would appear, then, that after his early cycle of messianic hope and disillusionment, Zola becomes involved in a second, more protracted one that basically follows the same pattern. His postadolescent confrontation with reality does not seem to have cured him: he is going round in circles.

It is this evident need to act out, over and over again, his oscillation between true and false messiahs that prompts the question whether Zola has not stumbled unawares into some form of compulsion or even neurosis. Readers may have noticed, in their own environment, that individuals suffering from what we may loosely call a "rejection complex," engendered by a real or perceived rejection in the past, tend to go through endless cycles in which they are confirmed in their sense of not being wanted. Psychologists tell us that such people actually create or provoke the situations in which, once again, they will experience rejection. The same pattern prevails in many other complexes: the person who considers himself a failure will unconsciously gravitate to situations that demonstrate an inability to cope. Individuals who have rejected their fathers or mothers may launch themselves into sustained rituals of adopting and then discarding parental figures. Those with a father or mother fixation will find themselves locked into pursuing a never-ending succession of father or mother substitutes and so on.

Does Zola fit into this pattern? With over a century elapsed since the period in question, any speculation would be hazardous, ... were it not for the survival of so many written documents in the form of stories or novels. Whether they admit it or not, artists may dream on paper, on canvas, or even on videotape. True enough, one should remember that paintings, works of fiction, et cetera have a life of their own; one should beware of drawing hasty conclusions from isolated or even repeated scenarios. However, when an author confesses that he has written a given work in his own blood, so to speak, we may be justified in taking a closer look. Now, this certainly applies to Zola's first novel.

Studies like Henri Guillemin's *Zola, légende et vérité* (1960) have made it clear that *La Confession de Claude* is largely an autobiographical work. John Lapp quotes from a letter in his possession, dated 14 November 1865, in which Zola refers to the novel as ". . . ces pages où j'ai mis beaucoup de ma chair et beaucoup de mon coeur"[1] (. . . those pages into which I have put so much of my flesh and so much of my heart). B. H. Bakker follows H. Mitterand's dating of Zola's letter to Baille (5 February 1861)—a document that creates the definite impression that the writer has personally experienced the disillusionment involved in trying to redeem a prostitute. In fact Zola is quoting the prostitute scenario to demonstrate to his friend the advantages of realism over fiction in the novel![2] How then may we reconstruct the background to *La Confession de Claude*? Back in 1861, twenty-one-year-old Emile, still a virgin, had taken pity on a fallen girl, Berthe, who was going through a nervous crisis and she had rewarded him in the only way she knew. Maybe to overcome his own sense of guilt, maybe in keeping with the idealism that would never forsake him, Zola set about to reform her, but she did not respond to his efforts and proved irredeemable. Readers familiar with the author's disenchanting adventure cannot help smiling with recognition as they follow Claude's story of his youthful idealism; his encounter with the sick young prostitute (Laurence); his vain attempts to restore her to the path of virtue, his own fall into guilt and a sense of death; her betrayal of him with his more pragmatic friend, Jacques; and Claude's fond efforts to put back in place his slipped messianic halo as he cares for Jacques's innocent mistress (Marie) and plans to return to the purity of his native Provence.

This is not the place to embark upon a full analysis of the novel,[3] but it is useful to review some aspects of the work that bear on the messianic theme. It should be noted then that, just like Sidoine, the failed messiah of *Contes à Ninon*, Claude is a stranger in a strange land and that there is a connection between his moral lapse and the fact that he is away from home. Zola is consciously transposing his own departure from Aix and his early traumata in Paris. What he may not have realized, at the time of writing, is that, in a novel or dream, leaving home or one's native district can become a symbol of leaving behind one's early values, of being unfaithful to one's social roots.

Whether or not this applies to Zola himself, it is evident that his *Rougon-Macquart* cycle features many a hero or heroine who arrives, or has arrived, in a strange place (like Saccard in *La Curée*, Florent in *Le Ventre de Paris*, Gervaise in *L'Assommoir*, Etienne in *Germinal*, and Jean in *La Terre*). Each sets out to achieve a goal—modest or grand—but eventually flounders, dies, or is eliminated as an unwanted outsider. The persistent myth of the failing stranger, then, is already operative in Zola's earliest novel. In the case of Claude, the ineffectual stranger will turn out to be a flawed or tainted messiah. His very name—Claude means "the lame or limping one" (Latin *claudus* = limping)—suggests this: the hero sets out to confess an experience that will cause him to limp for the rest of his days. In a sense, Zola himself will be limping as well, the point being that his traumatic involvement with Berthe was a fearful blow to his self-respect. It is tempting to conclude that, in order to compensate, he turns the fairly common messianic dreams of his adolescence into a full "messiah-complex." When his sense of realism and honesty make this impossible to sustain, when the repressed truth of his impurity, materialism, or ambition comes to the surface, the messiah complex will turn itself inside out—it will become an equally obsessive denunciation of false messiahs or antichrists—until the author finally is reconciled with human sexuality and human fallibility in general and is able to return to a more modest and serene form of the early messianic idealism.

There is little point in reviewing the tale of Claude's introduction to ailing Laurence by La Pâquerette (=Daisy!), a shriveled old hag (Fate)—a scene skillfully analyzed by Roger Ripoll[4]—and his yielding to his own instincts in a moment of inebriation: it is the morning after that interests us here.

Even before his sexual experience, Claude had picked up a sense of death in the fateful room and he had actually taken the girl's prostrate body for a corpse. Now he returns to the symbolic decor of his dark, desolate lodgings, where the candles have burned right down and where "le foyer [est] mort depuis longtemps" (chapter 4, p. 20)[5] (the fire in the hearth [is] long since dead). From now on, he thinks, all his dreams of love will be haunted by a vision of death: "Ce spectre pâle et flétri sera de tous mes rêves" (chapter 4, p. 20) [This wan, withered specter will haunt all my dreams].

Any reader of *Les Rougon-Macquart* will acknowledge readily that this confession applies not only to Claude but to his creator as well, but that theme does not concern us here. As Claude puts it in the next chapter, he has drunk from "une coupe souillée" (a sullied cup); he has betrayed his ideals. For the time being, he will try to give his fall a virtuous twist by passing it off as an attempt to redeem Laurence (note his recourse to the messianic myth). Partly out of pity, partly out of a sense of guilt and responsibility, he receives the penniless prostitute into his room. In spite of all his forced kindness, his patience and religious zeal, she does not change. The two simply become regular lovers, with Laurence soon slipping into boredom and indifference. All of Claude's efforts to redeem her are of no avail: he is no messiah, no savior of the fallen—just a sinner, like everyone else!

His unsuccessful attempt to rehabilitate Laurence is only one in a series of failed exploits by Zola's heroes. We have already considered Sidoine and Queen Primevère. In the same way, Silvère will not be able to rescue his love Miette from death in *La Fortune des Rougon* [The Rougons's Fortunes]; Florent cannot free the bourgeoisie from its overfed torpor in *Le Ventre de Paris* [The Belly of Paris]; Goujet cannot save Gervaise in *L'Assommoir*; Etienne will emerge from the mine-shaft in *Germinal* without his Catherine; Saccard is a very questionable savior in *L'Argent* [Money]; Napoléon, far from being a conquering hero like his famous predecessor, is a doomed, broken man in *La Débâcle*; even the noble Dr. Pascal cannot ultimately cure his patients in the novel that bears his name.

We are brought back to the basic thesis of this chapter: could it be that, through all these flawed saviors, Zola is projecting (i.e., unconsciously confessing), over and over again, his own sense of failure, his inability to live up to his youthful dreams? Here too, we may well have stumbled upon the real root of Zola's rejection of religion with its redeeming Christ: saying that salvation is not possible in the religious realm can be a way of projecting outside of oneself one's inability to regain a lost ideal. In the novel under discussion, Claude is approaching such a crisis of faith. In chapter 8 he can still resolve: "Je serai prêtre, je relèverai la femme tombée et je pardonnerai" (p. 27) [I shall be a priest; I shall raise up the fallen woman and give absolution]—just as Zola himself, a few years before writing La Confession de Claude, had recorded the following prayer in a letter to a friend: "Nous demandons à Dieu de nous envoyer une âme flétrie, pour la lui rendre jeune et blanche de notre amour"[6] [We ask God to send us a blighted soul, so that we may return it to him, rendered young and pure by our love]. Zola's text in chapter 8 virtually reproduces that prayer, simply substituting the word "morte" (dead) for "flétrie" (withered) (p. 27).

In his disillusionment, however, Claude is bitter enough to advise his friends: "Repoussez la Madeleine, niez ses larmes et son coeur, raillez toute rédemption. Voilà la sagesse" (chapter 8, p. 43) [Reject Mary Magdalen; deny her tears and her heart; jeer at any form of redemption. There is wisdom]. For Claude this is but a passing crisis of despair; he will get over his mortifying fiasco. Zola himself, however, will never be quite the same again. In his next two novels, he will try, maybe quite unconsciously, to regain a positive, messianic perspective, but starting from Thérèse Raquin, the reverse picture will dominate. The world of Les Rougon-Macquart too will be mostly a dark place where vice, egoism, and materialism prevail. Paradises will be evoked nostalgically, as in La Faute de l'abbé Mouret [Father Mouret's Error] or in Le Rêve [The Dream], but they do not last or they lack substance. Utopian dreams will prove ineffectual and their messiahs corruptible (Etienne in Germinal). It will take the onset of old age for Zola to allow himself, once again, to yield to dreams of human saviors and scenes of Heaven on earth—much to the detriment of his art: it is perilous for any writer to regress to a defunct myth.

To complete the overall perspective, we need to enlarge for a moment upon one of Claude's coping mechanisms—turning his fall into sordid sensuality into a mission to redeem Laurence. Zola himself, in his late novels, will indulge in the same myth on a larger scale: he will try to purify and save French society; eventually he will start drawing up his own "gospels" for the

3: FROM MESSIANIC DREAMS TO MESSIAH COMPLEX

salvation of the whole of humanity! All that, however, lies in the distant future. For the moment Claude, and Zola with him, will try to pick up the broken pieces of his dream and battle on. Like his creator, the hero is very courageous. He refuses to give in to despair. And so this first novel, like so many of Zola's desolate epics to come, ends up on a possibly rather forced note of hope: even after finally dismissing unfaithful Laurence, he can say: "Je me suis senti au coeur une force jeune, invincible, un espoir immense. . . . (chapter 30, p. 112) [In my heart there was a feeling of young, invincible strength, of immense hope. . . .]. He will head for his friends in Provence and there, he claims hopefully, he will grow young again. More than that, Claude cannot give up his faith in God. Night's inscrutable darkness, he tells us, yields at last to the promise of God's dawn:

> Tout le ciel s'est enflammé peu à peu . . . laissant voir Dieu à cette heure matinale et transparente. Frères, c'était l'aurore." (chapter 21, p. 112)

> [Little by little the whole sky began to blaze—revealing God in this transparent, early-morning hour. Brothers, it was the dawn.]

The mature Zola will not be able to follow Claude into that perspective of religious hope: he will develop a different faith, a faith wrested from many a struggle with darkness and depression, but our incurable messiah is certainly going to make the attempt—witness his next two novels.

On a first reading of Le Voeu d'une morte (A Mother's Dying Wish), one might well decide that the work shows little evidence of any messianic preoccupations on the part of its author. In fact the novel could be read as an allegorical expression of Zola's turning from romantic idealism to the virtues of truth, realism, and science. The basic plot details bear out this interpretation.

After the death of his foster-mother, Blanche de Rionne, a pure, serene, idealized figure, eighteen-year-old Daniel finds himself alone and without a home. Our twice-orphaned hero (he lost his real mother in infancy) wanders aimlessly into the Luxembourg gardens. There he encounters a robust, dynamic "protector" (in the style of the Gothic novel), Georges Raymond (his surname means "wise counsellor") who generously invites him to share his lodgings and scientific vocation (Zola has just run into his new self!). Daniel accepts: he steps out of his dreamy past and embarks upon a new career as he helps to compile a scientific encyclopedia.

However, previously he had taken on a responsibility with messianic implications: he had vowed to the dying Blanche that he would keep a watchful eye on her daughter Jeanne, aged six at the time, who must not fall into the ways of her weak, womanizing father, a man, moreover, tormented by the fear of death. Initially the girl is adopted by a socialite aunt who promptly dispatches her to a convent for twelve years. When she eventually emerges as a beautiful young woman, her aunt exposes her to the empty glamour of her own flippant, immoral, and corrupt milieu. To keep his promise, Daniel becomes secretary to the girl's uncle. Already in love with Jeanne, he rather clumsily and heavy-handedly, begins to act as her "chevalier noir" (black knight), her moral mentor, and chaperone. His efforts are not appreciated; his scientific research suffers.

During an idyllic riverside vacation in Normandy, Daniel finally gets through to the natural, unspoiled side of Jeanne, who had at first been inclined to ridicule this awkward, inferior specimen of manhood. In spite of that, he loses her to the calculating Lorin, who marries her for her money. The hero at last realizes the state of his affections and pines for his love by the seaside of his native Provence. While Daniel turns his back on science and reality, his friend Georges becomes a celebrity and moves into larger quarters. Daniel slowly pulls himself together and returns to Paris, to the former convent, and to his scientific pursuits.

At this juncture, Zola stages a coup de théâtre: Jeanne's worthless husband dies during a business trip. With Jeanne about to plunge into another undesirable relationship, Daniel pours out his heart to her in an unsigned letter that finally initiates her into the nature of true love and passion. Unfortunately for Daniel, she believes the letter to have come from Georges. When Daniel and Georges together call on a transformed, serene Jeanne, the more dynamic and articulate Georges wins her hand, aided by the self-sacrificing Daniel who acts as a go-between, before again retiring to the sea. He is heartbroken and nearly beside himself with grief, but he has kept faith with his adored foster-mother: Jeanne is saved; his sacred mission has been accomplished.

The moribund hero is visited by the young couple and learns that Jeanne loves him after all. Self-effacing as ever, he allows himself to slip into easeful death: in his last moments he hears Blanche calling him from beyond the tomb.

Le Voeu d'une morte is not quite as mawkish as this summary might lead one to believe, but even Zola himself agreed that it was no masterpiece. Why then should the novel detain us at all? Because, in its pages, an unconscious, repressed part of Zola indulges in a practice similar to that which, in the modern record-industry, is called "back-masking": the author, in other words, slips in a hidden message that integrates the work into his lifelong messianic aspirations.

On the surface, his novel contrasts the abortive emancipation of Daniel (who reverts to type) with the triumph of the more robust and enterprising Georges—both in the world of science and in the realm of romantic love. It is fairly obvious that Zola has written a parable about the battle within himself between a somewhat effete romantic idealism, which he is outgrowing, and a more virile and pragmatic openness to reality.[7] The denouement of the tale shows which side has prevailed.

However, there is a deeper level of meaning, a mythical message that contradicts the surface scenario. Even within the main plot—a tale of love with a half-heroic, half-tragic ending—one can discern a messianic strand: the portrayal of a hero who comes to the rescue of an erring, endangered individual and who lays down his life for his friends. And so we arrive at the paradoxical situation of an author who sets out to relate his own conversion to science but then, almost unwittingly, it seems, includes a mythical scenario very much in line with his old messianic dreams. The very title of the novel—Le Voeu d'une morte [A Mother's Dying Wish]—suggests that Zola is paying tribute to a past loyalty, idealized and dearly loved.

Unconvinced readers should take a close look at the opening page of the novel. Supposedly to explain Daniel's background, Zola quotes an item from a Marseille newspaper: a mother in the Provençal seaside village of Saint-Henri dies as she jumps from a burning house to save her baby. It seems likely that the author reports this incident by design to prefigure or match symmetrically Daniel's self-sacrifice at the end of the novel. However, writers given to myth and symbolism often crystallize their tales around a little fragment that is in itself a myth in miniature, a tiny microcosm foreshadowing the overall theme, and here we may well have a case in point: there has been a disaster and someone dies to preserve the life of another. What irony! At the threshold of a novel that supposedly shows a man turning from poetry to science, Zola wittingly or unwittingly makes a character act out a scenario consistent with the central messianic myth of self-sacrifice and redemption! And since Daniel will embrace a similar heroic destiny, we are faced with a novel that is framed at either end by messianic scenes.

To unearth an interesting clue about the link that persists in the author's psyche between his old messianic aspirations and his new dedication to realism and truth, we need to examine a minor detail that is offered to us at the end of chapter 4. When Georges first rescues Daniel from loneliness and perplexity, he takes him to his attic room, situated in a former convent, at 7, impasse (dead end) Saint-Dominique de l'Enfer. Now, why are we repeatedly given this information (quite a mouthful)? Is Zola telling us, in rather cryptic terms, that his new devotion to science is taking the place of a religious past (the former convent) that has become an impasse—a dead end? If so, his choice of the sacred number seven and the reference to St. Dominique, the Spanish preacher who tried to rescue the gnostic Albigensians from the flames of hell, suggests that, for all that, Zola considers Daniel's new career a "sacred mission" (metaphorically speaking).

Summing up the address-symbolism—admittedly a little far-fetched (the reader might prefer the prosaic explanation that Zola actually lived at 7, impasse Saint-Dominique, "un ancien couvent, aux longs couloirs voûtés" (a former convent with long, vaulted corridors), during his days with the publishing house Hachette, as Paul Alexis notes in his *Emile Zola*, p. 57)—one could say that Daniel, alias Zola, has entered upon a life of science, but that he does so under the insignia of religious ideals: dropping a religion does not necessarily mean that one abandons the old values involved. And so this minor detail may tell us a great deal about an author who will end his career composing two cycles of novels—*Les Trois villes* [The Three Cities] and *Les Quatre evangiles* [The Four Gospels], the first of which revolves around a hero, Pierre Fromont, who will renounce his priestly robes, but not his priestly ideals.

Priestly ideals (in fact the whole messianic myth of which such ideals are a key-element) are much in evidence in Zola's next novel, *Les Mystères de Marseille* (1867). We shall see however that, for the first time in Zola's literary world, those who incur serious guilt may be pardoned, but will not escape penance and punishment: the two lovers featured in the work will ultimately atone for their mistakes only in death.

If *Le Voeu d'une morte* leaves much to be desired as a novel, *Les Mystères de Marseille* is easily Zola's worst effort. As the author himself wrote to Jules Claretie, in the early stages of composition: "Je sais que l'oeuvre est mauvaise"[8] [I know that it is a poor work]. But then, what can one expect from a work that earned its writer two sous a line from the weekly *Messager de Provence*? The evocation of the Provençal landscape is not without appeal, but the plot is arbitrary, often sentimental or melodramatic; characters appear as if by spontaneous generation, to meet the needs of a given five-page installment or to fit the data of the newspaper archives on which Zola based many of his episodes. The general story line digresses, stagnates, or accelerates in the most unpredictable manner and the whole work lacks structure, direction, and unity.

Yet it is precisely the hasty composition and the lack of scruple that make the novel interesting from another point of view. Zola does not have the time or concentration to censor his writing and, every now and then, he drops his guard to such an extent that the discerning reader gains intriguing insights into the myths and ideals that inspire him, the fears and guilts, too, which continue to haunt him. In spite of the surface chaos of the novel, then, there is a hidden coherence that derives from the inner world of Zola, an unconscious pattern that brings to light aspects of the author of which his conscious mind may not always have been aware.

In the opening pages of *Les Mystères*, he seems compelled to act out, all over again, his troubling encounter with sexuality, presented this time in the guise of a seduction scene. Chapter 1 relates the elopement of naive Blanche de Cazalis (note the connotation of innocence both in her Christian name (Blanche = white) and in her family name (Cazalis = "house of the lily") with impetuous Philippe Cayol: ". . . elle péchait par ignorance," the narrator tells us, "comme Philippe péchait par ambition et par passion" (part 1, chapter 1, p. 231)[9] (. . . she sinned through innocence, just as Philippe sinned through ambition and passion). Zola, in his pre-Freudian innocence, is projecting onto his lovers the guilt he still feels over allowing his passionate self (Philippe) to run away with his naive, virtuous self (Blanche).

Then, in chapter 2, he resurrects the puny, clean-living hero of *Le Voeu d'une morte*, the incarnation of his ideal self, the self he meant to become before his 1861 misadventure. This time he makes him into Marius, significantly, the *younger* brother of Philippe, whose self-imposed mission it will be to save his erring brother and to atone for his sins. In dreams, Freudians say, we often project onto brothers or sisters conflicting aspects or successive stages of our personality. However that may be, it did not take our novelist long to revert to the messianic theme of salvation and atonement.

As the story unfolds, Blanche's wealthy foster-uncle. M de Cazalis, has the eloping lovers tracked down. For financial, political, and social reasons, he has Philippe, a Republican nobody, put in prison for five years and the latter looks set to stay there, unless he can be rescued by Marius and Fine, a flower girl infatuated with Philippe who soon begins to appreciate the superior qualities of the younger brother.

If the tale about Philippe's emprisonment conveys anything about the author, this takes the form of the traditional myth of crime and punishment, guilt and atonement. At this early stage, and again toward the end of the novel, when Philippe engages in revolutionary activities, he corresponds to the more radical side of Zola that tends to jib at conventional morality and hence to incur guilt. Accordingly we could interpret Marius's efforts to free his brother (by raising a ransom or obtaining a royal pardon) as a fictional reflection of Zola's desire to atone for his past. Any such desire would have been all the more intense because, ever since his adolescence, he had had a sense of a high, almost priestly calling, as can be seen plainly in the following extract from a letter he wrote to Baille on 10 August 1860:

> Dans notre temps de matérialisme . . . , le poète a une mission sainte: montrer à toute heure, en tout lieu, l'âme à ceux qui ne pensent qu'au corps et Dieu à ceux dont la science a tué la foi.[10]

> [In our age of materialism . . . , the poet has a sacred mission: at any time and in any place, he must reveal the soul to those who think only of their body and reveal God to those whose faith has been destroyed by science.]

Paradoxically, this religious vocation did not leave him after his "conversion to science"; witness his earlier heroes and, closer to home, the following comments he passes on Marius:

> Les malheurs qui l'accablaient grandissaient en lui l'amour de la vérité et la haine de l'injustice. Il sentait que toute sa vie allait être vouée à une oeuvre sainte. (part 1, chapter 7, p. 264)

> [The misfortunes that overwhelmed him increased in him his love of truth and his hatred of injustice. He felt that his whole life was going to be devoted to a sacred task.]

Many readers who, in the course of exploring Zola's work, have come to know the author intimately, have come to love and admire those very qualities in the man himself.

Corresponding to the two brothers, the erring Philippe and the virtuous Marius, there are two clerics in the novel through whom Zola dramatizes the same scenario of guilt and atonement in a more religious framework. Pierre Ouvrard, in his *Zola et le prêtre* (1986), briefly examines the historical and social implications of the two priests.[11] The present study aims to suggest that they also serve to help Zola sort out, in projection, his own Christian past.

The ironically named priest, Donadéi ("gifts of God"), unctuous, insinuating, and ambitious, not only refuses to help Marius rescue his brother, but even attempts to seduce the daughter of Marius's employer, Claire Martelli. Far from sharing in the messianic mission of Christ, he is out to glorify himself and to use or even destroy his fellows. In the work of Zola, he is the closest prototype we have encountered so far of Antichrist. Donadéi is unmasked by Marius, after a Tartuffian letter falls into the hero's hands, and is forced to head for the border, appropriately in the company of the aging prostitute, Armande (exeunt phony religion and illicit sex).

On the other hand, the humble, kind, devout priest, l'abbé Chastenier, a defender of the poor, lives up to the chastity suggested by his name. Unable to keep Philippe out of jail (genuine religion does not obviate the need for penance), he at least saves him from the pillory. He repeatedly takes care of pregnant Blanche whom he will encourage to enter the order of St. Vincent de Paul, where she will take care of the sick and dying (she too is made to go through a process of penance and will ultimately give her life for the cholera victims to whom she devotes herself).

Taken together, the two priests neatly encapsulate Zola's conviction that false religion is in league with immorality (cf. the religiosity surrounding his own Berthe involvement), whereas true religion, for him, is a matter of purity, humanity, and compassion for the sick and suffering. When, at the end of the novel, the good priest ministers to cholera victims and then dies in peace himself, pointing to the heavens, Zola may be saying, in part that, for him too, salvation (in the figurative, psychological sense of wholeness, fulfillment, and peace of mind) is to be obtained by devotion to noble causes such as championing the poor and oppressed. Many of his subsequent novels—*L'Assommoir* and *Germinal* are the most characteristic—show him to be involved in that kind of endeavor.

Zola's lingering belief that sins must be atoned for, unless a supreme pardon is extended from on high, emerges several times as we follow the fortunes of imprisoned Philippe. Fine, the flower girl, insinuates herself into the good graces of the jailer. In fact, she so moves him to pity, that he is willing to let Philippe escape, even without the promised bribe of fifteen thousand francs. The prisoner, however, has enough decency not to endanger the livelihood of his warder and refuses to leave unless the ransom is paid in full—a rather surprising twist in the plot, but one that makes sense on the deeper level of how an individual may feel about clearing himself of guilt. Significantly, Philippe never manages to pay the ransom himself: it is only when his brother saves the chastity of his employer's daughter, that the grateful father gives Marius the needed money. And so Marius atones for his brother's seduction of Blanche de Cazalis by playing messiah in two ways: not only by paying the ransom but, more essentially, by symbolically reversing the original seduction as he saves Claire Martelli from the hypocritical priest (the Christian Messiah, too, pays the ransom for sin and extricates believers from pharisaical religion). Interestingly, Zola himself will try to set his moral record straight by marrying an abandoned girl, Alexandrine Meley. That may well have been *his* way of attempting to reverse his original lapse.

At a later stage, Philippe is tracked down by the vengeful de Cazalis and two gendarmes and is about to be led back to prison when Marius arrives on the scene with a letter of pardon from the king. Surely Philippe's experiences in the novel (and the whole scenario of the virtuous brother who becomes an agent of royal pardon) warrant a suspicion in the reader that Zola is still heavily influenced by the messianic myth of atonement for sin. The plot details we have considered suggest that man may try to compensate for his past mistakes by penance (Philippe in jail) and virtuous actions (Marius saving Claire), but cannot save himself. He needs the merit earned by someone who is himself innocent (Marius) and it is that virtuous deliverer who procures ultimate pardon from a Higher Court (the king).

The only respect in which this mythical enactment differs from that in the preceding novel is that, in *Le Voeu d'une morte*, the hero actually gives his life for the sake of his guilty protégée. In *Les Mystères*, the good priest will give his life for the cholera victims, but Marius, the real savior, will live on in married bliss with Fine. However, both of the offenders, Blanche and Philippe, in spite of royal pardon and penance, will pay the ultimate price as they fall victim to cholera, even if, thanks to Chastenier, they die in peace.

The moral is clear enough. Zola, both in his life and in his fiction, needs to cultivate a messianic scenario to compensate for his past and present mistakes but, for him, the substitutionary death of Christ is no longer enough. The fate he reserves for Blanche and Philippe suggests that ultimate atonement is to be found only in death. His next two novels, *Thérèse Raquin* and *Madeleine Férat*, will make this abundantly clear. Is it because Zola can no longer see a definitive solution to the problem of guilt, that his novelistic world is about to plunge into darkness and that any perceived saviors will turn out to be agents of death and destruction?

Thérèse Raquin (1867) marks a new point of departure for Zola—a parting of the ways as far as his messianic aspirations are concerned. For the first time, in his novelistic world, religion is completely absent—at least on the surface, for a scenario of guilt and expiation (no longer guilt and atonement as in *Le Voeu* and *Les Mystères de Marseille*) becomes increasingly evident in the second half of the novel. On a metaphoric level, one could even continue to speak of a messianic scenario: the novel deals with a heroine who loses the dignity of her North African origins and drifts into a living death, until she meets a full-blooded individual, a pagan messiah, so to speak, who seems to promise deliverance from darkness and initiation into the fullness of life. However, it turns out that this restorer of life is also a bringer of death—to his murder victim, to himself, and to his mistress. In the end our pagan messiah is no more efficacious than the dying Jesus of Zola's tale "Le Sang."

As I have shown more fully in an article entitled "Can One Bury the Past,"[12] Thérèse's origins are not lacking in strength and dignity. She is the child of a tribal chieftan's daughter and a French soldier. On the death of her mother, she is confided to the care of an aunt whose home, on the Seine at Vernon, may be rather monastic and secluded but, for all that, is surrounded by green fields and flanked by a living river. No wonder the heroine almost chokes to death when her aunt steers her into marrying her puny, sickly, virtually impotent son, Camille, and then confines her in a musty haberdashery shop at the end of a dark and airless Parisian alley. Soon withdrawn into a state of dazed torpor, she sits through the weekly visits of a few familiars who seem to act out a mechanical and pointless danse macabre.

When sanguine, forceful Laurent breaks into this scene, he makes no messianic claims (in spite of the religious art in which he dabbles) and quotes no poetry, but Thérèse quickly yields to this incarnation of instinct who seems to hold out a promise of passion, vitality, and freedom.

There is no need to trace out the whole scenario of sexual bliss, frustration, murder, obsession with death, remorse, and suicide that many writers have covered from different perspectives. The only point that needs to be made here is that Laurent, the dropout law-student, the wastrel son cut off financially by his father, the casual dispenser of a religious art he no longer believes in, the somewhat brutal seducer of Thérèse, fails the messianic test at every stage (attitude to father, to religion, to sexuality). The heroine will realize to her sorrow that he is no genuine savior, not even a liberating Pan-figure, but rather an agent of destruction. Not only does he share the author's morbid obsession with death (witness his daily visits to the morgue as he anxiously awaits the retrieval of Camille's body from the Seine), but, after drowning the legitimate husband, he is no longer able to make love to Thérèse, is haunted by the face of his victim and, ultimately, can only join his new wife in death by suicide.

Clearly Zola no longer believes in messiahs—religious or otherwise—but why does he have to dramatize this so obsessively in his fiction? When a similar scenario emerges in his very next novel, the discerning reader may well observe: "Methinks, the lady doth protest too much!"

In *Madeleine Férat* (1868), the author at last begins to home in on an unpardonable sin,[13] a basic flaw, which does not only prove the undoing of his heroine, but may also suggest a personal reason for Zola's provisional rejection of messianic aspirations and of messiahs in general.

Before the principal characters of the novel meet, each of them is rescued by the person who will turn out to be a badly flawed messiah—cheerful, jovial, rugged Jacques. The latter is not lacking in kindness or courage, but both his moral conscience and his sense of responsibility are less than exemplary. Like the messianic king in Christ's parable of the talents or that of the vineyard, he leaves for a far country (Cochin-China) and even manages to virtually rise from the dead. His return, what we might call his Second Coming, however, does not exactly bring bliss and joy to his former protégés. By the end of the novel, both the hero (Guillaume) and the heroine (Madeleine) will face disaster because of their involvement with this selfish and unfaithful savior.

Madeleine is the orphaned daughter of a self-made man and a fragile, neurotic mother. At the critical age, she needs to flee from the sexual advances of old Lubrichon, a former fellow worker of her father's to whom she had been entrusted. She then runs into Jacques, about to complete his medical studies, who offers her shelter. Without much hesitation on her part, she becomes his in body and soul: "Elle se sentait devenir lui, elle comprenait qu'il prenait une entière possession de sa chair" (chapter 2, p. 715) [She felt herself turning into him; she understood that he was taking complete possession of her flesh]. Not long after Jacques's departure for overseas, she meets up with Guillaume, "le fils intelligent et affaibli d'une noble race" (chapter 1, p. 693) (the intelligent and enfeebled son of a noble race) who, unbeknownst to her, had been taken under Jacques's wing during his tormented school-days: "C'est lui qui est venu me défendre. Il m'a sauvé des larmes, il m'a offert son amitié et sa protection. . . ." (chapter 4, p. 796) [He is the one who came to my defense. He saved me from tears; he offered me his friendship and protection]. Guillaume is no literal orphan, but he is one emotionally. His father, an aloof scientist who locks himself up in his castle-laboratory (where he works on synthetic poisons) avoids him, while his mother, the one-time mistress of the scientist, refuses to recognize him on the rare occasions when she meets him in public. Geneviève, the aging Calvinist housekeeper, tries hard not to love this "child of sin."

The relationship that develops between Madeleine and Guillaume is an uneasy one, mainly because of Zola's much-discussed theory of impregnation—his belief, at the time, that a woman is marked indelibly by her first lover and will vaguely experience any subsequent involvement as adulterous. On top of that, there is Guillaume's need of a tender, maternal woman, which casts Madeleine into the uncomfortable dual role of mother and lover. Zola makes no bones about the situation: "Elle le considérait un peu comme un enfant" (p. 732) [She looked upon him rather like a child] the author tells us and, before the end of the chapter, he adds: " . . . il y avait dans ses baisers plus de maternité que de passion" (p. 734) [Her kisses were more maternal than passionate] and "Elle voyait une sorte d'inceste dans son double amour" (p. 737) [She saw a kind of incest in this double love]. The first problem is exacerbated by Madeleine's discovery that her original love was in fact Guillaume's best friend, but that situation eases as news reaches the couple of Jacques's drowning at sea.

Guillaume's father dies, leaving the hero more vulnerable to the Huguenot maidservant who is becoming quite fanatic. Already aware of Guillaume's irregular origins, she now begins to sense Madeleine's impure past as well. Her favorite saying: "Dieu le Père n'aurait pas pardonné" (chapter 7, p. 778) [God the Father would not have forgiven] will become a leitmotiv in the novel and so the messianic voice of those who, in earlier novels, stood for compassion and mercy is silenced and replaced by the harsh, unrelenting judgment of Geneviève, this caricature of the Old Testament Jehovah who threatens to visit wrath and condemnation on his helpless creatures.

When Jacques virtually returns from the dead—he had survived shipwreck—Guillaume welcomes him with open arms, while Madeleine desperately avoids him. Her life turns into a perpetual nightmare for, physically and emotionally, she still belongs to her first lover. Jacques has coarsened with time and experience; he has discarded any youthful ideals he may have had and is now satisfied to live purely for pleasure: " . . . il lui suffisait de contenter sa chair" (chapter 7, p. 785) [It was enough for him to satisfy his flesh]. Madeleine, daily tortured by her conscience, is much comforted one day, as Geneviève reads aloud of Jesus not condemning a repentant adulteress. The old servant, however, in her self-chosen role of prophetess of Jehovah, soon shatters her hope with the words: "Dieu est sans pitié. . . . La faute ne meurt pas" (chapter 7, p. 790) [God knows no pity. . . . An offence does not die] and again: "Dieu le Père ne pardonne pas" (p. 796) [God the Father does not forgive]. When Madeleine finally looks for relief by confessing her past to her husband, he too is overcome with guilt: Jacques was like a father to him and now he has married Jacques's mistress: "Il voyait là un inceste et un sacrilège" (chapter 8, p. 803) [He saw in this both an act of incest and one of sacrilege]. All the couple can do now is to launch themselves into an endless, headlong flight that will culminate in madness or death. Meanwhile Jacques, who has not yet set eyes on Madeleine again, pursues the couple without realizing the harm he is doing.

At this stage, as the decor around the haunted couple turns to winter and death, Zola puts some surprising words into the mouth of his hero: "Jamais il n'avait eu l'idée sotte de travailler à la rédemption d'une pécheresse" (chapter 9, p. 814) [Never had he been taken with the stupid idea of redeeming a fallen woman]—an attitude, we know, not always that of the author; witness his youthful prayers reported by Henri Guillemin, quoted earlier, and his whole involvement with Berthe. Zola himself must have been ill at ease over this projected denial of his desire to be somebody's savior, for he hastens to add, on the same page: "Ce sont uniquement les jeunes niais . . . qui forment parfois le projet de racheter une âme" (p. 814) [It's only the young and foolish . . . who sometimes conceive the idea of redeeming a soul]. Clearly the author is still in his antimessianic frame of mind, as is borne out by the doleful end of the story.

Madeleine is again told by the ever more fanatical Geneviève that God does not forgive: "Le repentir est inutile. Dieu ne pardonne pas les crimes de la chair" (chapter 11, p. 851) [Repentance is futile. God does not forgive the sins of the flesh] (a belief that does not match the experience of the Jericho prostitute, Rahab, who became an ancestor of Jesus, and that would have meant the end of King David after his sin with Bathsheba!).

In spite of these grim pronouncements, the heroine is drawn irresistibly back to Jacques (as Gervaise will be to Lantier, in L'Assommoir). She calls on him alone, supposedly to clarify the impossible situation, but ends up in his bed, as the child she has had by Guillaume, but who looks like Jacques, lies dying at home. All she can do, after that final degradation, is to stagger home and seek death: "Je vais me tuer. Tout sera fini" (chapter 12, p. 885) [I'm going to kill myself. It will all be over]. After facing her dead child, the symbol of her failed marriage, she comes upon Guillaume in his father's derelict laboratory, drinks a phial of poison and dies, leaving her husband to play hopscotch over her prostrate body. Geneviève has the last word: "Dieu le Père n'a pas pardonné" (chapter 13, p. 896) [God the Father has not forgiven].

In telling tales like this, Zola is homing in more and more on his own "unpardonable sin," metaphorically speaking—the irrational guilt feelings that can be experienced by individuals with a mother-fixation when they make love to any other woman or marry a mother-substitute. His Berthe affair was more than an adolescent sin against chastity, but that subject need not detain us here. In his last novel before the *Rougon-Macquart*, Zola has, among other things, exposed a flawed messiah—the protective, good-natured Jacques who seduces his innocent protégée and returns from the dead to haunt her with guilt. His second seduction of her constitutes, of course, a base betrayal of the husband who loves him as his savior and protector. Now that his messiah figures are fallen from grace, the author has raised up a rival figure that is equally destructive—the fanatic "believer" who denies the Gospel message of pardon and mercy and who, in the style of Flaubert's raving John the Baptist (Hérodias), proclaims a one-sided God of fire and brimstone.

Zola himself intends Geneviève to be an embodiment of fate. This emerges specifically when, just before her death, Madeleine faces the old hag with the words: "Vous êtes la fatalité, vous êtes le châtiment" (chapter 13, p. 888) [You are fate you are retribution]—a role plausibly elaborated by Roger Ripoll in his article "Fascination et fatalité".[14] It could be argued, however, that Geneviève is also a deformed remnant of Zola's old values (Guillaume significantly refers to her as a "legs sacré" (chapter 3, p. 791) (a sacred heritage left him by his father's mother)—values that Zola now prefers to exorcise by gross caricature. We all tend to denigrate people or values we can no longer love.

In the course of this chapter, we have seen Zola trace the failure of his messiah (Claude), attempt to resurrect him in Le Voeu d'une morte (Daniel), and in Les Mystères (Marius, Chastanier), only to disown him in Thérèse Raquin (Laurent), and particularly in Madeleine Férat (Jacques). Paradoxically, the inverse pattern will emerge from our perusal of relevant volumes of Les Rougon-Macquart, but that will be a slow, laborious process for Zola, until he manages to come to terms with his own "unpardonable sin." Basically his faith in messianic idealism will rise and fall (more correctly, fall and rise) with his acceptance of his own sexuality.

4
False and Flawed Messiahs

At two stages of his career, already, we have witnessed Zola becoming disillusioned with messianic figures. After the sorrowful renunciation expressed in "Le Sang," we saw him start a fresh cycle of hope in *La Confession de Claude* and reach new heights of idealism in *Le Voeu d'une morte* and in *Les Mystères*, only to revert to his focus on the moral failure of supposed saviors in *Thérèse Raquin* and *Madeleine Férat*. The last two novels set the stage for what is to be Zola's perspective over many years. All we can hope to find, in fact, in the first ten volumes of *Les Rougon-Macquart* (1871–81) is villains posing as messiahs or else ineffectual visionaries or weaklings who may look for a moment as though they will come to the rescue, but who lack the inner strength, capacity, or know-how to do so.

Yet all this simply amounts to the other side of the one messianic coin: in the same way that Zola does not stop being an idealist when he resolves to show up the hollowness and rottenness of the Second Empire, he does not abandon messianic aspirations when he persistently unmasks false messiahs. Bank officials hunting for false currency may seem obsessed with forgery, but we know that they are only trying to protect the genuine article. Much the same applies to Zola and to his passion for exposing hypocrisy, sham, and deceit. Usually the very volume that shows up criminal, immoral, or perverted behavior will contain that same antidote Gide told his shocked readers to look for in works such as *L'Immoraliste* and *La Porte étroite* [Strait is the Gate].

The opening volume of *Les Rougon-Macquart* is a case in point. *La Fortune des Rougon* [The Rougons's Fortunes] (1871) may be about "une famille de bandits à l'affût, prêts à détrousser les événements" (H. Mitterand's edition of *Les Rougon-Macquart*, la Pléiade, Gallimard, Paris (1960–67), vol. 1, p. 72[1] (a family of bandits, lying in wait, ready to pillage whatever comes to pass), as Zola tells us in very plain terms, but one of the three children mentioned on that occasion is said to be a noble soul, a doctor who combines integrity of spirit with charity and devotion to scientific research. Moreover, the book opens and closes on a couple of innocent young lovers, while the central chapters—those that have most intrigued commentators—home in on this idyllic and tragic tale of nascent love, mostly set in a mythical, nocturnal landscape of ruins, moonlight, and fragrant Provençal vegetation.

It is opportune to highlight for a moment the change that is about to come over Zola's messianic figures: from now on they are no longer just flawed, failing, erring heroes or the victims of naive admirers; many of them consciously set out to defraud, to deceive, or to exploit. They are, in the full sense of the word, false messiahs, following in the tracks of the one who, in Scripture, is said to go about "as a roaring lion, seeking whom he may devour" (1 Pet. 5:8).

One could not fall much lower than Pierre Rougon, when he cheats his own mother, the unstable Adelaïde, out of her property and disposes of his half-brother, Antoine, and his half-sister, Ursule. If his later heroic posturing is inspired and guided by others, this original exploit is purely his own idea. Besides being a heartless son and brother, he is a man without principle. Used at first as straw man by the legitimist marquis de Carnavant (the illegitimate father of Pierre's wife, Félicité)—a man said to get his directions through ecclesiastical channels—Pierre is ready to follow any political wind that promises a rich harvest. And his wife is no better. Referring to her determination to leave the old, working-class area of Plassans for greener pastures, Zola makes some ironic use of biblical language:

> Elle était décidée aux actes les plus extrêmes pour entrer dans la ville neuve, cette *terre promise* sur le seuil de laquelle elle brûlait de désirs depuis des années (1, p. 99, italics added by A. J. E.)
>
> [She was determined to go to any lengths in order to enter the new city, that promised land on whose threshold she had been burning with desire for years.]

Note the inversion of a biblical scenario: Félicité will commit any *crime* to enter her New Jerusalem—in the novel, the luxurious quartier of the nouveaux riches.

Husband and wife are advised by Carnavant to pose as public

saviors, when the coup d'état of December 1851 seems likely to provoke a short-lived republican counterattack. In the hour of danger, Pierre goes to hide behind his old mother's skirts, but the moment the rebel army has come and gone, our hero emerges from his shelter. He gathers a small band of helpers, manages to arrest his own half-brother (left behind by the Reds to keep Plassans in respect), and to disarm his drunken rowdies. By dawn our heroes have concocted some fictitious exploits, thanks to which Rougon will be regarded as savior of Plassans and provisionally appointed mayor.

The heroic farce is repeated a few days later, when the city, in fear of republican reprisals, withdraws its support of Rougon. The latter, secretly informed through his wife that the coup d'état has been entirely successful, alerts his guards for immediate engagement and makes a show of cool bravery. Antoine and his party, who have been allowed to escape, are duly recaptured, so that Rougon may once again show his valor. With the arrival of the Bonapartist army, Pierre is confirmed in office and decorated with the rosette of the Légion d'honneur. In a particularly wicked mood, Zola reveals that the rosette is improvised from some *blood-colored* satin, taken from the sash of Félicité's dress.

If we have left out of consideration, so far, the idyllic tale of Adelaïde's grandson, Silvère, and the very young smuggler's daughter, Miette (Marie)—"ces grands enfants, avides d'amour et de liberté" (1, p. 162) (those big children, greedy for love and freedom)—this is because, with them, Zola has regressed to a mythical time before the Fall, when there was no call for messianic figures. Protected by the author from "sullying" their growing intimacy, the chaste lovers move about in paradisiac innocence, on the edge of a mysterious realm where living nature and the shades of past lovers conspire to invite to the act of love.

It is no doubt significant that, while setting out to expose materialism, ambition, and deceit, Zola should take time off to revive his former adolescent dreams—dreams that are forever beyond realization after the Berthe affair and that he must content himself with idealizing in his fiction. Like the young Zola, in some respects, Silvère is a "naïf sublime" (a sublimely naive person). He has read some Rousseau and lives days of utopian ecstasy when the republic is proclaimed in 1848. Soon disillusioned by developments, he aspires to bring in universal happiness by force of arms. Together with his love, he joins a band of three thousand republican soldiers, but neither is destined to be a messianic deliverer. Miette will be shot by the approaching nationals, surviving just long enough to lament over her unsublimated love: "Elle pleurait sa virginité" (1, p. 217) [She wept over her virginity] while Silvère will be executed by the vengeful gendarme, Renegade, whom the boy had previously blinded in one eye during a scuffle.

And so the double plot of *La Fortune des Rougon* dramatizes the fragility of paradise, the mysterious kinship of love and death, the demise of naive messianic dreams, and the apparent triumph of the wicked. For Zola, nostalgic for his romantic self and inclined to fight his shadow—projections of his less admirable traits—the world is run by false messiahs.

To that perspective of villainy triumphant, volume 2 of the series, *La Curée* [The Scramble for the Spoils] (1872), will add the theme of moral decadence. Zola's focus will be mainly on the incestuous relationship of a stepmother and stepson, but since our present study calls for the highlighting of any messianic features, we shall concentrate on Pierre Rougon's son Aristide, whose minor role in volume 1 sets the stage for volume 2.

Far from being a genuine messianic figure, Aristide is clearly presented as a man who walks in the footsteps of his father: Zola is elaborating on the notion of "direct heredity" that he had absorbed from Dr. Prosper Lucas's *Traité de l'hérédité naturelle* [Treatise on natural heredity]. In one respect, however, the son does not resemble the father: unlike the hardworking Pierre, Aristide is at first portrayed as a parasitic idler. Once married to Angèle Sicardot, an army major's daughter, he lives at his parents' expense, before taking a mediocre job at the préfecture. To save the reader from being led astray by his promising name—Aristide derives from the Greek *aristos* = "best" or "most noble"—Zola introduces him as a starving wolf, constantly on the prowl to satisfy his desire for pleasure.

Like his father, Aristide lacks integrity. Through his envy of the rich, he becomes editor of a violently abusive Republican paper, but has second thoughts when he notices that his smart brother, Eugène, backs the future Napoleon III. After an eavesdropping scene in which he learns of the coup d'état, he promptly retrieves a revolutionary article from the paper and feigns a hand-injury to avoid having to join the republican band until the situation in Paris is clarified. The father, then, hides in his mother's cottage, while the son opts for malingering!

To crown his opportunism, he lets his mother persuade him to write an article in defense of the coup d'état, whereupon he calmly stands by as his half-cousin, Silvère, is being executed, to settle a personal score. The basic similarity of father and son is effectively dramatized as Zola has Aristide inform Pierre of Silvère's death. The hero of Plassans coolly remarks: "Ça m'évite une course.... Allons dîner" (1, p. 303) [That saves me a walk.... Let's go and have dinner]. A flashback in volume 2 shows Aristide on the prowl in Paris, where he senses an abundance of prey to come. His brother Eugène, not quite as "wellborn" as his name suggests, procures him a modest position at the mairie [town hall]. Aristide will put this post to good use in order to find out the lie of the land. At his brother's suggestion, he changes his name. He ends up by choosing Saccard, which sums him up perfectly, given the meaning of the French verb "saccager" (to sack or pillage). Actually, Aristide is thinking of bags of money ("des *sacs* d'argent): "Hein, il y a de l'argent dans ce nom-là" [Aha, there's money in that name] while Eugène associates the name with jailbirds: "Oui, un nom à aller au bagne ou à gagner des millions" (1, p. 364) [Yes, a name to go to jail with or to earn millions].

He may have been thinking of the expression "homme de *sac* et de *corde*" (= scoundrel).

As his wife, Angèle, lies dying, Saccard adopts his father's policy of posing as savior: his shady sister, Sidonie, suggests that he marry Renée, a girl in trouble. In return for saving the reputation of this rape-victim, Saccard will receive one hundred thousand francs from her aunt—an amount that the young messiah will manage to double. Angèle dies in full knowledge of her husband's scheme, but chooses to forgive him. After her demise, Saccard spends the night writing death-notices to his relations, interrupting the task to make financial calculations on scraps of paper (shades of Balzac's Grandet, when he does little sums in the margin of the paper that announces his brother's suicide). Having thus demonstrated his devotion to his wife, he insinuates himself with Renée's father, extricates a promise for half a million francs, and launches himself into speculation on the property market—a most lucrative pursuit in the Haussmann era if one had prior knowledge of areas to be expropriated.

To his great delight, Renée miscarries and begins to console herself with precocious, effeminate Maxime, the son Saccard had by his first wife. He encourages his spouse to buy and parade expensive jewelry (to boost his credit rating).

Before long, the selfless savior of the fallen has made a small fortune and is ready to set out on the second phase of his messiahship. Perhaps messiahship is not quite the right word and "Antichrist-apprenticeship" would be more appropriate, especially if one keeps in mind the new heights he will attain in Zola's *L'Argent* [Money]. At this early stage, he founds the Crédit viticole with an associated bank that will prove irresistible to the money-pressed city, particularly as he manages to give the building the grace and dignified appearance of a temple, a shrine of the new god of materialism. Zola does not actually call Saccard a high priest of Mammon, but he certainly implies it in passages like the following:

> Rien ne frappait le public d'une émotion plus religieuse que le sanctuaire, que la Caisse, où conduisait un corridor d'une nudité sacrée, et où l'on apercevait le coffre-fort, le dieu accroupi, scellé au mur, trapu et dormant, avec ses trois serrures, ses flancs épais, son air de brute divine. (1, p. 417-18)

> [Nothing inspired the public with more religious awe than the sanctuary, the bank strong room, reached by way of a corridor whose very bareness suggested holiness. There you would catch sight of the safe, the crouching god, welded to the wall, thick-set, asleep, with its three locks, its heavy flanks, its look of brutish deity.]

Saccard's true nature—his immorality and his rapacity—emerges further as he enjoys amorous escapades in the company of his son, Maxime, and as he and his sister, Sidonie, allow Renée to become ever more deeply involved in extravagance and debt, so that he may force her to sign over a large property holding that he craves for his speculation. Momentarily taken aback by his wife's incest with his son, he soon seems to condone it, finally extracting the desired signature when Renée is distraught over the news of Maxime's coming marriage with the rich but consumptive Louise. Maxime, who seduced his mother's femme de chambre at age seventeen, before making incestuous advances to his stepmother, is of course continuing his father's recipe of marrying for money. Father and son will remain the best of friends while Renée, ruined financially and overcome with a sense of shame and degradation, will die of meningitis the following winter. Just like the first novel in the cycle, *La Curée* ends on a desolate note of evil triumphant, of materialism, the Antichrist of the new age, firmly ensconced.

Is there no light in all this darkness, no witness to purity, innocence, and integrity? Very little in terms of human beings. One could mention Saccard's first wife, moribund Angèle, who is horrified to overhear her husband's plan of marrying Renée, but finds peace in the self-effacement of death, after forgiving faithless Aristide. Nevertheless, she is not so much a witness as a pathetic martyr-figure, dying without any hope except that of oblivion. More effective is Zola's use of symbolic decors. He manages to impose a perspective of paradise lost by contrasting the setting of Renée's upstairs room, in her father's house—a place of sunlight, flower-boxes and the singing of birds, a little "paradise" (Zola's word) overlooking the Seine, "la rivière vivante" (1, p. 412) (living river)—with the steamy, sensuous, counterfeit paradise of the "serre," the conservatory in her husband's showy residence, where she has her nocturnal trysts with Maxime, on a dark bearskin (symbol of man's dark, animal past), under the gaze of a black marble sphinx (destiny or death).

For a long time, the reader is led astray by the author into taking the unmoved, correct, disdainful footman, Baptiste, for a perennial symbol of integrity and morality. After all, every messiah needs his John the Baptist, to herald his coming. Whenever Renée sinks to a lower level, the lackey is featured for a moment as the uninvolved, incorruptible spectator of a decadent scene. We meet him briefly in chapter 1 where he lends perspective to an empty, boring party at the Saccards, and then again in chapter 4, just after Maxime has shrugged off responsibility for his involvement with his stepmother:

> Le grand valet, avec sa carrure de ministre, . . . avait, cette nuit-là, un visage plus correct et plus sévère encore que de coutume. (1, p. 484)
>
> [The great valet, with his ministerial breadth of shoulder, wore, on that night, an even sterner and more correct expression than usual.]

In the last chapter, however, Zola, somewhat cynically, explodes his sustained antithesis between decadent family and upright servant: it turns out that the solemn, irreproachable Baptiste is just a misogynist homosexual who carries on with the stable boys!

There is little room for saints, prophets, or messiahs in the Second Empire, where the very Tuileries palace, Zola tells us, stretches out its two wings into the dark "comme pour une embrassure énorme" (1, p. 435) [as if for a gigantic embrace] and where Napoléon III himself crosses the ballroom "d'un pas pénible et vacillant" [with a labored and unsteady gait], unable to keep his eyes off Renée (1, p. 439). From time to time, we shall return to the emperor, until Zola, in La Débâcle, will present him as a fallen messiah, a pathetic wreck of a man, manipulated by his wife and despised by the Prussian enemy.

Not only is there little room for saints or messiahs in Zola's vision of the Second Empire, but even when a rare one does appear, he is overcome by the system, or else the forces in place are determined to resist and eliminate him.

We have seen that ambition and greed tempt characters like Pierre Rougon and son to masquerade as public or private saviors. However, there were more insidious vices at work in Zola's world, one of which was the placid, one-sided physicality, the renunciation of spiritual, intellectual, or artistic pursuits that may come with material abundance. Zola's own life-style was affected by his rising income and his more settled homelife. Alexandrine, Zola's friends tell us, was an excellent cook and the author made a point of sharing his table with his less fortunate friends. Over the years, in fact, he would grow stout—a situation drastically remedied by a pure meat diet about the time of his setting eyes on a linen-maid named Jeanne. But that takes us to the years preceding Le Docteur Pascal.

Meanwhile Zola may well have told himself that he must not allow his unaccustomed prosperity to dull the flame of his reforming zeal. And so it is not surprising that, in Le Ventre de Paris [The Belly of Paris] (1873), he should have fastened on les Halles, the vast foodmarket of the capital, as a symbol of one of the factors that prove the undoing of a good man, called to be a prophet. Basically Florent, the hero of the novel, is a potential messiah who, for a number of reasons, fails to rouse the bourgeoisie from its self-centered, smug complacency, its uncritical support of a regime that lined its wallets and kept its cupboards larded. In his "Notice" to the 1979 Folio edition of Zola's Le Ventre de Paris, Henri Guillemin wittily refers to the plot of the novel as "l'histoire d'un proscrit ascétique, à sa manière nouveau Christ persécuté par les marchands"[2] (the story of an ascetic outlaw, in his own way a new Christ, persecuted by those buying and selling).

Unlike the Rougon, Florent is a caring, compassionate person—a man of loyalty and integrity. Zola's first description of him speaks of his "deux grands yeux bruns d'une singulière douceur, dans un visage dur et tourmenté" (1, p. 604) [two big, unusually gentle brown eyes in a hard, tormented face]. A flashback in chapter 2 informs us that, after the death of his widowed mother, he dropped his law-studies in Paris and took up teaching, so that he might look after his half-brother Quenu, whom he fetched from Le Vigan (in the Cévennes, down south). Back in the capital, he is little more than a rootless outsider, an uncomfortable misfit because of his half-finished education but, rather than brood over his lost prospects or yield to bitterness, he embraces the ideals of republicanism. And so it is not envy or rebelliousness, but utopian aspirations that prompt him to man the barricades in 1848.

Then he undergoes the trauma of his life—the shock that will determine his destiny: ever after he will be haunted by the young woman who dies beside him and whose blood, found on his hands, will lead to his wrongful conviction and transportation to Cayenne.

As far as the authorities are concerned, he is dead and buried. Florent will spend seven years of toil and deprivation in French Guyana, but then he manages to rise again. He escapes, takes on the identity of a dead fellow-sufferer, and finds his way back to France. Like many of Zola's heroes to come, then, he has a fresh start, a resurrection, so to speak, as he enters Paris in the vegetable cart of "la mère François" (mother François) (Freudians, take note!). To add a religious nuance to this vaguely messianic scenario, Zola lends the following comment to Gavard, the man who will share Florent's fate and who senses something gentle and priestly about him: " . . . c'est un curé, ce gard-là. Il ne lui manque que la calotte" (1, p. 847) [. . . he's a priest, that fellow. All that's missing is the calotte]. Starving, lean Florent is immediately nauseated by the mountains of food to which he is introduced visually by the equally bony but enthusiastic painter, Claude Lantier. In spite of that, he yields to the invitation of his now prosperous half-brother and his attractive, healthy wife, Lisa (daughter of Antoine Macquart) to take shelter in their butchery, amid the steamy, sickly smells that emanate from the smallgoods-room.

Initially Florent resists the offer of a job as supervisor at les Halles—a position which, he feels, would compromise his ascetic, pure life-style: a prophet should not be involved with the fleshpots of Egypt! Gradually, however, he feels himself succumb to a demoralizing torpor, "une lâcheté molle et repue" (a soft and sated slackness), until, late one evening, he does not protest when Lisa, on his behalf, accepts the post:

> . . . il glissait à la lâcheté heureuse de cette digestion continue, au milieu gras où il vivait depuis quinze jours (1, p. 695)

[. . . he slipped into the contented slackness of this continuous digestive process, into the well-fed milieu in which he had been living for the past fortnight.]

Clearly Florent is overpassive: he allows himself to drift into situations not of his own choosing. The same lack of initiative or dynamism stops him from winning the heart of his sister-in-law (Lisa)—both on the sexual and on the ideological level. That would have been a daunting challenge, anyway, for "la belle charcutière" [the beautiful pork butcher's wife], while not averse to a little discreet courtship, values her peace of mind. Likewise Florent's revolutionary ideas simply worry her, because they threaten her comfortable life-style. The pep talk she gives her husband, when he warms to Florent's dreams of practical reform, is an eloquent, if not very idealistic expression of bourgeois resistance to change (she is arguing the good sense of supporting a regime that enables them to sell their sausages in peace):

Reste donc chez toi, grande bête, dors bien, mange bien, gagne de l'argent, aie la conscience tranquille, dis-toi que la France se débarbouillera toute seule, si l'Empire la tracasse. Elle n'a pas besoin de toi, la France! (1, p. 759)

[So stay at home, you big silly, sleep well, eat well, earn money, have a quiet conscience, tell yourself that France can sort herself out (lit.: "wash her face") all on her own, if the empire bothers her. She certainly doesn't need you!]

Florent is protected from adultery, not so much by his sense of loyalty to Quenu as by his faithfulness to a memory: the girl who died beside him on the barricades. In several ways this regressive, idealistic head-love is to contribute to his downfall. Just as Lisa Quenu would not have informed, later on, on a man who had shown that he worshiped her from a distance, another woman, Louise Méhudin, "la belle Normande" (the beautiful woman from Normandy), who vainly tried to arouse him, would not have betrayed a more responsive lover. And this brings us to Florent's greatest flaw as an effective messiah: he is too much the romantic dreamer out of touch with reality. Scripture speaks of the Word that was made flesh and dwelt among us, but our hero is not properly incarnate on any level. The sexual-political parallel is not just an arbitrary association favored by Zola (he will use it again in *Son Excellence Eugène Rougon* [His Excellency Eugène Rougon] and especially in *Germinal*). Florent's inability or unwillingness to make advances to Lisa and Louise is matched by his inability to penetrate and fertilize the fleshly milieu in which he has landed himself.

The German critic, Friedrich Wolfzettel, in a thoughtful, stimulating article, elaborates on Florent as the ineffectual outsider, the detached, half-educated intellectual who cannot integrate properly into the real world:

> Florent ist realitätsfern, d.h. seine Träume sind überhaupt nicht in die Wirklichkeit transponierbar . . . er ist der Intellekt ohne Nährboden und ohne Wurzel.

> [Florent is remote from reality, that is, his dreams are totally incapable of being transposed into reality. He is the rootless intellectual without a soil to feed on, translated by A. J. E.][3]

Possibly Wolfzettel is reading more recent psycho-sociological insights into the novel when he goes on to link Florent's predicament with the increasing alienation of the individual in the mass-society that takes shape in the closing decades of the nineteenth century.[4] Would it not be closer to Zola's vision to suggest that Florent acts out the problem of the postromantic individual, lonely and out of place in a brutally materialistic milieu, who strives for integration, both in society and in his own psyche, because his one-sided emphasis on mind or spirit has estranged him from his instinctive, physical self, as well as from the increasingly prosaic and pragmatic world around him? If this is so, Zola's novel juxtaposes the double problem of a mind out of contact with evolving social reality and of a bourgeois society bereft of spirit. In his subsequent novels, Zola will dramatize repeatedly the problematic relationship of the reflecting, intuitive individual with the earth, the senses, or the instincts, represented by a milieu, a region, or a woman.

Let us note in passing the irony of Zola's reversal of scenario, when it comes to his messiahs failing: when the Claude of *La Confession* goes astray, it is because he loses his purity; Florent comes to grief because he cannot renounce a pure dream of the past, because he refuses to lose his virginity!

We have examined how Florent's trauma on the barricades locks him into a dead ideal that stops him from responding adequately to the present. There is yet further evidence of this when, on two occasions, the hero visits the Nanterre home and garden of the kind, strong, sensible Mme François. Her name suggests that she represents all that is best about France, in contrast to the self-centered, callous materialism of the new middle class. Intended by Zola as a standard of normal, wholesome humanity, the antidote to the problems he is about to broach, she is first described as "robuste et belle de sa vie en pleine air et de sa virilité adoucie par des yeux noirs d'une tendresse charitable" (1, p. 613) (strong and beautiful from her life in the open air, her mannishness tempered by black eyes filled with compassionate tenderness). Halfway through the novel, Florent and his painter-friend spend a day with her in the peace of her vegetable garden and the author makes sure that we note the difference between the right and the wrong way of using the gifts of nature:

> Alors les Halles qu'il avait laissées le matin lui parurent un vaste ossuaire, un lieu de mort où ne traînait que le cadavre des êtres. . . . La terre était la vie, l'éternel berceau, la santé du monde. (1, p. 803)
>
> [Then the Halles that he had left that morning seemed like a vast ossuary, a place of death where only the corpses of living things lay around. . . . The earth was life, the eternal cradle, the health of the world.]

Already Zola has profound misgivings about the retailing class that handles only the dead bodies of things, whereas women like Mme François, the essence of the old France that is close to the soil, remains in wholesome contact with natural and living things. In Florent's mind, she is associated with the earth, fresh air, open skies, and the scent of hay. Yet his faithfulness to his revolutionary ideals, crystallized around his memories of the dead girl, keep him from finding happiness in the miniature "paradise" (Zola's word) of Nanterre. Like the author himself, he needs to pursue a mission that somehow perpetuates a lost ideal.

It is only wishful thinking on the part of Zola that inspires Mme François's remark at the end of the novel, when Florent, after heading a secret society that prepares for the big day of revolution, informed upon by Louise and meanly betrayed by Lisa Quenu and the whole neighborhood, is arrested and sent back to Cayenne:

> On aurait pu être heureux. . . . C'est Paris, c'est ce gueux de Paris. . . . Il aurait dû m'écouter. . . . venir à Nanterre, vivre là avec mes poules et mes lapins. (1, p. 893)

[We could have been happy.... It was Paris, lousy Paris. He should have listened to me ... and come to Nanterre to live there with my hens and my rabbits.]

In the end many factors will have contributed to Florent's failure and second descent into hell: his romantic naïveté and lack of integration, his inability to cope with his sexuality, but especially, the obstinate resistance of a bourgeoisie that is unwilling to engage in critical self-appraisal, unwilling above all to imperil the soothing, comfortable delights of the fleshpots. Zola himself, in his Ebauche, sums up both the ideals of his ineffectual messiah and the besetting sin of the middle class of his day: "En somme, au fond c'est la bataille des Maigres et des Gras" [In short, it's basically the battle of the Fat and the Lean] and again:

> Florent, ce prescrit, ce maigre, cet affamé ... qui est la protestation de l'idéal, du rêve, de la justice et de la fraternité, tombe au milieu de la bombance du Second Empire, dans la satisfaction et le triomphe des appétits du ventre.[5]

[Florent, the thin, starving proscript—himself a protestation of the ideal, the dream of justice, and the brotherhood of man—lands in the midst of the Second Empire excesses that cater to the satisfaction and triumphal elevation of sensual appetites.]

After two false saviors (Pierre and Aristide Rougon) and one flawed potential redeemer (Florent), it only takes a prototype of Antichrist to complete the third cycle—an essentially negative phase—of Zola's orbits around the messianic myth.

As a study of Provençal society, Zola's next novel, *La Conquête de Plassans* [The Conquest of Plassans], traces how the hometown of the Rougon-Macquart, which had largely reverted to legitimism (faithfulness to the old Bourbon dynasty), is won back to the emperor's cause. Early in the novel, the heroine's husband, François Mouret, throws light on Zola's title when he guesses that the local Bonapartist clique will soon try to "faire la conquête de Plassans" (1, p. 934) [make a conquest of Plassans].

Much of the novel, however, has a more intimate focus. While covering a campaign of political subjugation, the author is really more interested in portraying a personal accession to power—a recurring scenario for Zola that will usually feature an intelligent, unscrupulous individual, endowed with energy and indomitable willpower, who will readily resort to hypocrisy, deception, and seduction. The priest in *La Conquête de Plassans* is just such a man. In his recent study, Henri Troyat neatly sums up both connotations of the title as follows:

> ... cette évocation de l'ascendance maléfique prise par un prêtre, l'abbé Faujas, sur une famille, sur une maison, sur une femme qu'il conduit à la folie, sur un village enfin. . . .[6]
>
> [this evocation of the sinister ascendancy gained by a priest, the abbé Faujas, over a family, a house, a woman whom he drives to madness, finally over a village. . . .]

The name of the villain could hardly have been chosen more aptly. Even readers little acquainted with French will sense there is something false about the name *Faujas*. Those with a more thorough knowledge of the language will associate the name both with "faux" and "jaser" [to chatter, to talk too much]—the priest is expert at "innocently" chatting up individuals to pump them for information or to win them over to his purposes). Only those familiar with the local scene, however, are likely to know that "jas" is an old Provençal term for "bergerie" [sheepfold], so that "Faujas" may be read as "false shepherd": the refuge he offers is illusionary.

We soon gather that the priest is an outsider from a poor peasant background and that he has fallen on hard times. His cassock is so threadbare that it brings a contemptuous smile to the lips of the locals, but that is not necessarily to his discredit: the Good Shepherd himself was poor and did not have a place to lay his head. Nevertheless, informed gossip in town has it that, in his last post at Besançon, Faujas had a hand in an industrial enterprise that failed and, more seriously, that he nearly strangled a fellow-priest.

To give him maximum involvement with the Rougon-Macquart, Zola makes him a tenant in the home of François and Marthe Mouret (née Rougon), both of whom have the by now insane Adelaïde as grandmother. It will transpire later that Faujas is virtually an electoral agent, sent down by his Parisian superiors to effect a swing in the right direction (according to Zola's views, the church hierarchy had espoused the imperial cause, in an attempt to maintain its power over French society).

To this official mission, Faujas adds a personal quest for power, partly inspired by the mocking glances that greeted his first arrival. In the early chapters we see him familiarize himself with the local scene and set out on a patient, calculating, Machiavellian campaign to ingratiate himself. Guided by his Bonapartist contact, the wicked Félicité Rougon, a worthy feminine counterpart to his scheming role, who advises him to "plaire aux femmes" [make himself agreeable to women], he wins the heart of his hostess, Marthe. Acquiring a new "soutane" (cassock), cultivating charm, tact, and gentleness, he founds a hospice for the girls of working parents (L'Oeuvre de la Vierge) [The Society of the Blessed Virgin] and a social meeting-place for the young (Le Cercle de la Jeunesse) [The Youth-Club] that impress the townspeople and even the hostile clergy. With time, he manages to manipulate the old bishop into making him curate and then vicar-general. After marginalizing his rivals and taming the bishop, he virtually runs the diocese. At election time, he is able to come up with a Bonapartist candidate—a move for which he has prepared the voters by reconciling the two antagonistic local factions under his apparently disinterested, benign, and constructive patronage.

Viewed from that angle, Faujas's portrayal does not go beyond the usual anticlerical cliché of the political priest, the underhand operator who tends to take over. When it comes to the priest's handling of Marthe, however, Zola departs from the seduction scenario he had at first considered. We are given instead a preview of the paradise myth in *La Faute de l'abbé Mouret* [Father Mouret's Error], with Faujas, rather than nature, playing the role of Satan. Zola sets the stage for this from his opening scene. Marthe is depicted in her tranquil, domestic paradise, her refuge from the world outside that threatens her frail personality. When she is apprehensive about Mouret's letting the upper floor of the house to a priest, he assures her that Faujas is no Devil. Having had a taste of Faujas's ability to extract confidential information, however, he repeatedly refers to him as "ce diable d'homme" (1, p. 926, 931) [that diabolic man]—a sentiment soon echoed by the local abbé Surin (1, p. 987). Just after his change of mind, the proud husband and father, in front of Faujas, imprudently defies the Devil to disturb the peace of his little Eden:

> Nous restons chez nous, nous autres; nous ne recevons personne. Notre jardin est un paradis fermé, où je défie bien le diable de venir nous tempter. (1, p. 932)

> [We people stay at home; we never have guests. Our garden is a closed paradise and I defy the Devil himself to come and tempt us there.]

Zola is not beyond appealing to popular superstitions, when it suits his purpose of building up a sinister perspective.

Faujas's demonic dimension has more than a little in common with that of Balzac's Vautrin, the tempter in Le Père Goriot (1835). Like him, he is a man of savage ambition and great willpower; like him, he uses a frail woman to attain his ends; like him—and the Antichrist figure in Dan. 11:37—he spurns "the love of women." In the latter respect, however, a basic difference emerges: it could be argued that both Faujas and Vautrin are projections of their creator's shadow—in Balzac's case that of the cult of ruthless power, in Zola's case that of his desire to dominate, his ambition to rise to glory, but where Vautrin's scorn for women stems from his homosexual orientation, Faujas sees women as the supreme temptation of his life. When Marthe finally confesses her love to him—a flame he had kindled through his show of tenderness and that he had tolerated to ease himself into Plassans society—Zola first reminds us of his contempt for the whole gender: " . . . il laissa tomber sur elle son mépris de la femme" [He turned on her all his contempt for women] and then puts into his mouth a passionate speech whose irony cannot fail to fill the reader with moral indignation:

> Oui, c'est l'éternelle lutte du mal contre les volontés fortes. Vous êtes la tentation d'en bas, la lâcheté, la chute finale. . . . Si j'échoue, ce sera vous, femme, qui m'aurez ôté de ma force par votre seul désir. Retirez-vous, allez-vous en, vous êtes Satan! (1, p. 1176)

> [Yes, it's the eternal battle between evil and men of strong will. You are the temptation from down below, weakness, the ultimate fall. . . . If I fail, it will be you, woman, who has robbed me of my strength, by your desire alone. Get back, depart from me, you are Satan!]

What is so fascinating about this self-righteous tirade, delivered by a total villain, is that it seems to reflect some of Zola's own views at the time of writing. Earlier in the novel, in a now famous maxim, Zola attributes Faujas's immunity to temptation to his wholehearted quest for power: "Les hommes chastes sont les seuls forts" (1, p. 1079) [Only chaste men are strong]. In his commentary, Pierre Ouvrard, himself a priest, points out that this maxim sounds suspiciously like the sentiments the author lends to Claude Lantier in L'Oeuvre [The Work]: "Le génie doit être chaste" (4, p. 347) [Genius must be chaste] and that Zola's contemporaries long applied to the author himself.[7]

It should be noted, then, that, once again in La Conquête de

Plassans, chastity is presented in an ambiguous light. Just as Florent, in *Le Ventre de Paris*, failed to redeem the Parisian bourgeoisie, because he could not give up his ideal of purity, and just as his excellency Eugène Rougon will fall from power for refusing to marry the Clorinde he keenly desires, Faujas indirectly brings destruction upon himself for keeping intact his clerical ideal of chastity. It is paradoxical but true that, for Faujas, sexual abstention marks the apex of his cruelty. After all, it is the priest who courts Marthe by his assumed gentleness and interest in her children. It is he who nurtures love in her by their long hours of intimacy on the terrace. It is he who fails to warn her of her incipient love that she sublimates into religious mysticism. Even when her growing devotion submerges her in an ecstatic, trancelike state, he merely bends her mind with his iron will and keeps her on the edge of hysteria. And finally, when her passion reaches its paroxysm and reveals itself for what it really is, he coldly disdains her adoration, rejecting it as utterly evil.

At that stage, Zola seems to suggest that the basest form of evil is to "lead on" a person, for purposes of personal ambition, without any intention of completing the natural process of desire and consummation. The unpardonable sin, in other words, is a sin against life in the biologic sense of the word, but Zola is not yet ready to articulate that belief that will ultimately become his firm conviction in the first of his *Quatre evangiles*. Meanwhile "Zola le chaste" remains caught in a dilemma, because he strives to pursue his adolescent ideal of "pure" love, while sensing more and more that his idealism is a trap that stops him from fully responding to life.

To return to our Antichrist scenario, according to which, at the end of the age, the Devil raises up a cruel master who imposes a harsh, treacherous regime, before being defeated and cast into the lake of fire, we must briefly consider how Zola concludes his story. Of late a number of writers have commented on the supernatural dimension of Faujas: following in the footsteps of Roger Ripoll, in his massive thesis,[8] Pierre Ouvrard in his *Zola et le prêtre* ("une sorte de personnage mythique, incarnation d'une puissance démoniaque"[9] [a kind of mythical character that is an incarnation of demonic power]) and Marc de Launay ("une sorte d'incarnation pernicieuse et sournoise de Satan"[10] [a kind of sly, malevolent incarnation of Satan]), draw attention to Faujas as a supernatural agent of evil.

Zola's earlier references to "ce diable d'homme" (that diabolic man) prepare the reader for the way in which the priest unmasks himself once he has completed his electoral mission. Faujas contemptously goes back to his threadbare cassock and unkempt squalor. In fact, he assumes all the characteristics that medieval artists and romantic writers of the Gothic variety attribute to rebellious Lucifer or to the harsh ruler of hell:

> Du prêtre souple se dégageait une figure sombre, despotique, pliant toutes les volontés. Sa face, redevenue terreuse, avait des regards d'aigle; ses grosses mains se levaient pleines de menaces et de châtiments. La ville fut positivement terrifiée, en voyant le maître qu'elle s'était donné grandir ainsi démesurément, avec la défroque immonde, l'odeur forte, le poil rousse d'un diable. (1, p. 1166)

> [From the pliant priest there emerged a somber, despotic figure who bent every will. His face, which had reverted to its former sallow complexion, had the (cruel) eyes of an eagle; his big hands were raised full of menace and chastisement. The town was positively terrified as it saw the master that it had acquired, growing like this beyond all measure, with the filthy, castaway clothing, the stench, the red hair of a Devil.]

We shall see shortly that, not only is the sinister paragraph just quoted constructed to end on the word "diable" (Devil), but that, more effectively still, the novel as a whole concludes on an evocation of the evil one that the reader is made to supply out of his own imagination.

In keeping with the twentieth chapter of the biblical Apocalypse, Zola has reserved a horrific end for Faujas and his tribe (his grasping peasant-mother; his sister, Olympe; and his base, repulsive brother-in-law, Trouche). François Mouret, who has suffered from his wife's wandering affections and growing neglect of her family, is wrongly styled a wife-basher when Marthe's fits cause her self-sustained injuries. Local persecution, countenanced by Marthe, leads to his most innocent actions being construed as signs of madness and to his being committed to the same asylum as his grandmother. There the poor man really goes insane. Allowed to escape by Antoine Macquart, at the instigation of Faujas's defeated legitimist rival, l'abbé Fenil, François incinerates his former home, Faujas, and his whole clan (actually Mouret strangles Faujas, before both roll down the stairs into the blazing inferno).

At the cost of a good deal of melodrama, then, poetic justice has been done, even if Mouret did not deserve such a fate. The author has symbolically disposed of his Antichrist by plunging him into hell, but his own ambition and, especially, his continuing repression of erotic love will prove harder to eliminate. For a long time yet, Zola will be as haunted by religion and apocalyptic judgment as consumptive Marthe is when, on her deathbed, she makes out her son Serge's black cassock against the red evening sky and presumably takes him for the Devil.

5
The Messianic Merry-Go-Round

With regard to Zola's involvement in the messianic myth, volume 5 of the cycle, *La Faute de l'abbé Mouret*, [Father Mouret's Error] brings us back to square one. On the human level, there are no messianic characters in the novel, and that for a good reason: the hero, Serge Mouret, who has been assigned the small country parish of Les Artauds (three kilometers southeast of Aix), abandons his veneration of the Virgin for what Zola calls "le culte de la croix" [the cult of the cross] (1, p. 1488)—a religion focused on death and suffering. The model Serge will ultimately identify with is not the resurrected Savior of Christianity or the Messiah of the Jews, but the same ineffectual martyr we first met in Zola's short story "Le Sang."

Accordingly, we may approach the novel as a variation on a theme, a reiteration of Zola's reasons for discarding the messianic myth. We must realize, of course, that it is bound to reemerge in later works: myths are not embraced or rejected simply by a conscious act of will or by an operation of the intellect.

Very early in the novel, the author comes up with his usual mythical microcosm: the church decor of chapter 2 prefigures what is about to transpire in the plot and what has already transpired in Zola's psyche. As Serge says mass in front of an empty church, the golden sunlight invades the building, falling resplendently on the statue of the Madonna and Child:

> Ce fut alors que des flammes jaunes entrèrent par les fenêtres. ... La Mère de Dieu, dans une gloire, dans l'éblouissement de sa couronne, et de son manteau d'or, sourit tendrement à l'enfant Jésus. ...
> (2, p. 1222)

> [It was at that moment that yellow flames came through the windows. The Mother of God, in radiant glory, in the dazzling splendor of her crown and her golden mantle, smiled tenderly at the baby Jesus.]

A few pages later, the author will explicitly associate the sun with nature, the life-force, "les fécondités de mai" (2, p. 1226) [the fecundity of May].

The sunlit Virgin and Child may be said to correspond to Serge's past life at home, the little "paradise" presided over by Marthe while she was still a caring, devoted mother. One might add that it also corresponds to Zola's own life in Provence that combined the enjoyment of the sun-drenched countryside with the tender care he received from his mother and grandmother.

To complete Zola's microcosm, the dazzling statue of Mary is contrasted with the image of Christ, significantly lost in the shadows where it expresses suffering and death: "Seul, au milieu de cette vie montante, le grand Christ, resté dans l'ombre, mettait la mort, l'agonie de sa chair. . . ." (2, p. 1222) [Alone in the midst of this upsurge of life, the great statue of Christ remained in the shadows, presented an image of death and the agonies of his flesh]. In principle, the young priest has already made his choice: troubled by the pagan sensuality of the village girls and the immersion in nature and instinct of his retarded sister, Désirée, we are told in chapter 4, Serge, like a desert-hermit, has turned away from life and "la nature damnée" (2, p. 1232) [fallen nature]. For a long time he will fight his sexuality; he will pray to become an inanimate stone beneath the Virgin's heel but, like the author before him, he will experience a lapse that will drive him from paradise. Suffering from amnesia as a result of illness, Serge will be initiated into the life of the senses by Albine, a true child of nature, adopted by the keeper of the mythical gardens of Le Paradou. He will experience all the joys of paradise, before regaining the knowledge of good and evil at the foot of the fateful tree, where he finally makes love to Albine (there is no need to spell out again how young Zola came to grief in a similar manner).

Returning to his parish, Serge abandons his "culte de la Vierge" [cult of the Virgin] (he gathers the dried-up flowers from her altar and casts them on the dungheap) and substitutes "le culte de la croix" (2, p. 1448) [the cult of the Cross]. The church now becomes a scene of death and suffering, as Zola highlights the stations of the cross (cf. 2, p. 1462). Pregnant Albine, for all her passionate pleas, will be abandoned along with the wild beauty of le Paradou. In the end it is she who drives away the man who fails to respond to her any longer.

And so Mary, the pure Virgin, has been dethroned and even pagan Pan has lost his appeal. And as for the Christ-figure, stripped of his Resurrection powers, he can only bring his silent message of death. What does that leave of messianism in Zola's novelistic universe? Only the caricature of the Old Testament Jehovah, "le dieu de colère, le Dieu jaloux et terrible" [the god of wrath, the jealous, terrible God], as Zola calls him in his Ebauche [rough outline].[1] From the very beginning, the author intended to incarnate this implacable god in Frère Archangias, the uncouth, unsavory teaching brother who drowns songbirds, hates women and courting couples, and whose thundering voice summons Serge from paradise. And no one in his right mind would suspect Archangias of messianic aspirations! Having become a dispenser of poetic justice, Zola takes a parting shot at the man who is anything but an angel, let alone an archangel: he shows all the contempt he feels for his obnoxious character by getting Jaubernat, the atheistic uncle and guardian of Albine, to cut off his right ear.

If there is no messianic potential in the characters of *La Faute*, how shall we rate the powerful politician and statesman who gives his name to volume 6 of the series, *Son Excellence Eugène Rougon?* (His Excellency Eugène Rougon)

Given the record of his father, Pierre, and his half-brother, Aristide, alias Saccard, we are immediately sensitive to the irony and bathos conveyed by the title: the honorific "Son Excellence" (His Excellency) and the noble sounding "Eugène" are followed by a common name already associated by the reader with greed, rapacity, and opportunism.

Clearly the hero is more impressive than his father and less base than his brother. After each political death, he manages to rise again: his serene self-control, patience, and cool strategy enable him to stage a double resurrection, but is he really a messiah? Surely not! He may be chaste, in the sense that he is no blind slave to his sexuality, but this is so only because he is possessed by a stronger impulse—the lust for power. Determined to preserve his sovereign independence at any cost, he declines to marry his female counterpart, the powerful Clorinde Balbi, a woman whom he craves and who has played a cat-and-mouse game with him for years (his refusal will prompt the Italian courtesan-adventuress to engineer his second fall from power). Eugène may look after his servile, self-seeking hangers-on and protect the interests of his political allies, but only because it satisfies his vanity, because he enjoys the adulation of lesser mortals at his feet.

His greatest flaw, the one that immediately disqualifies him from messianic pretentions, is his self-centered ambition, his desire for might and glory for their own sake or, as Paul Alexis puts it, as "une manifestation de sa propre force"[2] [a manifestation of his own strength]. In his own commentary, Zola suggests that his hero's grasping for supremacy smacks of Lucifer's desire to make himself equal to the Most High: "Sans vice aucun, il faisait en secret des orgies de toute-puis-sance" (2, p. 77) [Being without vices, he secretly went in for orgies of omnipotence]—omnipotence being the preserve of the deity. Where the traditional Messiah is sent by the Father whom he loves and glorifies, and where Christ tells his followers that he came, not to be served, but to serve, Eugène can be loyal only to himself.

Ruthless in his power, he compares himself to his aristocratic rival, de Marsy, in these terms: "Lui, sabre élégammant le monde, sans tâcher ses gants blancs. Moi, j'assomme" (2, p. 77) [He cuts down people with elegant saber-strokes, without even soiling his white gloves. I just pole-axe them]. Learning of an Italian plot to assassinate Napoléon III, he idly sits by and lets events take their course: he is quite prepared to risk the life of his sovereign, to make sure that de Marsy, minister for the interior at the time, will fall into disgrace.

Power isolates; it encourages egoism and lack of scruple, but it may also lend itself to sadism. Clorinde demonstrates this when Rougon has cornered her in his stable and she uses her horsewhip to good effect to cool the ardor of her panting pursuer. Eugène himself, too, is no stranger to sadistic motivation. After his first fall from power, he dreams of returning to his peasant roots, of being the absolute master of a farm where he would wield the whip:

> ... une ferme dans laquelle toutes les bêtes lui obéiraient. C'était son idéal, avoir un fouet et commander, être supérieur, plus intelligent et plus fort. (2, p. 42)

> [... a farm where all the animals would obey him. Ideally, what he wanted was to hold the whip and to give orders, to be superior, more intelligent, and more powerful.]

His dream is more than an idle fantasy: at the height of his power, he delights in keeping prefects waiting in his office and in becoming a repressive figure of terror who muzzles the press and orders arbitrary arrests:

> Cela l'amusait d'être une épouvante, de forger la foudre ... d'assommer un peuple avec ses poings enflés de bourgeois parvenu.... Et il jouait son rôle de Dieu, damnant les uns, sauvant les autres, d'une main jalouse. (2, p. 218)

> [He enjoyed being a terror, forging thunderbolts ... knocking people down with the swollen fists of a bourgeois parvenu.... And he played his God-role with a zealous hand, damning some, saving others.]

At the mention of the word "Dieu" [God], we recognize the myth that Zola is already attacking through Geneviève in *Madeleine Férat* and that takes shape more clearly through Archangias in *La Faute*. The allusion to Eugène hurling thunderbolts associates the Old Testament Jehovah caricature with the Greek vision of Zeus—a far cry from the Judeo-Christian ideal of the compassionate Shepherd-King.

When there is a tide of protest against Rougon's heavy-handed repression and he is increasingly compromised by his hangers-on, Eugène forestalls trouble by writing a letter of resignation. The author than uses an evocation of his hero's state of mind to make the Jove myth quite explicit:

> ... et il rêva une nouvelle incarnation, une résurrection en Jupiter Tonnant, sans bande à ses pieds, faisant la loi par le seul éclat de sa parole. (2, p. 327)

> [... and he dreamed of a new incarnation, of being resurrected as Jove the Thunderer, unhindered by a crowd of followers at his feet, creating law by the mere impact of his word.]

Hinduism ("incarnation"), Christianity ("résurrection"), paganism ("Jupiter Tonnant")—Zola is certainly coming up with a wide range of religions to serve as points of reference for his central character. In an earlier portrayal of Eugène, too, when the latter irritates his supporters by his serene, detached attitude to his first loss of office, Zola includes clear allusions to a Buddhist or Hindu ideal:

> Il jouait au *Bon Dieu*, disait encore l'ancien sous-préfet (= du Pozat). Ce *diable* de Rougon vivait comme une *idole hindoue*, assoupi dans la satisfaction de lui-même, les mains croisées sur le ventre, souriant en béat au milieu d'une foule de fidèles qui l'adoraient en se coupant les entrailles en quatre. (2, p. 191, italics added by A. J. E.)

[He played at being God, the former subprefect, would add. That devil of a fellow, Rougon, lived like a Hindu idol, immersed in self-satisfied slumber, with his hands folded on his belly, smiling beatifically in the midst of a crowd of the faithful who slaved their guts out in their adoration of him.]

The sous-préfet, in the same breath, refers to Eugène as "Bon Dieu" [God], "diable" [Devil], and "idole hindoue" [Hindu idol], as though he does not quite know how to categorize him. Possibly Zola himself had doubts, about ambition or the will to power in himself, about their nature, their direction, and ultimate focus. In any case, what in Eugène is only a pose or at most a passing dream, suggests that the author has undergone the fascination of a worldview that is the very opposite of the pursuit of temporal power. The deity with its hands folded upon its belly—the traditional pose of the contemplating Buddha—is not an incarnate messiah, actively coming to the rescue of his erring creatures, but rather a pointer to the peace of allowing oneself to be absorbed into a "whole," a cosmic spirit to whom earthly ambitions are but "maya" or illusion. One may speculate that, in Zola's psyche, this new Oriental perspective corresponds to a compensatory dream. Driven by a seemingly endless, ambitious project, deeply involved in the contemporary scene, caught in the agitation of staging his plays, he must have felt the need to satisfy a neglected part of himself. What else is he looking for when he potters about in his garden or looks after his pet rabbits? Why the frequent interludes in his novels that hark back to his adolescent openness to the enchantment of nature?

One may suspect further that, in metaphorically referring to Eugène as Devil, Jove, or pagan idol, Zola is trying to name, to pin down, to exorcise from his psyche the demon of power that might prevail, were it not constantly checked by balancing forces—genuine affection for his friends, sympathy and compassion for the deprived, noble social ideals, openness to the joy and beauty of life in the wider sense.

Zola's somewhat naive, but lovable friend, Paul Alexis, inclined to hero-worship the master, is perceptive enough to inform the reading public that Eugène stood for Zola, if he had become a minister of state:

Eugène Rougon, c'est pour moi Emile Zola ministre, c'est-à-dire le rêve de ce qu'il eût été, s'il eût appliqué son ambition à la politique.[3]

[As far as I am concerned, Eugène Rougon is Emile Zola as a minister of state, that is to say, a dream of what he might have been, had his ambitions been directed toward politics.]

It would be most surprising if Alexis had not first checked that intuition with his friend. In any case, Zola had no illusions about the perils of power. Beginning, himself, to act as leader of naturalism (though ever refusing to be called "chef d'école" [the leader of a school], as Alexis reports[4] and liking to surround himself with a group of friends and disciples that his enemies would soon refer to as "la bande de Zola" (Zola's gang), or worse, the author must have been aware, too, of the trap of vanity. What other conclusions can one draw from comments like the following that seem to stem from personal experience? (Zola is entering into Eugène's meditation, as he attends a charity-sale at the Tuileries (the imperial palace) and simply pockets, unopened, the letter in which Napoleon accepts his resignation):

Ses fortes épaules craquaient sous les responsabilités . . . qu'il avait prises à son compte, par une forfanterie de grand homme, un besoin d'être un chef redouté et généreux. (2, p. 344)

[His strong shoulders strained beneath the weight of responsibilities . . . that he had taken on with the boastful swagger of a great man, the need to be an awe-inspiring and generous leader.]

It is always dangerous to infer data from a literary text and then to project them back onto an author, but at least it is beyond doubt that Zola is aware of Eugène's faults and of the risks to which he exposes himself morally. For all that, he does not doom him to political extinction: there is no poetic justice, this time. After the charity-sale, in the course of which Clorinde flaunts the fact that she has become the emperor's mistress, Eugène returns home to dream of future exploits. The final chapter, three years later, reflects Napoléon's changeover from repressive to more "liberal" policies, which allow Rougon to reenter the scene as minister without portfolio. He knows that the new liberality is only a sham, but eloquently defends the sovereign when a rebel deputy clamors for a free press and genuine elections. And when, on top of that, Eugène espouses the very religious causes his earlier policies had tried to check, his future is assured: "Rougon, par son discours, venait de commencer la prodigieuse fortune qui devait le porter si haut." (2, p. 367) [With his speech, Rougon had just begun the prodigious sequence of good fortune that was to raise him to such heights]. Knowing, as we do, Zola's attitude to press censorship and ecclesiastical scheming, we realize that, in his eyes, his hero is a very ambivalent character. Clorinde's verdict, on the last page of the novel, may well convey something of the author's own fascination for power and powerful men: "Vous êtes tout de même d'une jolie force, vous" (2, p. 369) [You are, all the same, a force to be reckoned with] but, at the same time, the author has given us sufficient information to allow us to conclude that, all things considered, Eugène is just a more "classy," more dignified, and sanitized version of his father, Pierre, and his brother, Saccard.

In earlier volumes of the series, we may have admired Zola's arcadian sequences, his developing gift for panoramic social evocations, his colorful street-scenes, or his snatches of cutting satire, but *Son Excellence* is written by a man of growing stature, a novelist with a wider, more mature, and objective view of the world, a thinker who is more honestly coming to grips with his own gifts, faults, and limitations. Eugène is no messiah, and neither is Zola himself, but both remain impressive.

If ever there was a situation that needed redemption, which called desperately for a messiah—human or divine—it is the one that unfolds for Gervaise in *L'Assommoir* (1877), in volume 7 of Zola's cycle.

The heroine has recently arrived in Paris (she is the daughter of Antoine Macquart and "Fine"). Her idle husband, Auguste Lantier, has sqandered his maternal inheritance in a mere six weeks and has sent most household items to the pawnbroker's, before walking out on her and the children. To make ends meet, Gervaise turns washerwoman. Over the steaming tubs, she tells her fellow-workers of her lost paradise back in Provence:

Nous allions à la rivière. Ça sentait meilleur qu'ici. . . . Il fallait voir, il y avait un coin sous les arbres avec de l'eau claire qui coulait. . . . Vous savez, à Plassans. (2, p. 388)

[We used to go to the river [Zola could well be thinking of the Torse that ran past the back of his first school in Aix]. It smelled better than here. . . . You should have seen it: there was a spot under the trees with clear, running water . . . at Plassans, you know.]

This idyllic picture provides the reader with a point of departure, a standard against which future developments may be measured.

Through much of her short life, Gervaise will be under attack: from her predatory, parasitic husband; from petty, spiteful neighbors and in-laws; from her degrading milieu; from the machinations of fate and, above all, from the ever-present, all-pervading curse of alcoholism. The latter will be symbolized by Père Colombe's mysterious still, a kind of monstrous materialization of evil, a veritable "cuisine de diable" (2, p. 404) [devil's kitchen].

Gervaise, then, is beset with enemies and dangers. Hardly has she been delivered from Lantier, the smooth talker, the half-baked republican revolutionary, who seduces a series of women only to prey on their substance, than she has to confront the spite of Virginie, come to the washhouse to taunt her with Lantier's defection to Adèle (Virginie's sister). After marrying Coupeau and gaining a measure of security, Gervaise will be exposed to the jealousy of her sisters-in-law. Apparently, she will even run afoul of fate itself, in the form of the old woman who watches Coupeau at work on the rooftop of the hospital, hoping to experience the "grosse émotion" (powerful emotion) of seeing him fall: " . . . comme si elle espérait de le voir tomber d"une minute à l'autre" (2, p. 480) [. . . as though she hoped to see him fall, from one moment to the next]. After the accident, which will start Gervaise's slide from prosperity to ruin, the little old lady will calmly close the window on a task well done: "Cependant, en face, la petite vieille, comme satisfaite, fermait tranquillement sa fenêtre" (2, p. 483) [Meanwhile, across the way, the little old lady calmly shut her window, as though satisfied]. Many writers have traced the degrading effect on Gervaise of her steamy laundry and discerned the intangible, collective pressure of the neighborhood that virtually drives her back into the arms of Lantier (Virginie lending a hand). Commentators also stress the role played by alcohol that first traps convalescent Coupeau and finally overcomes his demoralized wife: caught in a situation apparently without issue, easygoing Gervaise has already lapsed into slovenliness and self-indulgence.

So much for the villains—personal, social, or supernatural—that play a part in Gervaise's slow decline into deprivation and death. Apart from these negative forces, there are what one might call the nonsaviors—the characters whose desire or whose duty is to offer help, but who fail to do so. Coupeau, Gervaise's second husband, means well: he has no intention of repeating his father's abuse of alcohol; at the beginning of the novel, he pledges support to abandoned Gervaise: " . . . elle était une bonne et brave femme, elle pouvait compter sur lui, le jour où elle serait dans la peiné" (2, p. 378) [. . . she was a good, kind woman; she could count on him if ever she fell on hard times]. The irony of that promise emerges all too clearly on a second reading of the text.

The priests featured in the novel may be placed in the same category of useless saviors. Pierre Ouvrard, in his *Zola et le prêtre*, is not proud of his fictional colleague, the shabbily dressed old priest who bargains with Coupeau over a five-franc nuptial mass[5] and then rushes through the ceremony, forgetful of his mission to bless and consacrate, as though the Almighty were absent at the time:

> . . . le prêtre à l'air maussade promenait vivement ses mains sèches sur les têtes inclinés de Gervaise et de Coupeau, et semblait les unir au milieu d'un déménagement, pendant une absence du Bon Dieu, entre deux messes sérieuses. (2, p. 436)

> [The sullen-looking priest moved his hands swiftly over the bowed heads of Gervaise and Coupeau, and it seemed as if he were blessing their union in the middle of moving house, while God was absent between two more important masses.]

The priest who officiates at the funeral of old Mme Coupeau will be just as mechanical, uncaring, and money-minded.

Ironically, Gervaise's own indulgence toward others' faults and her compassion for the helpless, will contribute to her downfall. At the critical moment, she fails to pull convalescent Coupeau into line; even as she begins her own descent into ruin, she offers her home to Coupeau's aged mother and takes pity on starving old Bru. Come the day, however, no one will offer her aid. The landlord, nouveau riche Marescot, shows her no mercy; the avaricious Lorilleux couple refuse to give her ten sous. Only Bazouge, the undertaker, after foreshadowing to her the deliverance of death at various stages of the plot, will speak a word of consolation over her dead body: "Va, t'es heureuse. Fais dodo, ma belle!" (2, p. 796) [There, you're happy. Sleep tight, my pretty one!] But we have forgotten Goujet, the kindly neighbor across the landing. His name contains the German "gut" (good) or even "Gott" (God), but it is also close to the French "goujon," meaning both "gudgeon" (= little river-fish, small fry) and "pin or "bolt," a possible allusion to his craft as a metalworker.

From the outset, he is presented as a paradoxical figure, a combination of strength and weakness. On the one hand, he is described as a colossus of Herculean strength, on the other as a timid, shy man who lives with his mother (in a "vraie chambre de jeune fille" [a veritable girl's room]) and is going to get married to please her. He begins his role as a potential messiah, when he saves Coupeau during the uprising of December 1861. Then, when Coupeau's accident has eaten up all of Gervaise's savings and she frets over her lost opportunity of acquiring her own shop, Goujet comes to the rescue a second time by offering her a loan. However, it is only when Gervaise visits her secret admirer in his workshop at the foundry that he reveals his godlike qualities. Zola marks the occasion by building up a scene full of mythological allusions. First the author reminds us of Goujet's gigantic strength, describing him as "un colosse en repos, tranquille dans sa force" (2, p. 527) (a colossus at rest in the quiet calm of his strength). Is Goujet a Herculean hero, we wonder, who can clean up the Augean stables of the Parisian slums and chain up Cerberus, the hound of death that bays at the Coupeaus? Then, as the robust worker is lit up by the fire of his forge, his short hair, his blond beard hanging down in ringlets, his whole face and massive neck are transformed into a resplendent head of gold and he truly enters into the glory of his nickname, Gueule-d'Or [Golden Gullet]: " . . . il faisait de la clarté autour de lui, il devenait beau, tout-puissant, comme un bon Dieu" (2, p. 533) [he projected light all around him, he became beautiful, all-powerful, like an image of God]. At that stage, the capital D in "bon Dieu" suggests that Gervaise is facing God the Father himself, but almost immediately he takes on a pagan identity. As Goujet works at his anvil, the sexual undertones of his hammering transfix and satisfy Gervaise, while the rain of sparks reproduces the shower of gold in which Zeus visited Danae and engendered his son Perseus. In the end, when Goujet and his companion, Bec-Salé [Saucy Gob], are vying for Gervaise's love and the former prevails by first producing a large bolt, Zola turns him into the god Vulcan—appropriately enough, given the smithy setting, but rather ironically too, if one remembers that Vulcan lost his love, Venus, to Mars, the god of war (Goujet is about to lose Gervaise to the returning Lantier).

Philip D. Walker is not deceived by this mythological parade and insists on seeing in Goujet a further embodiment of what he calls "the redemptive lover": ". . . as such he is given Christlike attributes and associated with . . . whiteness, light, true love, self-sacrifice, even the sacramental bread and wine."[6] (The last detail is an allusion to Goujet bringing in Gervaise from the cold and feeding her, after she has tried to prostitute herself.) This study espouses Walker's views.

Speculating for a moment on the sudden flowering of mythological allusions and the mingling of Christian and pagan references that we have already noted in Son Excellence Eugène Rougon, we could comment that, perhaps, Zola is trying to impress cultured colleagues, like the Goncourt brothers and Flaubert, with his classical expertise. In addition, the present writer inclines to the view that Zola, as a self-respecting agnostic or atheist, may be becoming self-conscious about his endless lineup of potential, flawed, or false Christ-figures and that he is introducing a classical Greek or Roman nomenclature to hide the embarrassing truth.

Goujet may win Gervaise symbolically, in his Vulcan disguise: "Il lui prit la main, comme s'il l'avait conquise" (2, p. 535) [He took her hand, as though he had made a conquest of her] but in his normal, down-to-earth persona, he can only offer her white roses for her name day or silently hold her hand when they have their poignant, pathetic love-scene under a dead tree, on a piece of wasteland, while a dismally bleating goat circles around the stake to which it is tethered. The symbolism of the scene may be left safely to the imagination of the reader: "Vrai, murmura Gervaise, on se croirait à la campagne. . . . Ils allèrent s'asseoir sous l'arbre mort" (2, p. 614) [It's true, murmured Gervaise, you would think you were in the country. . . . They went to sit down under the dead tree]. Admittedly, Goujet proposes to run off with Gervaise (to Belgium), but when she declines, he lacks the drive to convince her. Throwing dandelions into her basket certainly will not win the day! Before the end of the chapter, Lantier manages to seduce Gervaise—a situation to which Goujet can react only by pining and falling ill.

At the funeral of Gervaise's mother-in-law, he will be there to offer help, but his words—"Tout est fini" [Everything is over]—have a very different ring from Christ's dying words—"It is finished"—while his final kindness of offering her food does not save her from a wretched death. All he can do, at their last meeting, is to respectfully kiss her forehead, where a more virile and dynamic lover would have snatched her away in extremis from the realm of darkness, vice, drunkenness, and death. It is true, then, that Gervaise's tragedy is due as much to fate (the accident) and to the effeminacy of her platonic lover as it is to heredity and milieu.

Goujet is another one in the series of potential messiahs who fail because they are too pure, too weak, and too passive. As for the paradoxical evocation on which our analysis of Goujet opened—the powerful colossus and the mother-dominated "namby-pamby"—could it be that Zola is using his portrayal as a mirror in which to gain understanding of his own puzzling amalgam of strength and neurosis, heroic courage and emotional frailty, openness to the life-force and fear of death? Is Zola trying to ascertain, in fictional projection, whether he himself is a genuine, flawed, or false messiah? That certainly seems to be suggested by such an obsessively repeated scenario.

In his next work, Une Page d'amour [A Page of Love] (1888), Zola perfects the art of disguising his messiah: he presents him in the guise of the likable Dr. Deberle, a man no one, at first sight, would suspect of messianic dimensions, since he is a self-confessed atheist. A second Christ-figure, frail, neurotic, morbidly jealous Jeanne, who suffers from fits, seems to be an equally unlikely choice. The former ultimately fails to save anybody; the latter appears to prevail through her expiatory death, but it turns out that the new life she wins for the beneficiaries is an existence stripped of genuine self-giving and communion and, therefore, of content and meaning. Jeanne will cast new light on Zola's disillusioned vision of the crucified Christ.

The plot of this novel, the eighth in the Rougon-Macquart cycle, is summed up adequately by the author himself in his letter to Van Santen Kolff, dated 8 June 1892: " . . . un coup de passion, un amour qui naît et qui passe imprévu, sans laisser de trace"[7] [. . . a flash of passion, a love that comes into being and dies, unforeseen and without leaving a trace]. The love story features Hélène Grandjean (née Mouret), the widowed mother of young Jeanne. What Zola's synopsis fails to convey is the ravaging, disintegrating effect of passion on the life of a hitherto virtuous, devoted mother (cf. Marthe Mouret in La Conquête de Plassans) who is induced to err to the extent of neglecting and harshly treating her ailing daughter—in the words of Pierre Marotte: "On voit ainsi une mère aimante rudoyer et repousser sa fille"[8] [So we see a loving mother treat her daughter harshly and reject her]. When Hélène's affair has fatal consequences for her daughter, she repents, stifles her passion, and returns to her former respectable, but sterile, way of life.

Zola has struck upon a dramatic "entrée en matière" [exposition]: Hélène, peacefully asleep in her blue-tinged bedroom, is rudely awakened at 2:00 A.M. by the convulsions of her eleven-year-old daughter. The panic-stricken mother cannot raise her own doctor and chances upon Dr. Deberle who comes at once. He arrives in time to save Jeanne from a second fit:

> Elle était retombée au milieu du lit, le corps allongé, les bras étendus, la tête soutenue par l'oreiller et penchée sur la poitrine.

> [She had fallen back full-length in the middle of the bed, with her arms extended. Her head, which was propped up by the pillow, had fallen forward onto her chest.]

and in case we have not recognized the traditional pose, Zola adds: "On aurait dit un Christ enfant. . . ." (2, p. 806) [You would have said a youthful version of Christ]. Zola's "notes préparatoires" [preparatory notes] allow us to conclude that, at this stage, the Jeanne-Jesus association makes the child simply a symbol of human suffering, although we should note that it is precisely this suffering that has brought Hélène into contact with Deberle and that thus offers her a chance to escape from a life of virtuous, respectable tedium and emptiness. The strong, healthy, impressive, Juno-like matron has already roused the doctor's admiration:

> Mais ce qui étonnait le docteur, c'était la nudité superbe de cette mère . . . elle gardait une majesté, une hauteur d'honnêteté et de pudeur qui la laissait chaste sous ce regard d'homme, où montait un grand trouble. (2, p. 810)

> [But what astonished the doctor was the superb nakedness of this mother . . . she retained a majesty, a lofty air of uprightness and modesty that kept her chaste under the gaze of this man, whose eyes reflected his growing agitation.]

Subsequent chapters sketch in Hélène's Marseille origins and her short-lived marriage to a husband she did not love. We meet Deberle's flippant society wife and gather from the wise, kindly abbé Jouve that the doctor is a straightforward, charitable, faithful man, although not at all religious.

It would be tempting to trace Hélène's slow rebirth to life, the memorable scene on the swing when the woman, still unaware of her love for the doctor, symbolically makes love to the sun, the platonic stage of growing intimacy, the scheming of la mère Fétu (=fate), the old woman whose pious poses and matchmaking efforts are anything but disinterested, Hélène's sublimation of her love in religious fervor (Marthe Mouret style), her enlightenment by Abbé Jouve who has seen overardent ladies before, and her eventual surrender to the very night of passion from which she is trying to save adulterous Juliette Deberle—but all that can only be a background to the concerns of this study.

Of the five panoramas of Paris that Zola tries hard to integrate into his plot, we shall retain only the one where mother and daughter contemplate a "ciel de fournaise" [fiery sky] at sunset (just after Deberle has declared his love):

> Alors toutes deux, la mère et la fille, demeuraient muettes, en face de Paris incendié. Il leur restait plus inconnu encore, ainsi éclairé par les nuées saignantes, pareil à quelque ville des légendes expiant sa passion sous une pluie de feu. (2, p. 911)

> [Then both mother and daughter remained silent, watching Paris on fire. The city seemed stranger to them than ever, lit as it was by blood-red clouds, like some legendary town expiating its passions in a rain of fire.]

The allusion to burning Sodom not only prefigures Hélène's coming confrontation with the blaze of passion, but it introduces the theme of Apocalypse and expiation that will reach its climax at the end of *La Débâcle*. In that novel, as Paris burns, the whole nation will be seen to atone for the folly, extravagance, and immorality of the Second Empire. But that vision will not be recorded until some fourteen years later. Meanwhile Zola is already associating the loose life-style to which Hélène is being initiated by the Parisian bourgeoisie with the imminent destiny of France as a whole. Both for Hélène and for France, it will be a matter, metaphorically speaking, of a night of passion followed by a morning of ashes:

> Tout d'un coup, il y eut une reprise formidable de l'incendie, Paris jeta une dernière flambée qui éclaira jusqu'aux faubourgs perdus. Puis, il sembla qu'une cendre grise tombait, et les quartiers restèrent debout, légers et noirâtres, comme des charbons éteints. (2, p. 912)

> [All of a sudden the fire broke out again furiously. Paris threw up a last flare that lit up everything as far as the lost suburbs. Then it was as if gray ash were falling and the various zones of the city remained standing, weightless and charred, like burned-out coals.]

At this stage we must concentrate on the apocalyptic sunset's application to the heroine. The fire of passion, she will realize, can be an overwhelming experience, with its total suspension of time and place, its obliteration of personal identity, but it does not last and it is not love. The poetic passage, later on in the novel, in which Zola evokes the night of passion closes on the surprising obervation: "Jamais ils ne s'étaient moins aimés que ce jour-là" (2, p. 1023) [Never had they loved each other less than on that day]. A corresponding flavor of bitter ashes pervades the conclusion of the novel: the life-style to which Hélène will revert, after her forgetfulness of duty has indirectly caused the death of her child, is fittingly prefigured by the ash-covered, charred shells of city blocks that mother and daughter have discerned in the lurid fires of the evening sky.

If we seem to have digressed momentarily into the theme of Apocalypse and expiation, this is for a good reason: both in Scripture and in Zola's mythical cosmogony, renewal cannot come before a cleansing, expiatory conflagration. Messiah's kingdom must come by way of Apocalypse. The desolate note on which *Une Page d'amour* closes shows that Zola has not yet attained that more hopeful vision that will begin to emerge in *Le Docteur Pascal* and triumph in *Les Quatre evangiles*.

Meanwhile Zola's horizons are darkened by a messiah (Deberle) who fails and by a Christ-figure who brings a redemption of a most dubious sort. Jeanne may look like "un enfant Christ" [a child-Christ], but she hardly shows the gentle submission that Luke ascribes to the young Jesus who obeys his earthly parents and grows up in the favor of God and man (cf. Luke 2:51–52). Her morbid jealousy first fastens on to mild, naive M. Rambaud, the decent solid citizen whom l'abbé Jouve proposes to Hélène as a husband. After Deberle has saved Jeanne from a second, nearly fatal episode of convulsions, she senses the growing intimacy of mother and doctor and turns into a fully fledged tormenter, most attentive, now, to M. Rambaud, but cold and hostile to the doctor. In the end, when her mother is so taken over by her passion, that she roughly pushes aside her clinging daughter, the twelve-year-old, who is just entering puberty and is not at all ready for the glimpses of passion that have come her way, feels abandoned and betrayed. Capitulating to the forces of resentment, hatred, and death within her, she promptly falls victim to a form of galloping tuberculosis. This time the doctor, who has twice saved her in the past, remains powerless, for he has become part of the problem. How can one accept help from an adulterous messiah?

Jeanne has certainly had to walk a via dolorosa [sorrowful road to Calvary], but she is hardly a saint, let alone a genuine Christ-figure. In spite of this, her death could be construed as expiatory, since it becomes the main factor in her mother's giving up her illicit passion for the doctor and returning to the path of duty. "Allez-vous en," she whispers into her lover's ear, "vous voyez bien que nous l'avons tuée" (2, p. 1062) [Go away; you can see only too well that we've killed her].

As foreshadowed in the introduction to this section, the Jeanne-Jesus nexus is significant in that it casts fresh light on Zola's vision of the suffering Christ. When we glimpsed him dying in the early story "Le Sang" or stretched on the Cross contemplated by Serge in his Les Artauds church, he was just another symbol of human suffering or at most a failed redeemer. In the present novel, however, Zola seems to allow for suffering to have an atoning, expiatory effect. This impression is strengthened by a parallel development in the plot: the sudden death of the kindly and pure abbé Jouve, we are told, somehow helps Hélène to accept the hand of his half-brother, M. Rambaud—a decision that virtually restores her to her former life-style of sobriety and virtue. But let us not be deceived by appearances. Pierre Marotte is not altogether accurate when he claims:

> Quoique tout arrière-plan religieux soit absent, dans le cas d'Hélène, du moins explicitement, tout se passe comme si sa "passion" était compensée, punie et rachetée, par la "passion," le calvaire de Jeanne.[9]

> [Although there is an absence of any religious background, at least explicitly, where Hélène is concerned, everything happens as if her "passion" were compensated for, punished and redeemed by the "passion," the Calvary of Jeanne.]

Young Jeanne and the priest do not just redeem Hélène and Henri from a life of sin, but rather from life itself. For the woman, it is a matter of paradise lost, a return to youth and happiness thwarted, the prospect of a long and weary road ahead. Her "beau calme" [beautiful calm] is of the wintry variety, as suggested by the snowy backdrop of Paris. She has married Rambaud without love, in a state of distraught resignation. In the same way, the doctor has returned to his flighty, superficial wife (Juliette) and has actually given her a new child, but he hardly projects the image of a succesful messiah: he has not saved Jeanne from physical death, nor her mother from a living death. He has not even saved himself.

As we have followed Zola in his gyrations around the messianic myth, we have seen things old and new. Eugène's posturing as a great, messianic leader, we found, was simply a glamorized reenactment of the policies of his father, Pierre, and of his half-brother, Saccard. Goujet, the ineffectual savior in L'Assommoir, is no great improvement on his prototype, Claude in *La Confession* or on Florent in *Le Ventre de Paris*; Dr. Deberle, in *Une Page d'amour*, comes up against the same ill will (in Jeanne) that frustrated the messianic dreams of Queen Primevère in "Aventures du grand Sidoine et du petit Médéric." However, we have noted some innovations as well. The priest Serge Mouret turns away from a religion of grace and compassion to a cult of death and finds himself being pursued by the choleric, implacable Jehovah caricature of the Old Testament (Brother Archangias). Eugène absorbs some of that thunder and lightning in his style of leadership, as Zola studies the temptations of power and glory. Possibly embarrassed by his preoccupation with messianic figures, we speculated, Zola begins to mix in elements of pagan mythology—fittingly enough, in the case of his excellency Eugène, but somewhat surprisingly in the less than virile weakling, Goujet. The latter allowed us a possible insight into the enigma of Zola's own amalgam of greatness and emotional frailty.

The main innovation and, paradoxically, the most promising, is the author's emerging attraction to the theme of Apocalypse. The latter is not a cheering prospect in itself and, as yet, our author cannot look beyond its devastating implications, but it can become an element of atonement and rebirth. Zola will never have much taste for the nihilistic solution of "tabula rasa," wholesale destruction in the hope of a better world to come, but when Apocalypse takes the form of expiation, of a cleansing, purifying fire, the author will ultimately decide, it may become an instrument of renewal in the hands of Messiah. Dr. Pascal cannot sustain that role after the conflagration of *La Débâcle*, but the descendants of the new Pierre, Pierre Fromont, the one-time priest of *Les Trois villes*, will be untouched by the flaws, errors, and ulterior motives that disqualified most messianic candidates in *Les Rougon-Macquart*. It is they, the saviors of the new, resurrected France, the aging writer will proclaim, who are called to realize the messianic dream of fertility, prosperity, and social justice. The reader needs to keep this in mind, if he is not to be unduly depressed by the "Great Whore" (*Nana*), the great apostasy of laity and clergy alike (*Pot-bouille*), the upsurge of exploitative and soulless commercialism (*Au Bonheur des Dames*), and the vain struggle against death (*La Joie de vivre*) that will occupy our attention in the next chapter.

6
The Great Apostasy

ONE WOULD HAVE TO BE INGENIOUS INDEED TO DETECT THE PRESENCE of messianic characters in Zola's *Nana* (1880). With some twisting and straining, one could perhaps highlight the short-lived salutary effect of young Georges Hugon on Nana, while she is enjoying the unspoiled countryside of La Mignotte (near Orléans): "Et elle tomba en vierge dans les bras de cet enfant, en face de la belle nuit" (2, p. 1239) [Facing the beauty of the night sky, she fell into the arms of this boy as though she were a virgin] but, then again, that union does not exactly hold messianic promise for the boy (it is going to destroy him) and, in any case, Nana's metaphoric virginity does not last: a glimpse of the former courtesan, Irma d'Anglars, become a "virtuous," respectable church-going châtelaine, is enough to make her think again and opt for Count Muffat, for he has the means to make such a dream a reality. For Nana, the glamour of life outweighs the charm of youthful love. And as for the retired solicitor, Théophile Venot, whose names suggest both love of God and poison, the man by whom Muffat will finally be welcomed back into his numbing, repressive form of religion, he is another savior à la Jeanne (*Une Page d'amour*) with nothing to offer but a living death.

Why then should *Nana* be included in a survey of Zola's messianic aspirations? Because, as a mythical projection of irresponsible, dissolving, corrupting, destructive sexuality, she is one of the cardinal points of the author's notion of evil (the others being selfishness, materialism, and the lust for power). According to his first Ebauche, Zola intended to portray Nana as "une des formes éclatantes de loin et séductrices du mal" [one of the seductive forms of evil—one that is striking even from a distance]. (He is no doubt a little hyperbolic—as well as crude—when he adds: "Il n'y a que le cul et la religion"[1] [In life, there's only your ass and religion]. As sensuality incarnate, Nana is comparable to the Great Whore in the Book of Revelation who, together with

Antichrist (her male counterpart) and the False Prophet, inaugurates the last days and calls down the divine fire of Apocalypse that will cleanse the earth for the coming of Messiah. To Zola's mind, Nana symbolizes the decadence of the Second Empire that led to the apocalyptic disasters of 1870. We shall see, in addition, that Nana, who has nothing holy or redemptive about her, unwittingly plays a diagnostic, cathartic, and cautionary role, because she exposes the evilness of evil, because she helps to manifest the mystery of iniquity that is at work in the individual, in society and, for those with a metaphysical perspective, in the cosmos.

Given the complexity and the ambiguity of Zola's presentation of Nana, the most prudent approach is to impose some order by simply following Zola's scenario and to do so by the light of observations made by those who have already explored the field.

As soon as Nana makes her debut on the stage of the Variety theater in Paris, Zola mentions her inability to act or sing, but then concentrates on her disarming "charme de gamine" [mischievous, tomboyish charm]—the good-natured, playful side of the girl who does not seek evil and is not herself motivated by lust. Before long, however, he is making references to omnipotence and intoxication, as though Nana wielded a power that transcended her own sex appeal:

> ... cette grosse fille ... dégageait autour d'elle une odeur de vie, une toute-puissance de femme, dont le public se grisait. (2, p. 1113)
>
> [... from this big girl there emanated the scent of life, an all-powerful femininity that the audience found intoxicating.]

Does Roger Ripoll explain this mystery adequately when he comments in terms of "impulsions élémentaires" [basic impulses] or "l'action des forces primitives"?[2] [the working of primeval forces]. Is it just a matter of elemental forces such as sexual desire manifesting themselves through Nana or is something more cosmic involved? It is particularly during the final act of *La Belle Vénus*, that we pick up the disturbing shift in Nana from "bonne enfant" [a good-natured girl] to a dimension that opens up "l'inconnu du désir" (2, p. 1118) [the mystery of desire]. A little more hip-swaying on the part of our half-naked Venus, and she takes possession of her male spectators and turns into a living myth—the mystery of nature, beauty, and sexuality that holds sovereign power of life and death, creation and destruction, while itself remaining an impassive, uninvolved spectator:

Et Nana ... restait victorieuse avec sa chair de marbre, son sexe assez fort pour détruire tout ce monde et n'en être pas entamé. (2, p. 1120)

[And Nana ... was victorious, with her marble flesh, her sex that was potent enough to destroy this whole world and yet remain intact.]

Flaubert was quite right when, in his often-quoted letter, he asserted: "Nana tourne au mythe sans cesser d'être une femme"[3] [Nana turns into myth without ceasing to be a woman]. It is, of course, highly ironic that Zola should have set out to destroy the Romantic myth of the pure, tender-hearted, lovable prostitute— "toute cette sentimentalité, tout cet enguirlandage du vice[4] [all that sentimentality, all that decking out of vice with flowery garlands]—only to create a myth on a cosmic scale himself.

Chapters 2 to 5 introduce us to the sordid world of Nana's financial problems and her endless string of bedfellows. We meet Paul Daguenet, the current "regular"; the wealthy Jewish banker, Steiner, who pricks his finger on a pin in Nana's skirt without realizing that it omens a far more serious bloodletting to come; the comic half-shy, half-impetuous Georges Hugon; Marquis Chouard, the seventy-year-old walking skeleton who will later help to symbolize Nana's secret alliance with death; and Count Muffat himself, poised between his inhibiting upbringing and the powerful attraction of Nana. Rather oddly, the count has never been able to warm to his hitherto virtuous wife, even though she will be revealed before long as an aristocratic double of Nana. For the moment, Muffat is still being held back by his moral guide, Théophile Venot, but already he is unable to resist planting a kiss on Nana's neck when he visits her offstage in her dressing room. No wonder he already associates her with demonic temptation: "Nana, confusément, était le diable. . . ." (2, p. 1213) [Nana, in a confusing sort of way, was the Devil]. Out of nostalgia for the lost innocence of his youth, for the sake of perspective in the evolution of the plot and, maybe, to demonstrate that sexuality need not be linked invariably with adultery and promiscuity, Zola inserts the idyllic episode at La Mignotte, where Nana indulges in her evanescent dream of young love, motherhood, and closeness to nature. Perhaps Chantal Bertrand-Jennings goes too far when, in this fleeting compensation for a life of gross immorality, she discerns vestiges of "une noblesse de coeur" [a nobility of soul] or "certaines qualités des traditionnelles femmes honnêtes"[5] [certain qualities of traditionally decent women]. More appropriately, Roger Ripoll points out parallel interludes in *La Confession* and in *Madeleine Férat*:

> C'est la même rémission fugitive, le même retour à l'innocence au contact de la nature, le même bonheur aussitôt perdu que goûté.[6]
>
> [It is the same fleeting remission, the same return to innocence when there is contact with nature, the same happiness that is no sooner savored than lost.]

reminding us that Zola espoused the old myth according to which sexuality can bring both the Garden of Eden and the Fall, Heaven and hell. It is characteristic that Zola should close the idyllic chapter 6 on Nana finally sleeping with Muffat—"sans plaisir" [without any pleasure].

In chapter 7, the author begins to spell out his conscious intentions as Nana makes her new lover read to her Fauchery's article on "La Mouche d'or" [The golden fly]. For the journalist (alias Zola, his Ebauche shows us), Nana represents a "force de la nature" [a force of nature]. She avenges the exploited proletariat by passing on its acquired ferment of destruction to the higher classes:

> ... une mouche couleur de soleil, envolée de l'ordure ... qui empoisonnait les hommes rien qu'en se posant sur eux, dans les palais où elle entrait par les fenêtres. (2, p. 1270)
>
> [A fly the color of the sun that had taken off from the filth and poisoned men merely by alighting on them, in palaces where it flew in through the window.]

The vivid golden fly image carries Egyptian associations: it is vaguely suggestive of the mythical dung beetle (or sun-scarab) and evokes the biblical plague of flies that infested the peasants' fields and Pharaoh's palaces alike. Chantal Bertrand-Jennings gives an interesting slant to Zola's notion of Nana as avenger of the working class: she sees Nana as an angel of death who "s'en va châtier, dans une atmosphère de Jugement dernier, les bourgeois et les aristocrats du Second Empire" [who, in an atmosphere reminiscent of the Last Judgment, goes out to castigate the bourgeois and aristocrats of the Second Empire], before disappearing herself in the purifying fire.[7] Her comment is consistent with the view, expressed in the introduction to this section, that Nana may be seen as the female counterpart of Antichrist.

Zola continues in a mythical or biblical vein: the sustained "Mouche d'or" metaphor is followed immediately by the notorious scene of Nana posing in front of her mirror. Entering into the mind of the bewitched but guilt-stricken Muffat, the author reports that the count sees his mistress as a new Jezebel or as the personification of lust and church infidelity that St. John calls "the Great Whore": "Il songeait à son ancienne horreur de la femme, au monstre de l'Ecriture, lubrique, sentant le fauve" (2, p. 1271) [He thought about his former horror of women, about the lustful monster of Scripture, with her musky, bestial scent]. We have, of course, already met "Lubrica" in the lurid, fanatic imagination of Geneviève (*Madeleine Férat*) and she will be featured again, under a different name, in the late novel *Travail*, the second of the *Quatre Evangiles*, where she will meet her appointed end, leaving the hero free to realize his messianic dreams.

We shall pass lightly over Nana's taming by the actor Fontan, her falling upon hard times, and her lesbian involvement with down-and-out Satin—all of which Zola has included to cover the full range of a courtesan's life. Nana's disastrous attempt to play a respectable countess at the Variety theater serves as a symbolic prelude to the last stage of her life—her second ascension to glory and her lamentable end.

Having practically bled dry Steiner, Nana renews her depredations of Count Muffat who sets her up in a sumptuous Parisian mansion. Meanwhile Vandeuvres, another count, is helped along to bankruptcy as well. Zola is beginning to gather in his mythical threads for a spectacular finale. Nana's role as destroyer becomes increasingly obvious—a point not missed by Ripoll when he comments: "Pourrir, salir, casser, les termes reviennent sans cesse pour qualifier l'action destructrice exercée par Nana"[8] [Rot, sully, break—these terms recur continuously to describe the destruction wrought by Nana]. Her destructive frenzy is juxtaposed with a mythical divinization. Seated triumphantly in her flower-covered open carriage at the races, she is toasted by a crowd of worshipers: ". . . elle leva son verre plein, dans son ancienne pose de Vénus victorieuse" (2, p. 1390) [She raised her full glass in her old pose of Venus triumphant]. This fairly mild mythological allusion yields to a more intense scene, when the horse named after her has won its race:

> Et la cour de Nana s'élargissait toujours, le mouvement qui avait fait de sa voiture le centre de la pelouse, s'achevant en apothéose, la reine Vénus dans le coup de folie de ses sujets. (2, p. 1405)

[And Nana's court grew ever larger; the surge of excitement that had made her carriage the focal point of the public enclosure culminated in apotheosis—Queen Venus amid her frenzied subjects.]

Nana, then, is not only a destroyer, but she reigns as a queen and sits enthroned as a pagan divinity. Into this increasingly complex web, Zola now weaves his earlier mythical thread of La Mouche d'or—Nana as a spreader of corruption. Chapter 12 features a ball to celebrate the coming wedding of Muffat's daughter, Estelle. The activities, comments, and atmosphere evoked all proclaim the decadence of an epoch headed for collapse, Nana's spirit hovering over it like some gigantic vampire-bat:

> ... la valse sonnait le glas d'une vieille race; pendant que Nana, invisible, épandue au-dessus du bal avec ses membres souples, décomposait ce monde, le pénétrant du ferment de son odeur flottant dans l'air chaud, sur le rythme canaille de la musique (2, p. 1429–30)

> [... the waltz sounded the death knell of an old race, while an invisible Nana, spreading out her lithe limbs over the ballroom, made this world decompose, invading it with the ferment of her scent that floated on the warm air, on the vulgar rhythm of the music.]

Intensifying his mythical perspective yet again, in chapter 13, Zola is no longer content with metaphoric apotheosis for his central character. He now attributes to Nana the occultist dream of having a bedroom shaped like a tabernacle—the holy shrine of the Israelites where Jehovah dwelt between the wings of the cherubim:

> Nana rêvait un lit comme il n'en existait pas, un trône, un autel, où Paris viendrait adorer sa nudité souveraine. (2, p. 1434)

> [Nana dreamed of a bed the like of which did not exist, a throne, an altar where [all] Paris would come to worship her sovereign nudity.]

It should be noted that, by now, Nana has assumed into her person all four cardinal points that encompass Zola's notion of evil—selfishness, materialism, lust, and the quest for power. Interestingly, it is this passage that serves as a focal point for many commentators: "... le sexe de la femme présenté dans un tabernacle diabolique" [... female genitalia displayed in a diabolic tabernacle] writes Henri Troyat in his recent work on Zola.[9] And a century earlier, Paul Alexis, who usually does not think it is his role to analyze plot or philosophical content, homes in on this same dream of Nana's as the crux (no pun intended) of Zola's thought:

> ... montrer, dans une sorte de chapelle ardente, au fond d'un tabernacle, le sexe de la femme, et, autour, un peuple d'hommes prosternés, ruinés, vidés et abêtis, tel était son sujet.[10]

> [... to show, inside a tabernacle, in a sort of capella ardente [chapel ablaze with candles], the sex of woman and around it a crowd of men who had been ruined, drained, and rendered mindless—such was his subject.]

Phillip D. Walker, who knows his Bible, is moved by the same sacrilegious dream to make the bold statement: "Nana is the Red Whore of Babylon, sitting on the scarlet beast full of blasphemous names"[11]—another view in keeping with our own approach of treating Nana as a kind of female Antichrist, at home in a setting of Apocalypse.

In order to prepare the reader for Nana's occult alliance with death (and to exteriorize his own obsession with lust opening out into an au-delà of darkness and abysmal evil), Zola has Labordette, one of Nana's familiars, suggest the motif of "night unveiled" for one of her bed-ends: "La Nuit enveloppée dans ses voiles, et dont un Faune découvrait l'éclatante nudité" (2, p. 1439) [Night wrapped in her veils, with a faun disclosing her dazzling nakedness]. Simultaneously, the author has Nana step up her destructive campaign to legendary proportions. She has seduced Georges Hugon's brother, Philippe, and involves him in imprisonment for stealing regimental funds; madly jealous, Georges stabs himself with a pair of scissors, when she refuses to marry him; Vandeuvres burns himself to death in his stables and four other men are shown to be approaching ruin—all because of Nana.

Thereupon Zola is ready to reveal his innermost beliefs about the nature and scope of human sexuality, as he once again asserts the intimate nexus between orgasm and religious ecstasy. Muffat begins to understand that, for him, Nana has usurped the place of God. Zola clearly agrees: commenting on Muffat's desire for oblivion or self-obliteration, he equates his character's experiences of Nana with his experiences of God:

> La femme le possédait avec le despotisme jaloux d'un Dieu de colère, le terrifiant, lui donnant des secondes de joie aiguës comme des spasmes, pour des heures d'affreux tourments, des visions d'enfer et d'éternels supplices. C'étaient les mêmes balbutiements, les mêmes prières et les mêmes désespoirs. (2, p. 1459)
>
> [The woman possessed him with the jealous tyranny of a wrathful God, terrifying him, giving him seconds of joy as intense as spasms, in exchange for hours of dreadful anguish, visions of hell, and eternal torment. There were the same stammerings, the same prayers, and the same despair.]

The familiar ring of phrases like "le despotisme jaloux d'un Dieu de colère" [the jealous tyranny of a wrathful God] suggests that, maybe, Muffat's anguished experience of sexuality is not far removed from Zola's own at the time of the Berthe drama. That would be confirmed by the conclusion of the passage (not yet quoted) which perfectly matches the sentiment Zola expressed for his own benefit in his first Ebauche ("Le poème des désirs du mâle, le grand levier qui remue le monde. Il n'y a que le cul et la religion"[12]) [The poem of male desire, the great lever that moves the world. There is only religion and one's ass]: "Il (Muffat) s'abandonnait à la force de l'amour et de la foi, dont le double lévier soulève le monde" (2, p. 1459) [He surrendered himself to the power of love and faith, whose twofold lever raises up the world]. And so Chantal Bertrand-Jenning's felicitous phrase, "la hantise ... du péché de chair puni de mort"[13] [the obsession with carnal sin punishable by death] may well apply both to Muffat and Zola himself: the whole drift of Zola's fiction up to Le Docteur Pascal supports that view.

If this theory is correct, Thomas Mann's reference to Nana as the "Astarte du Second Empire"[14] [Astarte of the Second Empire] needs qualification. True, Nana is at the center of a pseudoreligious cult: her divinization as Venus enthroned allegorizes the hold of sapping, dissolving sensuality over a decadent society, but where the cult priests and priestesses (temple prostitutes) initiated Astarte's devotees into union with the principle of life and procreation, where the orgiastic festivities of the Dionysian cult pursued intoxication and orgasm to effect mystical contact with the divine, Nana can offer nothing but a reversion to base animality—she makes Muffat crawl on all fours—if not an escape into death.

That, in our opinion, is the deeper significance of Muffat's opting out when he catches Nana in bed with the skeletal old marquis Chouard. The count is no doubt disgusted that his mistress should sleep with his decrepit father-in-law (Chouard is the father of Sabine Muffat), but he also realizes that the woman, sprawled across the bed like some shameless idol, is both a carnal substitute for the infinite and a bedfellow of death. The problem for Muffat, however, is that his refuge from passion, the retired solicitor Théophile Venot, for all his religion, is just as dead and lifeless: Muffat is repudiating one form of death to embrace another.

Nana has reached the apex of her destructive career, but refuses to accept responsibility: "C'est leur faute! Moi, je n'y suis pour rien" (2, p. 1470) [It's their fault! I've got nothing to do with it]. Inasmuch as she represents an unthinking force of nature, that self-justification may stand, but the continuation of the passage leaves no doubt about Zola's abhorrence of a life-force that so blatantly feeds on death:

> Comme ces monstres antiques dont le domaine redouté était couvert d'ossements, elle posait ses pieds sur des crânes; et des catastrophes l'entouraient . . . (2, p. 1470)

> [Like those ancient monsters whose dreadful domains were full of bones, she trod on skulls and was surrounded by disasters.]

In the long paragraph that follows, Zola passes in review the various myths that he has embodied in Nana: he presents her again as a bringer of death, repeats his "Mouche d'or" [Golden fly] metaphor, partially justifies her as avenger of the poor, and closes by focusing on the same sublime detachment that characterized her at the end of her first stage-appearance (cf. 2, p. 1120):

> Et tandis que, dans une gloire, son sexe montait et rayonnait sur ses victimes étendues, pareil à un soleil levant qui éclaire un champ de carnage, elle gardait son inconscience de bête superbe, ignorante de sa besogne, bonne fille toujours. (2, p. 1470)

> [And while, in a blaze of glory, her sexuality rose and lit up her outstretched victims, like the rising sun illuminating a bloody battlefield, she herself remained as unaware as a fine-looking beast, unconscious of what she had brought about, still the same good-natured girl.]

Nana is as powerful, as prodigal, as irresponsible, as murderous, as beautiful, and unaware as nature at its worst.

In a passage such as this, Zola clearly takes over from Nana's self-justifying thoughts. Realizing, maybe, that this is not fitting for a champion of naturalism, he shifts his point of view to public perceptions of Nana. After starring in the play *Mélusine*, we are told, she suddenly disappears to Cairo and then Russia and becomes a legend in the popular mind: " . . . elle prenait le rayonnement mystérieux d'une idole chargée de pierres" (2, p. 1472) [she took on the mysterious aura of an idol loaded with jewels]. Almost immediately, however, friends report her return and her coming down with smallpox: she is said to have contracted the disease from her ever-sickly, ever-neglected little boy, Louiset. The juxtaposition of these two details—the exotic, popular illusion and the sordid reality of a hopeless mother, incapable of giving love or nurturing life (Nana has produced a stillborn child as well), suggests that Zola himself needs to discredit the myth he has created. Paris may always remember Nana as she appeared in her last role, sunlike, incandescent, "ainsi qu'un bon Dieu" (2, p. 1476) [like an image of God] but, for the reader, this does not survive the horror of her rotting face, graphically described by Zola:

> Vénus se décomposait. Il semblait que le virus pris par elle dans les ruisseaux sur les charognes tolérées, ce ferment dont elle avait empoisonné un peuple, venait de lui remonter au visage et l'avait pourri. (2, p. 1485)

> [Venus was decomposing. It was as if the virus she had picked up in the gutters, on those rotting corpses to which people turned a blind eye, that ferment with which she had contaminated a whole people, had just now risen to her face and caused it to rot.]

The savage, laconic comment "Vénus se décomposait" [Venus was decomposing] is effective enough, but the author chooses to close his novel on a burst of dramatic irony: through the chanting of the optimistic Parisian crowds in the streets—"A Berlin! à Berlin! à Berlin!" [To Berlin! To Berlin! To Berlin!]—he dramatizes the extent of national misapprehension. The reader knows full well that what lies ahead for France is not glorious victory, but apocalyptic judgment.

In terms of mythical significance, one could not imagine a more complex and ambiguous figure than Zola's Nana. In the same breath, we have found, the author presents her as life-force and agent of death, supreme dynamic principle and destroyer, "bonne fille" [good-natured girl] and incarnation of evil, golden sun, and Queen of the Night. The central "Mouche d'or" motif combines her resplendant beauty with her power of contamination and corruption. On the one hand she is the Great Harlot who desires to be worshiped as God, the seductress who dissolves and undermines the whole structure of society. On the other hand, she becomes an unwitting agent of justice who avenges the oppression of the poor, an agent of destiny who sets the stage for the cleansing fire of Apocalypse.

How did Zola come to write such a many-layered work? Probably his original plan simply got out of hand. He intended to present a panorama of decadence under the Second Empire; he wanted to place Nana at the center of this society to epitomize the forces that were destroying it from within. However, other forces came into play: Armand Lanoux lays no claims to great psychological expertize, but he has no doubts about the double origin of the Nana myth—conscious and unconscious:

> Mais d'où vient ce mythe? De la haine de Zola pour le Second Empire et la bourgeoisie, du refoulement de Zola à l'égard de la femme.[15]

> [But where does this myth come from? From Zola's hatred of the Second Empire, from Zola's repression with regard to women.]

Lanoux notes that the novel is an indictment of a corrupt age, but realizes that "chaste" Zola, somewhat hypocritically, uses his exposure of vice to indulge his own fantasies and obsessions. Jung would have commented that Zola is inclined "to project his own shadow" on a society that, no doubt, contained many immoral elements, but that was not wholly given over to decadence and corruption.

In spite of that ambiguous inspiration, the novel gains universal scope as "le poème des désirs du mâle" [the poem of male desire] (Zola's own phrase[16]) or, in the more precise terms of Chantal Bertrand-Jennings, as a projection of male desires, secret obsessions, and sexual guilt:

> C'est en elle (Nana) que l'homme projette, non seulement ses désirs, mais aussi ses hantises les plus secrètes, sa conscience coupable et son sens du péché. Ce rôle de bouc émissaire qui lui est assigné contribue à la métamorphose de Nana en inquiétante femme fatale.[17]

> [On to her (Nana) the male projects not only his desires, but also his most secret obsessions, his guilty conscience, and his sense of sin.

This role of scapegoat assigned to Nana contributes to her transformation into a disturbing femme fatale.]

A second factor that infiltrates Zola's original design is his prophetic perspective of Apocalypse that casts Nana into the role of Great Whore, gathering in herself all that is evil and allowing it to be dealt with. In that capacity, Nana restores the original, religious meaning of the term *scape-goat*, as used by Chantal Bertrand-Jennings. Zola's mythical figure is more than a convenient depository for individual or collective guilt. As a supreme expression of evil, she becomes an object lesson on the ultimate destination of those who pursue materialism, power, glamour, and selfish pleasure. A society less hypocritical than that of Zola's day could have recognized Nana as a hyperbole of its own sins—to be faced, confessed, eliminated from the psyche, and allowed to perish in the desert for lack of nourishment.

By design or by accident, then, Nana remains an ambiguous figure. She is a type of the destructive social forces in league with Antichrist: through her beauty and allurement, she constitutes a false focal point, a center that does not hold. For all her occult, subversive, corrupting qualities, however, she serves the cause of Messiah by manifesting or "heading up" evil, by unconsciously avenging it and symbolically prefiguring its demise.

Given a better understanding of his tendency to project his own hidden problems onto the world of Nana, Zola might well have been content with exposing the decadent aristocracy. After all, the author of *La Curée* and *Le Ventre de Paris* had not exactly allowed the middle classes to pass uncensored. Had he not lost, over a period of six months, first the art critic and novelist Duranty, then his admired friend Flaubert, and finally his own mother, the depressed, mourning author might not have felt the urge to write *Pot-Bouille* [Hotch-Potch] (1883) or, at least, he might not have turned it into such a damning, unmitigated castigation of bourgeois vice and hypocrisy.

Even as a work of art or a social corrective, the new novel is excessive. Zola's intimate, Céard, is quite discerning when, in his generally appreciative and supportive letter of 19 November 1882, he questions the validity of such a systematic condemnation:

> Philosophiquement, vous avez fait un roman vrai, cela est incontestable. Mais la vie, dans son train-train, a-t-elle cette rigueur de démonstration mathématique?[18]

[Philosophically, you have produced a valid novel; there is no doubt about that. But does life, in its daily round, really have the precision of a mathematical demonstration?]

Colette Becker, on the other hand, tries hard to justify Zola's approach: "Ces exagérations, ces outrances caricaturales, ces oppositions trop systématiques sont volontaires"[19] [Those exaggerations, those outrageous caricatures, those oversystematic contrasts are intentional] but the argument of Zola's following a policy by design does not, in itself, decide the issue: it is the result of the policy that should settle the matter.

The author's intentions, however, are clear enough: he had laid bare the wounds of the working class in *L'Assommoir*; he had portrayed the decadence of the upper classes in *Nana*; now it was the turn of the bourgeoisie. "Une maison bourgeoise neuve, opposée a la maison de la Goutte-d'Or" [A new middle-class house, contrasted witht the Goutte d'Or tenement] he writes at the head of his premier plan détaillé, [first detailed plan] and he goes on:

Montrer la bourgeoisie à nu, après avoir montré le peuple, et la montrer plus abominable, elle qui se dit l'ordre et l'honnêteté.[20]

[Show the middle class in the raw, after showing the common people and show the former to be more obnoxious, even though this is the class that claims to incorporate order and decency.]

Creating a bourgeois pendant to the famous tenement in *L'Assommoir*, Zola introduces his central character, Octave Mouret (brother to the priest, Serge, and simpleminded Désirée) to an impressive—if *not very solid*—building featuring shiny magogany doors and an *imitation*-marble paneled stairwell. Even if, on a first reading, the reader does not pick up the little symbolic hints, he soon realizes that the tenants do not live up to the dignified decor of the rue Choiseul.

It falls beyond the subject of this study to analyze the evolution of the many characters that grace the building, but a shortened list of the main offenders will demonstrate both the aptness of Céard's comments and the magnitude of the immorality portrayed.

The fast-living Octave, we soon discover, chases women for sport, pleasure, and self-advancement. His host, Campardon, stresses the respectability of his tenants, but betrays his own adulterous life-style from the opening pages. Overprotected, naive Marie Pichot, easily seduced by Octave after her rereading of George Sand's *André*, demonstrates the likely results of inadequate instruction and a diet of romantically idealized literature. Somewhat unstable, fiery-eyed Valérie Vabre, pursued in vain by Octave, takes lovers to make up for her impotent husband and has already had a child by a butcher's boy to safeguard an inheritance. Unscrupulous Mme Josserand goes husband hunting for her daughters and martyrizes her own spouse in order to be able to make a good impression socially and to live beyond her means. Her daughter, Berthe, once she is safely married to a selected victim (Auguste Vabre), repeatedly sleeps with Octave to get her debts paid, while her sister, Hortense, is trying to net a lawyer whom she must first wean from his mistress of some fifteen years' standing. The girls' calculating brother, Léon, drops his aging mistress, Mme Dambreville, to marry her young Créole niece, but accepts the arrangement of the couple moving into the old lady's home. Octave's friend, Trublot, alias Paul Alexis (who later used the name Trublot as his pseudonym) sleeps with all the maids, and the whole clan is crowned by the adulterous judge Duveyrier. This noble champion of justice cheats the Vabre brothers out of their share of an inheritance and then condemns a mother to five years in prison for having killed her illegitimate child in a moment of despair. Suffice it to say that Zola's choice of characters was not made to delight the bourgeois section of his readership and that any character in the novel with messianic aspirations would have faced a daunting task.

Céard's criticism does not take into account a few individuals who do not conform to the prevailing pattern. As usual, Zola reserves one wholesome, somewhat stylized character for purposes of moral perspective and, maybe, to profess his faithfulness to an old ideal going back to the days of *Le Voeu d'une morte* and beyond. In *Pot-Bouille*, that role is played by the calm, noble, impressive, and beautiful Mme Hédouin. Octave has his eyes on her from the start, but she quietly resists his advances until her husband has died and Octave has proved his worth as an innovative, creative businessman. She does not save anyone, but it is her lifeblood, spilled on the literal foundations of Octave's fashion-emporium, that will mark the beginning of his partial redemption. (On a deeper level, Zola might be telling himself, in projection, that his ideal of the noble, untainted mother-figure must be sacrificed, if he is to be reconciled to the modern world of industry, progress, and enterprise.)

On a less exalted moral level comes the martyrized M. Josserand, the husband of a dominating wife and the father both of simple Saturnin and of three other scornful, misbehaving, and ungrateful children. After working at a crystal glassworks in the daytime, he slaves away at copying address-labels at night, to finance his wife and daughters' unwarranted luxuries. Tormented by scruples over a false dowry prospect, invented by his wife, he lacks the backbone to insist on honesty and integrity. He eventually dies in sorrow, without having touched the hearts or even the awareness of his selfish family. He does not save anyone either.

We need not dwell on the straitlaced concierge, M. Gourd, a former valet to a duke. He is so fanatically attached to keeping up standards, that he takes offense at one of his underlings bringing home his own wife (in service elsewhere) after-hours. Not intended as a serious champion of values, this ironic creation of Zola's officiates over a milieu of appearances and empty show.

Perhaps the character closest to the author's heart is not the noble Mme Hédouin, who personifies a rather remote ideal, but the humble, sensible old doctor Juilleret. He does not agree with the priest's notion of God's having forsaken the parish, casting the blame for the state of affairs rather on the narrow convent-education of girls, poor mental health, the political regime, and the prevailing ethics of propriety and hypocrisy. After such perceptive remarks, which he seems to have studied in Zola's Ebauche [plot-outline] and that the author himself styles "des observations justes de vieux praticien" [the accurate observations of an old practitioner], he comes out with some of the first intimations of Zola's own prophecies about a doomed bourgeoisie, avenging herds of barbarians, and a Utopia to come (we shall hear more on the subject in *Germinal* and in the late novels). Note how the author disguises his own views by presenting them as the ramblings of an old radical:

> ... dans son emportement de jacobin, [il] sonnait le glas entêté d'une classe ... dont les étais pourris craquaient d'eux-mêmes. Puis il perdait pied de nouveau, il parla des barbares, il annonça le bonheur universel. (3, p. 363)

> [Carried away by his Jacobin enthusiasm, he sounded the persistent death knell of a class whose supports were cracking of themselves. Then he lost track again; he spoke of the barbarians; he announced universal happiness.]

Ironically, the likable, decent doctor is an unbeliever, while the whole clan of fornicating, cheating, money, and vanity-driven delinquents go to mass, frequent the clergy, or at least show the outward veneer of religion. It is this unholy combination that, in biblical terms, merits the label great "apostasy" (= rebellion or falling-away), especially as it covers laity and clergy alike. Philippe Hamon, in his article dedicated to l'abbé Mauduit, goes a little far when he claims:

> ... le curé est, dans le système zolien, le garant hypocrite de l'hypocrisie d'une société, il en est l'incarnation et le symbole. . . .[21]
>
> [... in Zola's system, the priest is the hypocritical guarantor of the hypocrisy of a society: he is both its incarnation and its symbol.]

although, admittedly, his name smacks of "maudit" (cursed) or "mal conduit" [badly led or badly behaved].

However, the problem in the priest is not a love of deceit; he is not lacking in kindness, tolerance, worldly wisdom, and even devoutness of a sort. Like the tormented Josserand, he is in a position of weakness—an impossible situation, in fact, with which he tries to cope as well as he can. Forced by his office to act as a master of ceremonies over this "bourgeoisie gâtée" [spoiled bourgeoisie], faced repeatedly with festering sores and scandals that have the potential of rocking the whole parish structure, he chooses to please man rather than God, to smooth things over as decorously as possible: "Encore une plaie vive . . . sur laquelle il lui fallait jeter le manteau de la religion" (3, p. 150) [Yet another open wound over which he must cast the mantle of religion]. He indulges his personal passion for architectural renovation and expects great things from the "irresistible" light-effect on his new calvaire [crucifix] at Saint-Roche but, alas, it is not stone or mortar that will renew his parish and neither will anything else. Zola brings this out symbolically, when he has Mauduit minister to moribund old Vabre or Josserand—people on the way out—or when he shows him bringing about a reconciliation between Auguste Vabre and adulterous Berthe that is built on nothing more substantial than another false promise of money.

Overwhelmed by all the evil and corruption that he has condoned, the priest retires to his church where he has a vision of Christ crucified (on his new calvaire) rather like that of Serge in *La Faute de l'abbé Mouret*. Jesus, for Mauduit, as for Zola himself, is no longer the atoning Redeemer but "le symbole divin de l'éternelle douleur" (3, p. 365) [the divine symbol of eternal suffering]. He asks for pardon for his lies and for his craven indulgence and pleads for guidance: " . . . que fallait-il faire au milieu de cette société finissante, qui pourrissait jusqu'à ses prêtres?" (3, p. 365) [What must he do in the midst of this moribund society whose rottenness extended even to its priests?] There is no answer, however, and the priest can only weep over the empty heavens and the death of truth, whereupon Zola closes his poignant scene on another allusion to a Christ who is powerless to save: "Au fond des marbres et des orfèvreries, le grand Christ de plâtre n'avait plus une goutte de sang." (3, p. 366) [Behind all the marble statues and the goldsmith's work, the big plaster Christ had not even one drop of blood left]. And so Mauduit sees no alternative but to continue his decorous cover-up of an unrepentant, corrupt society. The priest has ended up with a form of salvation that is purely organizational and has nothing to do with the message of Jesus. Mauduit means well and knows better but, all things considered, he is a pathetic, some might say, a farcical messiah. One can but concur with Colette Becker when she claims that Zola has written a pessimistic novel "sans laisser pressentir un monde nouveau de justice et de bonheur"[22] [without giving any inkling of a new world of justice and happiness]. Depressed writers make no better messiahs than despairing priests.

In the early stages of planning *Au Bonheur des dames* [For Your Pleasure, Ladies] (1883), Zola had no intention of turning his hero, Octave, into some form of devious cult leader (metaphorically speaking) or the store into a Juggernaut that mangled and crushed every obstacle in its way. Octave, Zola writes in his Ebauche, will be "un garçon sans trop de scrupules, que je ferai honnête relativement dans le succès"[23] [a young man without too many scruples whom I shall make relatively decent in success]. (Colette Becker rather overstates the situation when, in her profile of *Au Bonheur des dames*, she claims: "Mouret est un héros presque parfait que son amour malheureux rend encore plus sympathique" [Mouret is an almost perfect hero, rendered even more likable by his unhappy love] and again:

> Le romancier accumule sur lui les qualités physiques et morales . . . ce méridional est ce que Zola n'est pas toujours et qu'il voudrait être.[24]

[The novelist generously endows him with physical and moral virtues . . . this man from the south of France is what Zola is not always and what he would like to be.]

True with regard to Octave's appearance and to his positive, dynamic and creative approach to life, Colette Becker's assessment does not reflect Zola's explicit attitude toward his hero's dubious morals.

No reader of the Ebauche could fail to notice that Zola desires to shake off his depression and to create "le poème de l'activité moderne" [the poem of modern-day activity]. He clearly intimates that he wishes to celebrate the energy and cheerfulness of life's self-renewal—"la joie de l'action et le plaisir de l'existence"[25] [the joy of being active and the pleasure of existing]. Pursuing another line of thought, he plans to demonstrate that the man who exploits women will, in the end, be overcome by them: "Octave exploitant la femme, puis vaincu par la femme" [Octave exploiting women and then being defeated by women] he jots down, still in his Ebauche, adding as an afterthought "le triomphe de Vénus"[26] [the triumph of Venus]. The completed novel is true to this initial, conscious vision, but it becomes much more than that. Mitterand does not exaggerate when he presents Octave, standing on the metaphoric bridge of his ship (the store), not just like an admiral but like "le démi-urge ordonnateur d'un monde mi-réel, mi-fantastique"[27] [the demi-urge, directing a half-real, half-fantastic world]. It will be shown that Octave's store becomes the ambiguous amalgam of a temple or cathedral and a golden calf, that is, a center for a new religion as well as an object of false worship. At the same time it will be suggested that Denise's initial persecution and symbolic death (her dismissal from the store) lead onto an eventual glorification, even to a partially redemptive role. Here again, however, Zola's presentation of the heroine remains ambiguous. Could this first sketch of a possible new messiah, who says yes to life, hint at a viable scenario for a future where progress and enterprise would be tempered by the eternally feminine à la Goethe (the maternally protective and compassionate side of man balancing his need for struggle and conquest)? Or is the glorification of women, in a shrine of their own, as engineered by Octave, merely a transparent pretext for seduction and exploitation? Is Denise's apotheosis, too, simply a cynical, facile ploy for putting a human face on a basically evil and destructive system?

A brief survey of the novel, from the point of view of its messianic relevance, should enable us to come to a well-informed judgment on the questions raised. Incidentally, too, it should cast light on two new insights on the part of the author—the relationship between the loss of an ideal and the quest for power and the intrinsic need in power triumphant to cast itself in submission before the resurrected ideal: Zola has glimpsed the ultimate conclusion of his personal myth.

The author needed to eliminate Octave's first wife, the former Mme Hédouin, both to simplify the plot (he did not want to become entangled in a scenario of jealousy and rivalry) and to make Octave the sole head of a male world, out to exploit women. Reference has already been made to the symbolic implications of Caroline's death. Starting from that same incident, Colette Becker, in her profile of the novel, shows how the themes of martyrdom and ritual sacrifice run through the whole novel, for instance in the death of Geneviève Baudu and her mother and in the attempted self-immolation of Robineau, a ruined rival store-owner. Unlike other commentators, however, she presents the incidents in question in a positive light:

> ... vèritables sacrifices rituels de fécondation et de fondation, ces violences sont bénéfiques: elles sont à l'origine du magasin qui annonce ... la société future.[28]

> [... genuine ritual sacrifices connected with fertility and foundation rites, these acts of violence are beneficent: they mark the origin of the department store that announces ... the society of the future.]

Rather like Florent in *Le Ventre de Paris*, orphaned Denise immediately demonstrates her willingness to nurture and care by arriving in Paris with two young brothers under her wing. Her initial involvement with the Baudu and with other declining textile retailers does not concern us here. Unkindly, grudgingly received by the staff at le Bonheur, she instantaneously proves attractive to Octave: " ... il sentait chez cette jeune fille un charme caché, une force de grâce et de tendresse ignorée par elle-même" (3, p. 441) [He sensed in this girl a hidden charm, a power emanating from her grace and tenderness, of which she herself was unaware]. The author then makes a point of contrasting the melancholy Paul de Vallagnose, a world-weary, ruined nobleman who has read too much Schopenhauer:

> Toujours il concluait à l'inutilité de l'effort, à l'ennui des heures également vides, à la bêtise finale du monde. (3, p. 451)

[His conclusions were always the same: the futility of exertion, the boredom inherent in hours of uniform emptiness, the ultimate stupidity of the world.]

with his dynamic, enterprising friend, Octave, who may enjoy chasing women, but prefers the joy of creative action:

> Puis, ce ne sont pas encore les femmes, dont je me moque après tout. Vois-tu, c'est de vouloir et d'agir, c'est de créer enfin. (3, p. 451)

> [Besides, it's not even women [whom I'm after]; in the long run I couldn't care less about them. It's to do with wanting and doing things, in short, with being creative.]

Zola, who is pulling himself together, after his mourning-induced depression and obsession with death, is juxtaposing, in projection, his ailing self of the last eighteen months and the new self he has resolved to become.

Soon, however, he adds a darker shade to Octave's motivation. First Zola has his hero win over the banker Hartmann by flaunting his policy of rapid turnover and that of exploiting women's vanity. After that the author shows him in action as he captivates his female audience by his intimate fashion-talk and his cultlike religious aura:

> ... elles se sentaient pénétrées et possédées par ce sens délicat qu'il avait de leur être secret, et elles s'abandonnaient, séduites; ... (3, p. 468)

> [... they had a feeling of being penetrated and possessed by his sensitive understanding of their secret being; and they let themselves go and were seduced!]

Octave is not just an innovative businessman, then, but also a calculating seducer.

Then the author's focus shifts to Denise. Against the background of the Monday sale, which Octave has planned like a military campaign, the heroine sets out on a long via dolorosa. Treated like dirt by her colleagues, mocked and criticized by her customers and her superiors, she is almost universally scorned. Particularly on a second reading, one notices the messianic touch of "the suffering servant," "despised and rejected" by the very people whose lot she will one day help to improve. It is only Octave's pity, tinged with physical attraction, that saves her.

Next the author establishes Denise's innate virtuousness and associates her with the freedom, fertility, and freshness of nature (she is nostalgic for the sunshine and the greenery of her native Cotentin, in Normandy):

> ... elle étouffait, prise d'un besoin de plein ciel, rêvant de grandes herbes où elle entrait jusqu'aux épaules, d'arbres géants dont les ombres coulaient sur elle comme une eau fraîche. (3, p. 521)
>
> [... she was suffocating, gripped by the need for open sky, dreaming of tall grasses where she entered up to her shoulders, of giant trees whose shade flowed over her like fresh water.]

Her life-style of virtue and innocence, added to her identification with the protective, nurturing, smiling side of nature, helps us appreciate the injustice of further persecutions that come her way. At first, she is protected by Octave, who has by now added a certain fear to his feelings for the girl. After resisting the amorous advances of the store-inspector Jouve, however, Denise is summarily dismissed, on some pretext, and reduced to a starvation job in Bourras's small umbrella shop. This leads on to her accepting to work for Robineau, a former floor manager of Octave's who unsuccessfully tries to set up a rival store. Soon, however, her steady ascension to glory begins with Octave apologizing to her and reinstating her at a higher wage.

Zola has timed Denise's rehabilitation to coincide with the grand opening of the extended store. As the author describes the new entrance in terms of a "porche d'église" (3, p. 611) [church porch] and then the store itself as "la cathédrale du monde moderne" (3, p. 612) [a modern-day cathedral], he encourages us to see the whole complex as a new center of worship, an institution that fills the gap left by the declining church.

At the same time, he lays bare Octave's ulterior motives in raising a temple to the glory of women:

> Mouret avait l'unique passion de vaincre la femme. Il la voulait reine dans sa maison, il lui avait bâti ce temple pour l'y tenir à sa merci. (3, p. 612)
>
> [Mouret had a single passion: the conquest of woman. He wanted her as the queen of his house; he had built her this temple in order to keep her there at his mercy.]

It is quite ironic, then, that Octave should be the elder brother of Serge Mouret. Where the young priest felt he needed to flee women in order to devote himself to his ministry, Octave virtually makes himself high-priest of a new religion centered on women. Faced with the machinations of Octave, the modern reader cannot fail to note the parallel with latter-day false messiahs—cult-leaders who use the alibi of religion to hide their pecuniary interests, sexual exploitation, or quest for power.

In the midst of all this dubious activity, Denise preserves her integrity. Promotion to "seconde" [assistant floor manager] does not blind her to her employer's promiscuity and she rejects his advances along with his playful offer of a handful of gold: sensuality, power, and money have no hold over her. Meanwhile the banker Hartmann warns Octave, as he has done before, that exploited women have a way of getting even with their exploiters—a theme that will prove to have profound implications toward the end of the novel. Denise's ascension to glory is momentarily checked, when Octave's spurned mistress, Henriette Desforges, attempts to humiliate her rival, but the scene Henriette provokes redounds only to the heroine's glory.

The conversation between Mouret and Vallagnose that follows is rich in implications for those who wish to understand Zola's deviation from the messianic myth to the quest for power. In addition it foreshadows the ultimate futility of all such quests. (The two friends discuss the respective value of love and action. Vallagnose rejects money and possessions if they cannot even buy the woman one loves, whereas Octave believes in the consolation of enterprise, struggle, and achievement):

Je la veux. Je l'aurai. . . . Et si elle m'échappe, tu verras quelle machine je bâtirai pour me guérir. Ce sera superbe quand même. . . . Agir, créer, se battre contre les faits, les vaincre ou être vaincu par eux, toute la joie et toute la santé humaine sont là!

—Simple façon de s'étourdir, murmura l'autre." (3, p. 697)

[I want her. I will have her . . . and if she eludes me, you'll see the kind of machine I'll build to cure myself. It will be tremendous all the same. . . . Doing things, being creative, pitting oneself against circumstances, conquering them or being conquered by them, that's where all human health and happiness lie!
—Just a way of drowning one's sorrows, murmured the other.]

Within the immediate context, this exchange helps to explain Octave's grandiose undertakings after the death of his first wife and their evolution, on an ever-expanding scale, while Denise continues to elude him. In the wider context of Zola's orientation in life, it may well cast light on the author's recourse to ambition, action and creative effort as compensation after the collapse of his messianic ideals. Vallagnose's sober rejoinder, while not to be taken as a strong refutation, is validated by later developments. The least we can say is that the discussion shows Zola to be aware that energetic action does not hold all the answers. When the very next chapter goes on to trace Octave's obsession with Denise and his powerlessness to elicit signs of her affection, when he becomes a harsh ruler (just like Eugène Rougon in similar circumstances), it becomes clear that the author has seen through his own motivational dynamics and is not overimpressed. Both Octave and his literary creator, one suspects, survey their respective empires and find that they are not satisfying. Zola uses the fiction of his hero to take stock of his own untiring efforts, his literary renown, and his prestige as the leader of naturalism and seems to come to the conclusion that wholeness and fulfillment may well lie elsewhere.

If Denise resists all of Octave's attempts to win her, this is not for want of love (witness her upset over his various love affairs) or even out of respect for the dictates of virtue. Rather, Zola informs us, she is moved "par un instinct de bonheur ... et pour satisfaire son besoin d'une vie tranquille" (3, p. 724) [by an instinct for happiness ... and to meet her need for a quiet life].

Appointed floor manager of the new children's section, Denise truly comes into her own, as she finds an outlet for her strong caring instincts. Kind to all, she pushes through a series of reforms that improve the life of the workers. Without seeking power or glory, she begins to reign as a beloved sovereign. In a sense this brings us back to the gentle messianic myth of the shepherd-king—the very opposite of Octave's pursuit of power (in order to hide the spiritual bankruptcy of his way of life). Given Denise's nonreligious status, however, it may be more appropriate to see her, as Jean Borie does in his *Zola et les mythes*, as "vierge-mère" [virgin mother] and to equate her beneficent reign with "le tendre despotisme de la maman"[29] [the tender tyranny of a mother].

Whatever the correct nomenclature for the myth involved—shepherd-queen or virgin-mother—Denise's power has its limits. She cannot stop her anemic cousin, Geneviève Baudu, from pining to death when her calculating fiancé repeatedly defers the wedding-day, nor can she save the tottering textile-retailers from falling into the path of Octave's Juggernaut (the department store):

> ... mais le colosse gardait son indifférence de machine lancée à toute vapeur, inconsciente des morts qu'elle peut faire en chemin. (3, p. 740)
>
> [... but the colossus remained as indifferent as a locomotive charging full steam ahead, oblivious to the dead bodies it may leave along its route.]

During the evening that follows Geneviève's funeral, Octave persuades Denise of the need for the new to take over from the old. Lying in her own bed, later that night, the heroine meditates on what she has come to see as the sad truth of life—the cycle of nature whereby today's dead make up the fertile soil of tomorrow's living:

> Etait-ce donc vrai, cette nécessité de la mort engraissant le monde, cette lutte pour la vie qui faisait passer les êtres sur le charnier de l'éternelle destruction? (3, p. 747)
>
> [Was it really true, then, that death was necessary to make the world fertile; must there be this struggle for existence that made all living things end up in the charnel house of eternal destruction?]

Apart from throwing light on the opening decor of *La Fortune des Rougon* (the lush grass growing in the former cemetery of l'aire Saint-Mitre), this passage reveals the old problems that persist beneath Zola's somewhat forced optimism. Denise's grief over her inability to help no doubt matches the author's own sadness over a very imperfect world:

> Mon Dieu! que de tortures! des familles qui pleurent, des vieillards jetés sur le pavier, tous les drames poignants de la ruine. (3, p. 748)
>
> [Heavens! what terrible suffering! families in tears, old people thrown out on the street, all the poignant dramas that accompany ruin.]

With the use of phrases such as "la lutte pour la vie" [the struggle for existence] (just quoted), Denise's meditation has turned into a social Darwinian tract. If we did not have the wisdom of hindsight, we might well conclude that her words to follow constitute Zola's formal admission that messianic endeavors are counterproductive—a view similar to the Marxist notion that individual charity only serves to superficially legitimize and perpetuate inhuman systems:

> Et elle ne pouvait sauver personne, et elle avait conscience que c'était bon, qu'il fallait ce fumier de misères à la santé du Paris de demain. (3, p. 748)
>
> [And she couldn't save anyone; she was aware that this was as it should be, that this manure of misery and suffering was necessary for the well-being of tomorrow's Paris.]

If sorrow and resignation had been Zola's definitive reaction to the grim realities of life, he clearly would not have conceived Pauline in his next novel, (La Joie de vivre), [The Joy of Living] the Mme Caroline of L'Argent, [Money] or the Clotilde of Le Docteur Pascal. It remains true, nevertheless, that, at least during the composition of Au Bonheur des dames, he comes close to a total renunciation of messianism. As for Octave's being the new hero after Zola's heart, however, nothing could be further from the truth, unless there is a total disparity between the philosophy of Zola's heroine, Denise, and his own point of view: summing up in her mind the merits and faults of Octave Mouret, Denise passes in review the early, calculating romances of this "aventurier de l'amour" [adventurer in love], his cultivation of fleeting sexual pleasures, his "génie de la séduction commerciale" [genius for commercial seduction], and his scorn for the women he exploits. It is only then that she does justice to his creative spirit of enterprise and considers him redeemed through the sufferings of love (cf. 3, p. 748).

But the novel does not end there: ambiguity will be maintained to the very end. Dramatizing the myth of Shiva the Destroyer, Zola has Denise chance upon Octave's rival, Robineau, after the latter has just thrown himself under the wheels of an omnibus and has escaped with a broken ankle. This sets her thinking again about the nature of Octave's creation:

> Mouret avait inventé cette mécanique à écraser le monde . . . et elle l'aimait quand même pour la grandeur de son oeuvre. (3, p. 761)
>
> [Mouret had invented this mechanism for crushing the world . . . and yet she loved him for the grandeur of his enterprise.]

Within the same context, Zola refers to the department store as "un colosse" [a colossus] that has devoured a whole quartier, as "l'ogre des contes" [the fairy-tale ogre] whose shoulders threaten to burst through the clouds and as a "monstre" that leaves Paris looking diminished (3, p. 763). The author is clearly in two minds about the achievements of his unscrupulous entrepreneur.

The conclusion of the novel is built up around Octave's latest inspiration, his "Exposition du blanc" (Display of white [garments]), and brings together a number of complex themes. On the one hand, Zola treats us to his poem of whiteness. Taking lyrical flight with evocations of snow, ermine, glaciers, white stars, swans, and shivering lace, he works these elements into a vision that is both religious and sensuous: the store decor becomes both "tabernacle and "alcôve." The climactic "apothéose du blanc" [apotheosis of white] is meant to dazzle us with a pure paradise of light, fit to celebrate the wedding of the "reine inconnue" [unknown queen], but this scene, too, is wrapped in a cloud of sensuality, where the shimmering of a pink knee is said to ravish the world.

Accordingly, ambiguity prevails: the store is like a virginal bed awaiting its spotless white princess, but it is also the pagan temple where Octave's seduced women-customers lie prostrate at his feet. Zola evokes "cette folie dernière de la clientèle conquise, abattue aux pieds du tentateur" (3, p. 790) [that final madness on the part of his vanquished customers, lying prostrate at the tempter's feet].

On the other hand, the author elaborates the paradox of the defeated conqueror. At the moment of his greatest commercial victory, Octave experiences the fear of collapsing on top of his millions and being broken "comme une paille par l'éternel féminin" (3, p. 773) [like a straw by the eternal feminine (principle)]. Our genius of seduction has a vision of a proud, avenging Denise planting her heel on his throat. And this, metaphorically speaking, is exactly what comes to pass at what one might call the mythical climax of the novel. At sunset, just as the hero is looking back over his triumphant day, he feels something momentous transpire within him:

> Mouret, les regards perdus, venait de sentir passer en lui quelque chose de grand; et dans ce frisson de triomphe dont tremblait sa chair, en face de Paris dévoré et de la femme conquise, il éprouva une faiblesse soudaine, une défaillance de sa volonté, qui le renversait à son tour, sous une force supérieure. C'était un besoin irraisonnable d'être vaincu, dans sa victoire, le nonsens d'un homme de guerre

pliant sous le caprice d'un enfant, au lendemain de ses conquêtes. (3, p. 799)

[Mouret, gazing vaguely into the distance, had just felt something great transpire within him; and in that thrill of triumph that made his flesh tremble, in the face of all this achievement—he had devoured Paris, conquered woman—he experienced a sudden feeling of weakness, a flagging of his will that brought him down in his turn before a superior power. It was an irrational need to be conquered, in his [moment of] victory, the absurd situation of a warrior yielding to the whim of a child, the morning after his conquests.]

If Jung had read this passage, he would have been delighted with this eloquent illustration of one of his theories—the notion of a repressed or neglected aspect of the personality taking its revenge at the very moment that the opposite aspect celebrates its greatest victory. As may happen at the climax of a physical relationship, where the "conquering" male experiences the need to submit to his partner, the overassertive male principle in any man, Jung believes, needs to surrender to the female principle or "anima" within his own psyche. Behind the fiction of Octave, Zola, the seasoned warrior, is astonished to see himself yield to the caprice of the child within him, with its need to submit to the gentle authority of the mother.

For Zola, then, there are some deep truths concealed in the popular belief that scorned or exploited women will have their revenge—a truth of which Octave has been warned three times. On the level of Zola's personal destiny, we could take the mythical denouement of the novel for a prophetic preview: the ambitious writer, with the world at his feet, will one day joyfully yield to the charms of a young servant-girl, Jeanne Rozerot. On a more philosophical level, the present novel foreshadows that the author's myth of power will one day be replaced by the old ideal of caring, guiding, and protecting—an atttitude that will allow him to revert to his half-forgotten messianic myth. In *Docteur Pascal* already, the old scientist gives up his efforts to save his clients, when he discovers the higher ideals incarnate in Clotilde, a potential mother of the world's new messiah. Similarly, in Zola's late novel, *Travail* [Work], it is the hero's love for a simple girl that inspires him to take up the cause of the suffering workers and to create a Utopia. At the stage in his life when he wrote *Au Bonheur des dames*, Zola, we might say, glimpses the bridge that will take him back to his most authentic self, but he is not yet able to cross it.

And so the final focus of the novel is not on the self-humbling or abnegation of the conqueror, but on the ambiguous nature of Mouret's new cult, the product of a man who both creates and destroys, who charms and seduces, who, in true Antichrist style, puts himself in the place of Christ. Zola now articulates, in his own name, his earlier suggestion that clothing stores fill the gap left in women's hearts by declining religion. He alludes in passing to the old rivalry between husband and God or priest, now revived as husbands have to cope with the financially seductive power of Octave ("lutte renaissante d'un dieu contre le mari" (3, p. 797) [the revival of the old battle between husband and god]; he hints at an explanation of the new "culte du corps" [cult of the body] by referring to "l'au-delà divin de la beauté" (3, p. 798) [the divine beyond of beauty]—the elusive, transcendent dimension that often shimmers just beyond the edge of physical possession.

Zola cannot resolve the enigma of conquest and self-prostration, seduction and divine purity, physicality and spirituality, and this is reflected in his final use of religious imagery. Note how he evokes the effect produced on Octave's employees as the day's takings are carried to the safe in solemn procession:

> Au premier (étage), les confections, la parfumerie, les dentelles, les châles s'étaient rangés avec dévotion, comme sur le passage du bon Dieu. De proche en proche le brouhaha s'élevait, devenait une clameur de peuple saluant le veau d'or. (3, p. 800)

> [On the first floor the ready-made dresses and costumes, the perfumery department, the laces and scarves had been lined up with devotion as though waiting for God to pass by. Step by step the hubbub grew louder, becoming the clamorous roar of a people hailing the golden calf.]

What at first is meant to remind us of a Corpus Christi procession and the faithful's reverent adoration of the passing host, merges into the noisy clamor that greeted the unveiling of Aaron's golden calf—the idolatrous, pagan cult-object that brought divine wrath on thousands of Israelites as they crossed the desert on their way to the Promised Land.

Given this double-edged conclusion to the novel, can we really share Jean Borie's misgivings about Zola's attempting to legitimize Octave's commercial world by placing it at the feet of a virgin-mother?[30] After all, Zola himself is not wholeheartedly on the side of his hero and maintains an equivocal perspective.

We may be tempted to accept Henri Guillemin's ironic comment on Denise's being the patron saint of a paternalist, humanitarian approach to high commerce,[31] but is it fair to impose a twentieth-century point of view on socioeconomic problems that still needed to be worked through in the 1880s?

The novel as a whole, admittedly, features a glorification of the entrepreneurial spirit—a form of false messiahship that has fallen into disgrace of late and that Zola tries hard to see in a positive light, because it is part of the dynamic, modern world, part of the reality one has to come to terms with, if life is to be viable. But we may assert, with equal justification, that Zola effectively juxtaposes an exploitative, false cult—the cult of Antichrist—with the positive, redemptive role of a good, pure woman, who shows some attributes of a genuine messiah.

The happy ending of the last few paragraphs of the novel is, perhaps, a little too conventional and lacks conviction. The two lovers may get married, as announced, in a month's time, but how long is Octave, the inveterate skirt-chaser, likely to remain faithful? And what about the whole dream of commerce and industry with a human face? Zola's detractors may well object that multinationals, in particular, have not shown much evidence lately of allowing "l'éternel féminin" [the eternal feminine principle] to arrest their wholesale pursuit of Mammon [the false god of materialism].

As we have seen, writers like Jean Borie and Henri Guillemin find a certain shallowness in the philosophy underlying *Au Bonheur des dames*, a parti pris of optimism that does not altogether convince, because it is based on little more than sheer courage and exercise of will. Zola has not yet had time to come to terms with his recent bereavements or to work through his troubling reactions.

While acknowledging the reservations of critics, we might argue in Zola's defense that, given the severity of his "symptoms," he had to do something fast and was brave enough to put up a provisional framework, even if his foundations remained a little shaky.

He must have had some misgivings of his own; witness the ambiguity of his hero, Octave, and the ambivalence of his denouement. Putting a brave face on things, hauling oneself up by one's own bootstraps, is one thing; taking fresh stock of one's assets and liabilities, facing the harsh realities of life and then choosing cheerfulness, generosity, compassion, and forgetfulness of self, rather than despair, is quite another. And that, essentially, is what Zola attempts to do in *La Joie de vivre* (1884). As Henri Mitterand puts it in his notes on the "Origines" of the novel:

> Il n'est pas déraisonnable d'interpréter la mise en présence de Pauline et de Lazare comme une confrontation des deux Zolas, l'un tentant d'exorciser les démons familiers de l'autre.[32]

> [It is not unreasonable to interpret the bringing together of Pauline and Lazare as a juxtaposition of the two Zolas, with the one trying to exorcise the other's demons.]

Henri Mitterand[33] and, more recently, Colette Becker[34] have dealt exhaustively with the causes of Zola's depression and with his conscious desire to define his own nervous problems, notably his demoralizing obsession with death. The reception given to the finished novel, both at the time and in our own day, shows that Zola has managed to universalize his personal trauma into the portrayal of a basic human fear, likely to confront us in every age.

What concerns us here, however, is to examine how Zola's major assessment of life and death fits into his messianic perspective. Has the author renounced the messianic aspiration of saving or redeeming the lost—as seemed to happen at one point in Denise's deliberations in *Au Bonheur des dames*—or is he continuing in the old vein with the complete spectrum of flawed, failing, false, and more or less genuine messiahs?

One failing messiah in *La Joie de vivre* immediately springs to mind—l'abbé Horteur who, rather significantly, does not play a major role in the novel. As his name suggests (Latin *hortus* = "garden"), he is more interested in his lettuces than in his erring parishioners (admittedly, an unsavory and unpromising lot). Unable to frighten them into decency or true piety, he is satisfied if they keep to the bare minimum of external observances. The author sums up his selfishness and total lack of messianic zeal in the line: "Personnellement, il soignait son salut; quant à ses paroissiens, tant pis s'ils se damnaient" (3, p. 849) [Personally, he looked after his salvation; as for his parishoners, too bad if they damned themselves]. His only effect on the person who was his model candidate for confirmation, Zola's heroine, Pauline Quenu, is to put her off going to confession by his indiscreet questions.

Lazare, the central male character is better intentioned than the priest, but fails almost as totally in saving anyone (he does manage to rescue a baby from a burning cottage).

As Zola himself admitted in an article published in the American review *Bookman*, he had put a lot of himself into Lazare.[35] Like his central character, who has not yet chosen a profession eight months after leaving school, Zola took a long time to find his vocation. Like Lazare, too, he initially frustrated his mother's ambition that he should be the family messiah.

In the same way that Lazare changes his projected Paradise Symphony into a "Symphonie de la douleur" [Symphony of Sorrows] youthful Zola had changed his inspiration from a planned epic celebrating creation to the kind of disillusioned evocations of universal evil, bloodshed, suffering, and futile self-sacrifice we have considered in chapter 2 of this study. The author writes about this espousal of sorrow to Van Santen Kolff in his letter dated 6 March 1889:

J'ai longtemps eu l'idée d'écrire un poème en prose sur la Douleur. Ce sont les débris de ce poème qui se trouvent dans *La Joie de vivre*, notamment dans la symphonie de Lazare.[36]

[For a long time I've had the idea of of writing a prose poem on the subject of pain and sorrow. It's the fragments of that poem that are found in *La Joie de vivre*, notably in Lazare's symphony.]

In the course of this study we have already had occasion to refer to Zola's obsession with death—an affliction he now projects onto Lazare. A vision of the starry sky, one summer evening on the beach, is enough to fill him with dread and to make him sob: "Oh! mourir, mourir!" (3, p. 884) [Oh, dying, dying!].

Where Zola failed to obtain his Baccalauréat, Lazare drops out of second-year medicine. At this point, however, the parallelism between author and character is cut short for, where Zola comes to his senses, embraces rugged reality, and begins to carve out a career for himself, Lazare continues to be the weak, ineffectual dreamer that Zola, in his worst moments, must have feared becoming.

Lazare's studies in Paris, besides turning him into a profligate spender, make him bitter and cynical. On his return home, however, daily contact with his cousin, Pauline, exposure to sea, sun, wind, and weather, improve his morale. Hoping to extract enough bromide from seaweed to heal all the nerve-sufferers of the world—a choice bit of irony on Zola's part (Lazare is indulging in what one might call symbolic problem solving)—he turns his attention to chemistry and eventually invests seventy thousand francs of Pauline's inheritance into a project that will come to nothing. So far, then, he has saved neither the family patrimony nor the neurotics of the world. He is not being much of a messiah!

Without such compensations for his frail, mother-dominated personality, he slips into morbid idleness and into a universal skepticism à la Schopenhauer—a condition not unlike Zola's state of mind after his repeated bereavements of 1880.

With time and further support from Pauline (who loves him), he recovers enough to take up a new cause. Having witnessed the periodic ravages the sea inflicts on the tiny village of Bonneville, he dreams up a coastal-defense scheme involving an "estacade," a system of sturdy stakes to break the violence of the waves. Initially there is an element of altruism in his project. The author concedes: "Il entrait aussi, dans cette entreprise une part de philanthropie" (3, p. 903) [A certain amount of philanthropy also came into this scheme]—a measure of messianic aspiration, but it transpires at once that his deepest motivation is to avenge himself for his earlier industrial fiasco by humbling the sea. Thanks to modern insights into the condition we now call "male menopause," we can comment that, at an unconscious level, perhaps, Zola is dramatizing his own attempts to flout the disintegrating powers of death that face a man from afar, just as he is beginning to reach the apex of his career. Zola, through his monumental literary creations, and Lazare, with his breakwater scheme, are essentially attempting to achieve the same thing:

> Et quelle plus belle vengeance que d'arrêter [la mer] dans sa destruction aveugle, de lui crier en maître: Tu n'iras pas plus loin. (3, p. 903)

> [And what sweeter revenge than to stop the sea in its blind, destructive course, and to shout to it as its master: You shall go no further.]

Looking after Pauline, during her critical illness, temporarily numbs his dread of mortality, but the horrible death of his mother (based closely on Zola's own recent trials) and the ocean's smashing of his defense system plunge him back into depression and paralysis of will. He even tries to recapture the simple faith of his childhood—a "temptation" that seems to have come Zola's way as well, when he could not cope with the idea of having utterly lost his mother.

After this series of major traumata, Lazare may develop a short-lived enthusiasm for politics and the world of finance; he may briefly forget his fears in a passionate relationship with the girl, Louise, whom Pauline persuades him to marry, but such diversionary tactics are not enough to permanently still his dread of the tomb. (He does not truly love Louise, anyway): "C'était la mort qu'ils retrouvaient au bout de leurs baisers" (3, p. 1053) [Ultimately, what they came back to in their kisses was death]. There are echoes there of the situation of couples in *Thérèse Raquin* and in *Madeleine Férat*. We know from the testimony of friends and acquaintances of Zola that the writer himself found that his marriage with Alexandrine was not enough to keep his demons at bay in the early 1880s.

Lazare may save someone else's baby, on the spur of the moment, but he pessimistically predicts gloom and doom for his own—the frail child whom Pauline has saved from death. It becomes evident that nothing or no one can save Lazare from himself. While it was said of Christ on the Cross, "He saved others; himself he cannot save," the only conclusion we can come to with regard to Lazare is that he is an ineffectual dreamer, a totally unsuccessful messiah who can save neither the world nor himself. Emasculated by a selfish, domineering mother, paralyzed by his morbid obsessions, lacking in genuine commitment to others, unable to cope with the trials of life or the prospect of death, he is doomed to futility.

None of these negative traits show in Pauline, Zola's heroine, whose only fault, from a literary point of view, is that she is "peut-être un peu bien angéliquement séraphique d'âme" [just a little too angelically seraphic in spirit] (Huysmans, in a letter to Zola, dated March 1884[37]).

Pauline is the orphaned daughter of the Quenu, the "charcutiers" [pork butcher couple] we have met in *Le Ventre de Paris*. As soon as she joins the Chanteau household in the tiny coastal village of Bonneville, she demonstrates her positive rapport with nature: she has no fear of the family dog and generously shares most of her dessert with the family pets—perhaps not the most tactful thing to do on first arriving at one's relations' home, but Zola is clearly intent on demonstrating her need to give of herself.

Noting her cheerful devotion, as she attends to her uncle during one of his gout attacks, Dr.Cazenove, who will turn out to be Zola's main spokesperson in the novel, remarks: "Voilà une gamine qui est née pour les autres" (3, p. 837) [There's a lass born to help others] thus highlighting a potential messianic trait. It is Pauline who gives Lazare a gentle push in the right direction—the direction of preserving life—as she encourages him to take up medical studies in Paris, even if this means that she will lose his treasured company. Her wholesome acceptance of her physicality, when she has her first period without prior instruction from Mme Chanteau, her keen efforts to enlighten herself with the help of Lazare's medical books, reflect a personality that welcomes life in all its manifestations:

> C'était la vie acceptée, la vie aimée dans ses fonctions, sans dégoût ni peur, et saluée par la chanson triomphante de la santé. (3, p. 857)
>
> [This was the acceptance and love of life in all its functions, without disgust or fear; this was life hailed in a triumphant song of good health.]

Her security is not bound up with things, but with people: she readily lends Lazare money for his schemes, does not reproach him when he fails, but rather opposes her laughter and good sense to his discouragement and fear of the grave.

In spite of her awakened sexuality and her wholehearted love for Lazare, she is willing to sacrifice herself for the sake of his health: at a time when she is too sick to take him on invigorating walks, she encourages him to go out with her rival, Louise. This selfless devotion to others remains her rule of life. Subsequently she takes care once again of ailing Chanteau and tends his dying wife—the woman who had not only misappropriated funds from her inheritance on a regular basis but who, in spite of Lazare's engagement to Pauline, had treacherously urged her son to court Louise (unlike Pauline's depleted patriomony, Louise's inheritance of two hundred thousand francs was still intact).

Similar trials come to Lazare and Pauline, but her positive outlook and her ability to look away from herself help her through every crisis. Her noblest quality is her devotion to others—not for the sake of results, reward, or recognition, but purely because she finds such a way of life satisfying in itself. This emerges particularly from her regular sessions with her "petits galopins" [little urchins] from the village whom she feeds and patches up. Zola awakens the reader to the futility of Pauline's charity, objectively speaking: the band of lying, depraved youngsters, sent out by their grasping parents to exploit Pauline, are clearly beyond redemption. In full knowledge of this, our heroine mothers them all the same, for the pure pleasure of loving, of giving of herself. And so, where Denise, in Zola's previous novel, realizes that individual charity is counterproductive, but does her best to humanize Octave's cruel commercial machine, Pauline has no illusions about her "galopins," but is able to pursue her charitable endeavor for its own sake, because it constitutes her way of fulfilling herself.

Whatever Huysmans may have thought, Pauline is not too good to be true. Even when she convinces herself that it is better for Lazare to marry Louise, she has to battle against feelings of jealousy. There is a particularly poignant scene as she stands naked in front of her mirror and contemplates her unfulfilled potential for motherhood. She is sorely tempted to let Lazare make love to her when they draw together after Lazare's disillusionment with nervy, highly strung Louise. We might comment that, like Christ, she is "tempted in every way, yet without sin," but that would not be true in every respect. Her gravest fault is actually her need to sacrifice herself, when a little more reflection on the part of this otherwise sensible girl would have convinced her that, robust, cheerful, and healthy as she is, she would have made a far better wife for Lazare than Louise could ever be. A. A. Greaves is quite correct when he points out, in an article entitled "Religion et réalité dans l'oeuvre de Zola":

> Elle (Pauline) est tellement pressée de se sacrifier pour les autres, qu'elle ne prend pas le temps de penser à ce qui conviendrait le mieux à leur situation.[38]
>
> [She (Pauline) is in such a hurry to sacrifice herself for others, that she does not take time to think out what would be best for them in their particular situation.]

Nevertheless, she amply compensates for such unwise and compulsive self-effacement by her heroic devotion to Lazare and by Louise's virtually stillborn baby, whom she wrests from the jaws of death. Not only does she coax little Paul back to life, an action worthy of messiah, but she reconciles the arguing, fighting couple, continues to care for the local urchins, and makes life bearable for declining Chanteau.

The novel ends with two effective antitheses that convey a great deal about Zola's themes and intentions. The first is the argument between Lazare and Pauline about the future of the frail baby Paul:

"—Bah!" murmura-t-il, "il aura la goutte comme papa et ses nerfs seront plus détraqués que les miens. . . . Regarde donc comme il est faible! C'est la loi des dégénérescences."
—"Veux-tu te taire!" s'écria Pauline. "Je l'élèverai et tu verras si j'en fais un homme!" (3, p. 1129)

["Go on with you," he murmured, "he'll have gout like Papa and his nerves will be in an even worse mess than mine. . . . Look how weak he is! It's the law of degeneration."
—"Will you be quiet!" cried Pauline. "I'll raise him and you'll see whether or not I make a man of him!"]

One's past and the laws of heredity, in other words, might lead one to despairing conclusions, but one can also choose to ignore negative data, devote oneself to others' welfare, and make the best of things. Pauline's having the last word shows that Zola has resolved to let the caring, compassionate, courageous part of himself win the day.

The second contrast opens on Véronique, the old maidservant who rallied to Pauline's defense in her various trials (the way her legendary namesake, St. Veronica, consoled Christ on the road to Calvary by wiping his face with a cloth). Unjustly reproached by Louise, however, Véronique hangs herself on a pear-tree in the garden. In contrast, helpless, pain-ridden, immobilized, moribund Chanteau, for all his suffering, desperately hangs on to life. Zola lends brilliant irony to his indignant rejection of Véronique's suicide: "—Faut-il être bête pour se tuer!" (3, p. 1130) [You'd have to be an idiot to kill yourself!]. Like Pauline, herself reduced to the role of a servant, and like St. Veronica, who found fulfillment in her humble devotion to Christ, Véronique has shaped her life around service to others. Unlike the other two women, however, she is not selfless and, once her value as a servant is challenged, her whole world disintegrates. Old Chanteau has no such problems: he demonstrates that, even when existence becomes pure agony, one can still choose to live on. Suffering humanity on the whole, Zola wants to show us, prefers life and instinctively rejects death.

Although Chanteau's exclamation represents Zola's parting shot, it is Pauline whom one remembers, as she stands on the veranda, cradling the baby in her strong arms before the setting sun (a painless, harmless symbol of death) and the polyvalent sea that can stand for virtually any aspect of nature or human experience—life and death, beauty and horror, poetic gentleness and malevolent violence, smiling serenity and roaring fury.

In the final analysis, Pauline is no true messiah. Admittedly, she is virginal in every sense of the word and she gives life to a baby born without hope of survival, but she fails in most aspects of her mission. She brings lasting contentment or happiness to no one—certainly not to Lazare and Louise or to Mme Chanteau, who dies in spite of her tender care. Yet she herself finds contentment of a sort. By choosing to align herself with nature—even when it causes given life-forms to sacrifice themselves in order to produce new life—she finds and propagates peace. By espousing the smiling, cheerful, maternal side of the life-force, she exorcises the terrors of time, change, suffering, and death. She makes life feasible.

If it be permitted to read between the lines, this may be restated as follows: in the midst of all his perplexities, his fears, and his neuroses, Zola has triggered off or released the "anima" in his own nature—what Jung defines as the archetype of life in every individual, the part of us that is at peace because, like nature, it is sufficient unto itself or, if we can follow Jung all the way, because it can become the bearer, repository, or tabernacle of the spiritual, the eternal. Zola is certainly not ready for this spiritual dimension, although he allows Pauline to retain faith in a just, all-powerful, wise divinity that rules the whole course of nature. There are intimations, however, that he can embrace the peace of nature when old Dr. Cazenove (Zola's mouthpiece) speaks of his inclination to let nature take its course or when he comes out with memorable maxims like the following: "Mais vivez, est-ce que vivre ne suffit pas? La joie est dans l'action" (3, p. 994) [But live! Isn't it enough to be alive? Joy derives from action].

Zola is obviously struggling to maintain his messianic myth, to defend or justify his irrepressible sense of being called to guide, warn, and improve the society of his day. He has shown in *Nana* that glorified sensuality and pleasure-seeking are a source of corruption and disintegration that will call down the Apocalypse of avenging, cleansing fire. Nana, the high-priestess of this false cult, is shown ultimately to share in the death and corruption she has sown. The almost universal immorality of *Pot-Bouille* and the guilty connivence of the clergy suggest that both the bourgeoisie and the church are doomed to destruction for, apparently, there is no messiah to save them. Modern commercialism, *Au Bonheur des dames* reveals, may be a substitute for religion, but it is essentially exploitative—a golden calf that cannot guide Israel out of the desert and into the Promised Land.

Suffering and death are all around, *La Joie de vivre* proclaims; the storms of chaos will carry off the last few houses of the defenseless human village—a village worthy of destruction, anyway—but there is always Pauline's solution. The latter does not try to fight nature, but serenely accepts it in all its diverse functions. She makes the best of life by joyfully denying herself, allowing the life-force to act through her and challenging others to follow her example. There are false divinities, failing priests, false prophets, and false messiahs, but there is hope of salvation through those who will sacrifice possessions, romantic dreams, and their very selves for the sake of the life-force that transcends all other ends.

7
Messianic Myth in Crisis

IN THE PREVIOUS CHAPTER, WE FOUND THAT ZOLA'S MESSIANIC MYTH was under pressure, but survived in an attenuated form. Denise, in *Au Bonheur des dames*, we noted, accepted the rightness of not being able to rescue small businesses (in the name of progress), but managed nevertheless to soften the harshness of Octave's regime. In the same way, we saw Pauline become wise to the futility of her charity, but persevere with it anyway, because it represented an exercise worthwhile in itself or because it was an essential part of her that called for fulfillment. It is tempting to conclude from this parallel scenario that, at the time, Zola himself entertained doubts about the feasibility of messiahship in the modern world, but could not really abandon it without abandoning part of himself, part of his raison d'être.

At the same time, we traced the emergence or the elaboration of two themes that the author called to the rescue of his fading messianic dream—on the one hand the vision of Apocalypse, foreshadowed in *Nana* as a means of purification, as a process setting the stage for messianic restoration; on the other hand the deification of the life-force. The latter may be both lifegiver and life-taker, apocalyptic destroyer, and redemptive messiah, but Pauline, while accepting its darker side, tends to embody its consoling, nurturing, healing aspects. In that role, she moves on the border of a sublime humanism and on a tentative form of pantheism.

The crisis of Zola's messianism will only deepen in his next four novels. *Germinal* portrays a world that needs to be saved, but is not, because of a remote, evil divinity, a flawed messiah, and the cruel dreams of a nihilistic Antichrist. Yet the work closes on a vaguely pantheistic dawn of hope. *L'Oeuvre* [The Work] features the fatal error of a painter (Claude) who confuses life and art, as he tries to encompass the whole of nature and reality by superimposing a fine portrait of his wife (Christine) on a view of Paris and the Seine. Rather than loving, embracing, and propagating life in the real woman, he deifies his art. As a result his at first lifelike portrait of his wife turns into a grotesque idol reminiscent of Nana's sacrilegious dream of being a bejeweled godess, sprawled across the bed of her tabernacle—a monstrosity in which the despairing artist recognizes only his own insatiable desire. Potentially a prophet of the life-force, Claude becomes guilty of idolatry, realizes this, and escapes into death—a mistake that Zola is determined not to copy.

Through the myth of "l'éternel retour" [eternal return], in *La Terre*, [The Land] Zola celebrates the unending cycle of the seasons, the eternal round of self-renewing nature, but contrasts this with the narrow goals of peasants, capable only of grasping and loving the material fiber of life or blindly following its most basic drives. Significantly such a primitive milieu has no room for a more refined and less brutal hero (Jean) who is eventually excluded. Ironically this more sensitive man, who has little taste for the nihilistic dreams of the teacher Lequeux (hordes of Cossacks or Chinese purging the land of its vermin) will move on to play a humble part in the vast apocalyptic drama of *La Débâcle*.

Clearly Zola's view of humanity has not evolved greatly since he depicted the destruction of the vice-riden hamlet of Bonneville in *La Joie de vivre*. Just like his hero, Jean, in *La Terre*, he is not inclined to accept the radical solutions of nihilism. Feeling like a stranger in a strange land, he prefers to retreat momentarily to the idealized world of *Le Rêve* [The Dream]—a fairy tale of innocent young love, a faithful prince charming and a man of God who seems to have the messianic gift of restoring life. When the story ends in death for the heroine, a death masked behind a sublime vision of spring sunshine, Zola reveals the lack of substance of his idyllic romance. Was Schopenhauer right after all, when he claimed that life was but an illusionary dream?

Germinal (1885), besides being one of Zola's greatest novels, may be considered as a provisional "summa"—a summing up of his current attitude to the messianic myth. Practically every aspect of the myth that we have considered in chapter 6—the destructive but cleansing fire of Apocalypse (*Nana*); the doom of a conniving, apostate church (*Pot-Bouille*); the false cult of materialism propagated by a type of Antichrist (*Au Bonheur des dames*); a failing messianic figure, contrasted with the persistent hope of one who espouses the life-force (*La Joie de vivre*)—reemerges in the epic canvas of *Germinal*.

7: MESSIANIC MYTH IN CRISIS

The very title of the work is a polyvalent symbol: borrowed from the "calendrier révolutionnaire's" name for the first month of spring, it aptly brings together the season of germinating seed and the idea of social revolution. The events portrayed in the novel may amount to little more than a false spring, but the novel as a whole is meant to prefigure an apocalyptic upheaval that Zola half-expected to occur at the end of the nineteenth century. The Ebauche makes clear the author's prophetic intentions. Having formulated one of his themes as "la lutte du travail et du capital" [the struggle between labor and capital], he reminds himself:

C'est là qu'est l'importance du livre, je le veux prédisant l'avenir, posant la question la plus importante du vingtième siècle.[1]

[That's where the importance of the book lies: I want it to foretell the future and formulate the most important question of the twentieth century.]

He hoped the revolutionary event would herald the dawning of a new age. On a more metaphysical level, the rising spring sun of the novel's conclusion may reflect the author's evolving belief in the self-perpetuating life-force we have already encountered in *La Joie de vivre*. If we read the symbolic decor of the novel's last pages correctly, this life-force itself could favor and energize the germination of social forces, renew the face of the earth, and set the stage for a future messiah.

The hero, Etienne, broaches this complex theme as he dreams aloud in front of the coal-mining family, the Maheu, with whom he lodges:

Mais, à présent, le mineur s'éveillait au fond, germait dans la terre ainsi qu'une vraie germe; et l'on verrait un matin ce qu'il pousserait au beau milieu des champs; oui, il pousserait des hommes, une armée d'hommes qui rétabliraient la justice. (3, p. 1277)

[But, at present, the miner was waking underground, germinating in the depths of the earth like real seed; and one fine morning you would see what was growing fair in the middle of the fields; yes, there'd be men springing up there, an army of men who would restore justice.]

Etienne will revert to this prophetic imagery, when he delivers his harangue in the moonlit forest. Like germinating seed, bursting from the ground "un jour de grand soleil" (3, p. 1383) (on a day of bright sunshine)—note how the life-force energizes the children of the revolution—the proletarian army will one day deal with capitalism and its cruel, remote god. Finally the author himself will round off the theme in the epilogue. In a setting of spring and dawn, featuring a soaring lark, he proclaims: " . . . le vieux monde voulait vivre un printemps encore" (3, p. 1588) [the old world wanted to live through yet another spring]. Merging the evocation of bursting seeds and the miners tapping away at the coal seams, deep underground, he prophesies about "une armée noire vengeresse" [a black avenging army] that will arise at the end of the century.

This consistency of theme, imagery, and setting is aesthetically satisfying in itself. It is very likely, however, that Zola used these mythical allusions to intensify his bourgeois readers' apprehension about a revolution that was as sure to occur as the coming of spring or the breaking of dawn. Such a hidden purpose is supported by the following prophetic warning, addressed to "les heureux de ce monde" [the fortunate ones of this world], which Mitterand quotes from Zola's *Correspondance:*

> Hâtez-vous d'être justes, autrement, voilà le péril: la terre s'ouvrira et les nations s'engloutiront dans un des plus effroyables bouleversements de l'histoire.[2]

> [Make haste to become just: otherwise there is the danger that the earth will open and the nations will be engulfed in one of the most dreadful upheavals in history.]

In this instance neither Zola nor his mouthpiece Etienne have proved to be false prophets: their predictions have been validated by history.

Apocalyptic prefigurations are, in fact, scattered throughout the work. One of the most pregnant instances of such imagery is found just before the climax of the novel, as the engineer, Paul Négrel and the mine-manager's wife, Mme Hennebeau, nervously watch the streams of miners tramping across the countryside, on their way to create havoc and destruction:

> C'était la vision rouge de la révolution qui les emporterait tous, fatalement, par une soirée sanglante de cette fin de siècle. . . . Des incendies flamberaient, on ne laisserait pas debout une pierre des villes, on retournerait à la vie sauvage dans les bois, après le grand rut, la grande ripaille. . . . (3, p. 1437)

[It was the red specter of revolution that would be bound to sweep them all away to their death, on a bloodstained evening of this end of a century. Fires would flare up; not a stone of the towns would be left standing. There would be a return to the primitive life in the woods after the great rut, the great orgy.]

The expression "fin de siècle" may be just a cliché, but it is a key-phrase in Christ's discourse on "the last things" in Matt. 24—the biblical chapter that also speaks of no stone being left on another. Could Zola be exploiting the emotive value of biblical phrases—phrases that matched the fears of many bourgeois of his day? Is he using mythical allusions as trigger mechanisms to make the reader believe in the reality of his "vision rouge" [red vision or specter]? It would seem so. To make sure that no one is left unaffected—not all readers are sensitive to religious terminology—he throws in a vague atavistic memory as well, an allusion to the specter of death and chaos that terrified our ancestors, at the onset of the dark ages: "leur poussée débordante de barbares" [the great, surging wave of barbarians] (3, p. 1437). The reference to barbaric hordes is all the more effective because, as a symbolic statement, it activates those deep-seated fears about chaos and breakdown of communication that we usually manage to keep suppressed.

When Zola speaks of the coming revolution in terms of "le grand rut, la grande ripaille" (the great rut, the great orgy), he goes back even further to the orgiastic Dionysian festivals that marked the death of the old year and mythically re-created the original chaos from which civilization arose. Passages like this keep us guessing whether Zola is simply threatening affluent bourgeois with rape and plunder (for purposes of stimulating social reform) or whether he half-believes the pagan and biblical myth that order is born out of chaos.

Death and destruction are only the dark side of Zola's myth of birth and renewal. It is perhaps hazardous to take the views propounded by Etienne in front of the spellbound Maheu for Zola's own, but, but when, on a given subject, the views expressed by the hero are very much in line with the general "mythical drift" of the novel—the sequence leading from cleansing catastrophe to renewal or rebirth—such an identification seems reasonable enough. According to Etienne, the germinating seed may violently crack open the soil, but Utopia will rise from the dust of the old order. He goes on to evoke a humanist equivalent of the heavenly Jerusalem that St. John writes about in the

Book of Revelation (the second volume of *Les Trois villes, Rome* (1896), shows how seriously the author will eventually take such views). Formulating the vision Etienne has but recently absorbed from his haphazard reading of socialist pamhlets, tracts, and newspapers, Zola writes:

> Une société nouvelle poussait en un jour, ainsi que dans les songes, une ville immense, d'une splendeur de mirage où chaque citoyen vivait de sa tâche et prenait sa part des joies communes. (3, p. 1278)

> [A new society grew up in a day, the way things happen in dreams, an immense city, as resplendent as a mirage, where every citizen made a living from his work and had his share of communal joys.]

While insisting, through Etienne, that the man-made Utopia must replace the Christian notion of a heavenly paradise, Zola repeatedly draws parallels between the idealistic hopes of his miners and the faith of the early Christians "qui attendaient la venue d'une société parfaite, sur le fumier du monde antique" (3, p. 1279) [who were waiting for the coming of a perfect society, on the dungheap of the old world]. However, his use of words such as "songe" [dream] and "mirage" in this context suggest that he is not altogether convinced that the workers' mythical dream will be realized. Later in the novel, when the miners' faith rises to fever-pitch in the course of Etienne's nocturnal harangue, Zola refers to this as "le coup de folie de la foi" [faith's moment of madness or frenzy] and compares it to the insane exaltation of a religious sect which, tired of waiting for the promised miracle, resolves to provoke it (cf. 3, p. 1384). The author seems to share the reserve of the passive moon overhead:

> Et la lune tranquille baignait cette houle, la forêt profonde ceignait de son grand silence ce cri de massacre. (3, p. 1385)

> [And the quiet moon bathed the surging tide of men, the deep forest enclosed, in its great silence the shouts of mass murder.]

Zola, in fact, is rather skeptical about the efficacy of revolution. That is why, after the abortive revolt of the miners, he introduces a much more sinister myth—an alternative prophetic scenario that centers around the nihilist Souvarine: where Etienne aspires to be a savior, a messianic deliverer, the Russian opposes his views to the extent that, near the apocalyptic climax of the novel, he will let him and his love descend into the sabotaged mine where they are likely to perish. This somber, brooding anarchist had turned bitter during his prerevolutionary days in Russia, when his mistress was publicly executed by the authorities. As he lives among the miners, he indulges in dark dreams of mass extermination, in the vague hope, perhaps, that a better world may arise from the smoldering ashes—"on verra ensuite" (3, p. 1257) [after that, we'll see]—but in reality to avenge himself for the loss of his ideal (his mistress seems to have been his personal symbol of life, hope, and tenderness).

For a while he manages to contain his destructive anger, as he strokes the ever-pregnant white rabbit on his knee, "cette douceur tiède et vivante" (3, p. 1254) [this warm, soft, living thing], his new, unconscious symbol of purity, fertility, and life. Coral Fuller argues very plausibly that the white rabbit, Souvarine's "surrogate mistress," acts as a restraining influence on his destructive impulses—until the animal's demise—in the same way that La Maheude (mother of many children) is at first a soothing influence on her husband.[3] On a deeper, mythical level, this notion of tranquilizing sexuality could be taken to reflect Zola's belief that natural, life-affirming activities tend to restrain human destructiveness. After the rabbit has been tortured by the miners' children, can no longer bear its young, and is finally eaten, Souvarine turns into Shiva the Destroyer. In terms of this study, we may call him a type of Antichrist: he plans and executes the horrendous mine catastrophe that is clearly a small-scale enactment of the end of the world. We last glimpse him as he disappears into the night to exterminate humanity. In the following quotation, it is worth noting how Zola confirms a myth he has just dramatized in a character of fiction, without realizing that, in doing so, he breaks his naturalistic stance of detachment and objectivity:

> Ce sera lui, sans doute, quand la bourgeoisie agonisante en-tendra, sous elle, à chacun de ses pas, éclater le pavé des rues. (3, p. 1548)
>
> [He'll be there, no doubt, when the bourgeoisie in their death throes hear, with every step that they take, the cobble stones shattering beneath them.]

And so it would appear that, at least at the time of writing, Zola had more faith in the end of the world than in the dawning of a new age.

But old beliefs die hard: parallel to his contrasting visions of

Utopia and Apocalypse, Zola features, within the wider setting of *Germinal*, a little Heaven and a little hell. The latter takes the form of Le Tartaret, an aptly named subterranean region of smoldering peat and coal seams, a sulphurous "cuisine de diable" [Devil's kitchen]. According to old tales, the heroine (Catherine) tells Etienne that depraved miners' girls are punished there forever for their sexual misdemeanors.

Philippe Lejeune's alternative interpretation of Le Tartaret as a graphic picture of the miners' poverty and of "la violence politique qui couve au sein de la classe ouvrière" [the political violence hatching in the bosom of the working class] lacks conviction. Not only does his association of the word "Tartaret" with "les Tartares" [Tartars] and "les barbares" [the barbarians][4] seem superfluous, when the allusion to Greek mythology is so obvious, but Zola himself makes his intentions plain enough in his Dossier préparatoire [preporatory dossier]. Referring to the underground fire, he comments: "Je n'ai plus qu'à montrer Catherine dans cet enfer ou plutôt dans un enfer semblable."[5] [All I have to do now is to show Catherine in this hell, or rather, in a similar hell]. This equivalent of the mythical Tartarus (and the biblical hell) performs several functions in the novel. Not only does it offer some insights into miners' superstitions and provide a focus for Catherine's lingering sense of sexual guilt, but it seems appropriate enough that the living hell of the miners should be matched by a realistic microcosm, an emblem of their world.

When it comes to La Côte verte (The green slope), Zola's equivalent of paradise or Heaven, it is more difficult to define its function in the economy of the novel. Philippe Lejeune's claim that La Côte verte is an allegorical landscape representing the bourgeois life-style, precariously based on the proletarian vulcano[6] must be rejected. Zola's stress on the fertility of the region is in flagrant contradiction to the sterility of the bourgeois women (Cécile dies a virgin; Mme Hennebeau is childless), whereas phrases used by Zola such as "éternel printemps" [eternal spring] are clearly inappropriate for an imperiled society threatened with extermination. Why then does the author take some time off to describe this "miracle d'éternel printemps" [miracle of eternal spring]—an idyllic mountain-slope paradoxically situated over the very top of Le Tartaret (which heats it from below), where the grass and the beeches are always green, where one can grow three crops a year and nature is beyond the ravages of frost? (cf. 3, p. 1395–96). Why have a realistic, tangible counterpart to the insubstantial dream of Utopia—a dream that Zola obviously has doubts about? Has the author retained from his Catholic childhood the dim notion that no world-picture is complete unless it features both a Heaven and a hell? Or does the very act of analyzing in detail a depressing, infernal nightmare, like the life of the miners, prompt in him the need to formulate the opposite dream as well? Is his curious idea of situating paradise on top of hell, as in the medieval three-decker universe, a pictorial way of showing that the compensatory vision of paradise is nurtured by the actual experience of hell—a psychological mechanism that we have already seen at work in La Joie de vivre? It is certainly true that, for all his championing of realism and determinism, Zola continues to be an idealist who is haunted by a mythical landscape of paradise.

From the contrasting strands of Apocalypse and Utopia, it emerges that Zola's faith in the myth of "Germinal" (crisis leading to rebirth and renewal) is not very solid. One reason for this could be that, subconsciously, he entertains doubts about the precise identity of the enemy. The surface-reality, looming at the center of the novel, is the all-devouring mine, Le Voreux, but does not this greedy monster show that ambiguity, that polyvalence that often characterizes myth? On one level, it is simply capitalism overrunning the modern world, oppressing the workers, and swallowing up the individual. At times, however, one gains the impression that the dark mine symbolizes death or, more precisely, the dread of mortality—a fear that obviously haunts not only Lazare in La Joie de vivre. Then again, Zola seems fascinated by the idea of presenting Le Voreux as a kind of dragon or hollow idol—the local manifestation of a remote, inaccessible, cruel divinity that preys upon humanity.

The struggle between capitalism and the proletariat is gripping enough in its own right to hold our attention. Yet there is more to the novel than class-warfare: as a mythical tale with universal implications, it seems to portray the unrelenting battle between light and darkness, life and death. Why do we share Etienne's fascination, early in the novel, as he watches the endless chain of miners descending into the abyss?

> ... Cela s'emplissait, s'emplissait encore, et les ténèbres restaient mortes, la cage montait du vide dans le même silence vorace. (3, p. 1154)

> [It filled up and filled up still and the darkness remained lifeless; the cage rose from the void in the same voracious silence.]

Is it not the perspective of death that closes in upon us, as we then join Etienne in his fearful descent into the pit, his personal initiation into the living death of the miners?

Just as, in general human terms, the experience of hell often provokes an affirmation of paradise or Utopia, the threat of death may prompt the reassertion of life. Among Zola's miners this takes the form of a purely instinctive reaction: their only recourse against encroaching death is rampant sexuality. That is why the author presents the promiscuity practiced around the abandoned mine-shaft of Réquillart as "une revanche de la création" (an act of revenge on the part of creation), suggesting, in the surrounding setting, that nature is playing the same age-old mythical game:

> ... une végétation drue reconquérait ce coin de terre, s'étalait en herbe épaisse, jaillissait en jeunes arbres déjà forts." (3, pp. 1239–40)

> [... dense vegetation was regaining a hold on this piece of land, spreading out as thick grass, bursting forth as young trees that were already sturdy.]

Similarly, the miners' festival day, La Ducasse, turns into an orgiastic affirmation of life, with the aptly named widow Désir officiating as high-priestess:

> Un souffle ardent sortait des blés mûrs; il dut se faire beaucoup d'enfants cette nuit-là ... [La veuve Désir] se vantait aussi que pas une herscheuse ne devenait grosse, sans s'être, à l'avance, dégourdi les jambes chez elle. (3, p. 1268)

> [A hot breath emanated from the ripe corn; there were sure to be a lot of babies made that night.... The widow Desire prided herself that not a single female miner became pregnant without having first loosened up in her bar.]

Life, then, asserts itself in the face of death. Yet it is characteristic of Zola's Weltanschauung in *Germinal* that he has no more confidence in the ultimate triumph of life than he has in the future of Utopia. When, at the height of the famine, the white mother-rabbit is first maimed and then eaten, the author may well be suggesting that starvation eventually gets the better of procreation. When the pit-horse, Bataille, a symbol of the miners' fighting spirit and their will to survive, tries to flee from the rising flood, is trapped in a dark, narrowing shaft, and finally drowns (and how desperately we wanted the brave horse to escape!) this is an ominous mythical enactment of defeat. It is one thing to call one's novel *Germinal*, but unless one accepts the metaphysical implications of that word, how is one to believe in the ultimate victory of life? Zola may derive a certain comfort from the cyclical pattern of nature, where spring ever follows winter, where life ever renews itself, but what does that amount to for a man without religious faith, without children, a man who is rapidly approaching "the wrong side of forty"?

Far from considering Christianity as a fortress against death, Zola can only see a church that identifies itself with the comfortable middle class and with the oppressive masters of capitalism. In the plot of *Germinal*, this finds its echo in the ineffectual abbé Joire who is on the best of terms with the establishment (in André Wurmser's words, he is "complice de César"[7] (in cahoots with Caesar). On the other hand, the newcomer, l'abbé Ranvier, may take the part of the starving miners, but has nothing to offer but an invitation to come to mass and trust in the Lord's provision. Frightened by this progressive priest, the bourgeoisie sees to it that he is promptly removed from the scene.

Zola's hostility toward the church is also reflected in the religious aura he sometimes creates around M. Hennebeau, the mine-manager, and around the mine itself. Just as la veuve Désir [the widow Desire] virtually acts as high-priestess during the miners' Dionysian affirmation of life, M. Hennebeau, Zola hints, is a priest to a distant, remote Parisian divinity. While the miners' deputation is waiting uneasily in the manager's drawing room, the author draws attention to the altar-front drapings that cover the chimney and to the chasuble (priest's vestment) embroideries on the doors. For good measure, he sums up the decor in the phrase "luxe de chapelle" (3, p. 1319) [chapel-style luxury]. The intention of this ecclesiastical setting (Hennebeau is obviously not a religious man) becomes clear toward the end of the chapter in question (part 4, chapter 2), when the author formulates how the miners view the Parisian board of directors, the infinitely remote body that controls their destiny:

> ... cela se reculait dans un lointain terrifiant, dans une contrée inaccessible et religieuse, où trônait le dieu inconnu, accroupi au fond de son tabernacle.... (3, p. 1324)
>
> [... (the scene) receded into an awe-inspiring, distant region, at once inaccessible and religious, where the unknown god sat enthroned, crouching in the depths of his tabernacle.]

As early as the opening chapter of the novel, the old miner, Bonnemort, had expressed similar views when Etienne asked him about the owner of the mining enterprise:

> Sa voix avait pris une sorte de peur religieuse, c'était comme s'il avait parlé d'un tabernacle inaccessible, où se cachait le dieu repu et accroupi auquel ils donnaient tous leur chair et qu'ils n'avaient jamais vu. (3, p. 1141)

> [His voice had taken on a tone akin to religious dread, as if he had been speaking of an inaccessible tabernacle, in which was hidden the crouching, sated deity to whom they, all of them, gave their flesh and whom they had never seen.]

In the remainder of that first chapter, the mine takes on the form of a vast, voracious monster, a Moloch-like idol (sun-god of the ancient Phoenicians), that preys on the miners. The idol, of course, is eventually destroyed and Zola delights in depicting its horrific death-throes, but the evil deity it represents lives on.

In the light of this imagery—the phrase "divinité cruelle et inaccessible" (cruel, inaccessible deity) virtually becomes a leitmotiv—would it be too farfetched to see *Germinal*, in part, as a mythical allegory of the human condition? Is Zola toying with the idea of man as the victim of a callous, remote God who reserves the pleasures of heaven for a few favorites, but who relegates his countless victims to the tortures of hell? If this is so, Zola has completely reversed the situation that prevails in the Book of Revelation. Its author, St. John the Divine, also features a mythical monster—the dragon of old, the real power behind an idolatrous image—but, according to his visions, it is Christ who destroys the image and the archangel Michael who incarcerates the dragon.

We are now in a position to grasp the connection between Zola's ambiguous use of the mine symbol and the pervasive pessimism of his tale: since he associates capitalism with all-powerful death and with a cruel, evil god, it is small wonder that he can only indulge in wishful thinking when it comes to the new dawn of his concluding chapter.

Consistent with the novel's negative, depressing perspective, the hero himself can be seen as a false or flawed messiah—such failing messiahs, of course, being the only variety that Zola is likely to feature at this stage of his career. Once again, Zola can be shown to partly follow and then to invert a biblical scenario.

My findings in this field agree only in part with those of Pierre

Aubéry in his "Imitations de Jésus chez Zola: *Germinal.*"[8] Aubéry goes to unreasonable lengths in pursuing his comparisons. His parallel between the twelve-year-old Jesus astounding the doctors of law in Jerusalem and Lantier conversing with Souvarine and pubkeeper, Rasseneur (p. 34) is forced, to say the least. When he attempts to identify Jesus' encounter with Mary Magdalene with Etienne's furtive adventure with La Mouquette (p. 37), he would have done better to point out the inverted scenario (Christ redeems a fallen woman; Etienne betrays his true love by yielding to the promiscuous La Mouquette). Aubéry's remark that "Lantier, monté à Paris, va siéger à la droite de son père Pluchart. . . ." (p. 40) [Lantier, after going up to Paris, will sit down at the right hand of his father, Pluchart] is clearly the conclusion of someone who has made up his mind to assert, by hook or by crook, that Etienne resembles Jesus, rather than to demonstrate it through an objective analysis of the facts: foppish, smart operator, Pluchart is never presented in godlike terms and Etienne, at the end of the novel, may be dreaming of rhetorical triumphs in Paris, but is not very sure of his reception by the crowds: "Déjà, il se voyait à la tribune, triomphant avec le peuple, si le peuple ne le dévorait pas" (3, p. 1589) [Already he could see himself on the rostrum, being a great success with the crowd—if the crowd did not devour him]. Admittedly, Aubéry himself expresses doubts about his thesis: he can see, for instance, that Etienne's desperate decision to join the miners in their confrontation with the soldiers is not exactly the action of a lamb that offers its life for the redemption of the world (cf. p. 38). In the end he is prepared to concede that the hero is "un messie égoïste qui n'a assuré véritablement le salut que d'un seul, lui-même. . . ." (p. 46) (a self-centered Messiah who, in actual fact, ensures the salvation of only one person—himself) and he is no more satisfied with Etienne than the Marxist writer Philippe Lejeune who writes him off as a swollen-headed, poor organizer, "une sorte de messie rouge" (a sort of red messiah) who has dazzled people with a shimmering dream.[9] Nevertheless, Aubéry structures most of his article around the premature conclusion that Zola is following the life of Jesus, whereas, in fact, more often than not, Zola departs from that model.

Like the Christ of the Gospels, Etienne comes in from the outside to share the life and condition of the oppressed. Both proclaim a message of hope—Jesus about the coming Kingdom, Etienne about his earthly Utopia. This, however, is where the resemblance stops and where Zola departs, not only from the biblical pattern, but also from the usual mythical messianic scenario favored by Semites, Persians, and Indians. During his temptation in the wilderness, Christ resists the allurements of materialism, pride, and power, whereas Etienne, among his miners, begins to relish his popularity, decides it is time to indulge in some linen shirts and fine new boots, and swells with vanity and pride as he fancies himself becoming the pivotal point of a new creation: "Ce furent des satisfactions d'amour-propre délicieuses. . . ." (3, p. 1281) [His self-esteem was flattered in very pleasurable ways. . . .] ". . . surtout devenir un centre, sentir le monde rouler autour de soi, c'était un continuel gonflement de vanité. . . ." (3, p. 1328) [. . . above all, becoming a center, feeling the world turn around one, was a continual boost to one's vanity. . . .]. Christ's "Sermon on the Mount" could be said to correspond to Etienne's forest harangue—after all, Zola does refer to his eloquent hero as "l'apôtre apportant la vérité" (3, p. 1378) [the apostle bringing truth]—but his revolutionary message is the very antithesis of Christ's promise that "the meek shall inherit the earth." While Christians celebrate the ultimate success of Christ's mission, there is little doubt about the failure of Etienne: crushed by the burden of responsibility, he becomes the "chef angoissé" [anguished leader]; losing control over the uprising, he has to face the remorse of not having been adequate to his task, to suffer the scorn and disgrace of a failed leader. Pierre Aubéry is even wrong when he says that Etienne saves himself: he is saved by the heroic perseverance of the engineer, Paul Négrel. Far, then, from reenacting, through Etienne, a myth of deliverance, salvation, and victory, Zola has created what one might call an "antimyth" that reflects his skepticism about messianic hopes and ambitions.

The flawed messiah scenario becomes more obviously mythical if we compare it to the parallel symbol of the horse Trompette. As a new arrival from the world of light, this animal brings the mine-horse, Bataille, the long-forgotten smell of sun-bathed grass. For all his trumpet calls of hope, however, he will pine away in the dark mine, becoming a symbol of confinement, death, and defeat.

It is remarkable, however, that Zola will not allow his messiah to fail altogether: he may die as a popular leader, but he experiences some kind of resurrection in the concluding chapter of the novel. Dawn, the season of spring, the rising lark, all match the resurgence of Etienne's hopes of being a socialist orator.

In fact, it seems quite likely that the final decor of *Germinal* is meant to suggest more than just a second chance for a failed messiah. In the year that Zola first published the novel, 1885, the tentative vision of pantheism, already discernible in *La Joie de vivre*, appears to be taking clearer shape in the author's mind. In March 1885, Zola writes to Jules Lemaître in vaguely pantheistic terms:

> L'âme que vous renfermez dans un être, je la sens épandue partout, dans l'être et hors de l'être, dans l'animal dont il est le frère, dans la plante, dans le caillou.[10]

[The spirit that you imprison in an individual, I sense diffused everywhere, in the individual and outside the individual, in the animal to whom he is brother, in plants, and in stones.]

and, four months later, Gustave Geoffroy comments on the spring scene in the final chapter as follows: "... n'est-ce pas assez pour montrer en Emile Zola le poète qu'on se refuse généralement à voir, le poète panthéiste? ..."[11] [Is not this sufficient evidence of the poet in Zola, that people generally don't allow themselves to see, the pantheistic poet?] Guy Robert, does not actually use the term *panthéisme* in 1951, when he discerns a perspective of hope in the luminous conclusion of the novel, but he refers to "l'oeuvre de la vie sans cesse en travail"[12] [the ceaseless activity of life, which is forever at work] and points out that the mine-disaster prepares the way for "les temps à venir" [times to come]: "En effet, au-delà de l'image de la Catastrophe s'est dressée celle de l'Espérance, qui s'associe déjà à celle de la Fécondité."[13] [Indeed, beyond the image of Catastrophe there has risen the image of Hope, already associated with that of Fertility]. Philip D. Walker, on the other hand, quite boldly refers to "la glorieuse vision panthéiste sur laquelle se ferme *Germinal*"[14] (the splendid pantheistic vision at the conclusion of *Germinal*).

And so, maybe, we should allow for an alternative vision of Etienne. There is merit in Rachelle Rosenberg's depiction of our strike-leader as a partly successful "solar hero" who is matured by his experience at the bottom of the mine and whose resurrection seems to bring fertility to the land. She stresses, however, that he is not a full-fledged hero, because he has neither freed the miners from their enslavement nor brought in a new spiritual dimension (she is referring to what she calls a "higher fertility" that involves a conquering of all fear of death through the perception of a living psychic center within man himself).[15]

In his major work on Zola's recourse to myth, Roger Ripoll takes a similar stand, as he suggests a link between Etienne's slaying of his rival, Chaval, the strike-leader's figurative death and resurrection and his initiation into fertility:

> Etienne, après avoir cédé aux impulsions héréditaires en tuant Chaval, passe par l'expérience de la mort au fond des ténèbres de la mine. A partir de là, il est possible de renaître, de connaître une nouvelle et miraculeuse fécondité.[16]

> [After giving in to hereditary urges when he kills Chaval, Etienne goes through an experience of death deep in the gloomy depths of the mine. From that moment on, rebirth becomes possible and he can come to know a miraculous new fecundity.]

It would appear then that, once again, Zola has left room for a certain amount of ambiguity. Is Etienne a failed messiah, a solar hero, or an initiate to pantheism? The quandary in which the reader finds himself probably corresponds to the author's position of ideological uncertainty or transition—a phenomenon that Philip D. Walker detects in the whole of Zola's religious thought:

> En somme, nous trouvons dans *Germinal* la même ambiguité ... le même caractère incertain, nébuleux, que dans l'ensemble de la pensée religieuse de Zola.[17]

> [In short, we find in *Germinal* the same ambiguity ... the same vague, nebulous quality as in all of Zola's religious thought.]

He has told the story of a failed uprising, a failed leader, and a failed lover—a man who fought, in the end, to win his Catherine from the bestial Chaval (Zola's own shadow?), but who emerged from the mine without her.

Yet our potential messiah, now white-haired like one of the sages of old, rises, phoenixlike, from the ashes of despair to pursue a new dream (or is it the old one?). This defeated hero upon whom light has dawned may yet walk into a future where he can serve the all-pervading, quasi-divine life-force. In this novel that amounts to a "summa," Zola has acted out the myth of modern man: he does not believe (as yet) in Utopia, but cannot forget his dreams of paradise; he fears Apocalypse, universal strife, and chaos, but clings to his ideals of light, justice, and community; he fears that he has little to look forward to but death, but remains fascinated by myths that promise redemption and rebirth.

Thanks to the work of Mitterand and others, it is now well established that *L'Oeuvre* [The Work] (1886) was not intended as a repudiation either of Cézanne or of the enthusiastic band of artists that Zola frequented and championed in the 1860s. The hero, Claude Lantier, who already played a secondary role in *Le Ventre de Paris* as the friend of Florent, may show qualities shared by Cézanne, the great companion of Zola's youth, and the novel as a whole obviously incorporates many memories dear to Zola and his early friends, but its prime focus is on the author's own dreams, trials, and torments as an artist. If, indeed, Cézanne was offended with "l'auteur des *Rougon-Macquart*" [the author of the *Rougon-Macquart*]—which is not certain—he would have done better to remember Zola's lifelong record as a good and faithful friend.

More relevant, perhaps, to our study of Zola's messianic myth is the author's repeated assertion that *L'Oeuvre* contains much autobiographical material. The very first page of Zola's Ebauche offers that information. No sooner has the author stated the theme of "la lutte contre l'Ange" [the struggle with the Angel], Philip Walker points out, than he adds: "En un mot, j'y raconte ma vie intime"[18] [In a word, it's my inner life that I'm talking about there]. Mitterand confirms this self-revelatory intention by quoting from Zola's letter to Van Santen Kolff (6 June 1886), written as the novel was still in its early stages:

> Je me suis mis à mon prochain roman. . . . C'est toute ma jeunesse que je raconte, j'ai mis là tous mes amis, je m'y suis mis moi-même. . . .[19]

> [I've started work on my next novel. . . . I'm writing about the whole of my youth; I have put all my friends in it and myself as well. . . .]

and by reproducing Zola's press-release for *Bibliographie de la France* (2 April 1886):

> L'auteur a mis ce drame dans le milieu de la jeunesse, il s'y est confessé lui-même, il y a raconté quinze ans de sa vie et de la vie de ses contemporains.[20]

> [The author has set this drama in the middle of his own youth; he has confessed his own sins there, covering fifteen years of his own life and that of his contemporaries.]

Note how, in the first two quotes, Zola shifts from "ma vie intime" [my inner life] to "toute ma jeunesse" [the whole of my youth], as though he wants to convince himself and the reader that, while Claude reflects the author's youthful ambitions and illusions, the painter's writer-friend, Sandoz, shares Zola's more mature and more humble realization that an artist cannot compete with the Creator, that he has no hope of capturing, on his restricted canvas, the whole of life, nature, and reality. Any such rationalization or alibi on Zola's part needs to be challenged, if we are to appreciate how the end of the novel, in particular, reflects the author's vision of himself as a messianic prophet or otherwise. One clear-sighted critic, Gustave Geoffroy, did make just such a challenge shortly after the novel's publication:

> Ce n'est pas seulement, en effet, par Sandoz que Zola s'est représenté. N'a-t-il pas aussi mis une partie de lui-même en ce Claude Lantier?[21]
>
> [In fact, Zola has not presented a portrait of himself in Sandoz alone. Hasn't he also put part of himself in that Claude Lantier?]

A more recent critic, Antoinette Ehrard, assesses very clearly the extent to which Sandoz's destruction of Claude's monstrous painting reflects Zola's doubts about his own enormous "canvases," his own "sin" of substituting art for life:

> Il est permis de penser que Zola détruit, à travers le geste violent de Sandoz, son oeuvre à lui, devant laquelle il doute. C'est lui-même qu'il venge: c'est lui le "travailleur héroique", "l'observateur passionné dont le crâne s'était bourré de science", qui a "donné sa vie entière" à la tentative de création, dont l'oeuvre dévore la vie.[22]
>
> [It is permissible to think that, by way of Sandoz's violent gesture, Zola is destroying his own work, about which he has doubts. It's himself that he takes vengeance on: he is that "heroic worker," "the passionate observer whose head had become crammed with science," who "gave over his whole life" to the attempt at creation, whose work eats up his life.]

In fact, we may add Christine, the young girl who becomes Claude's mistress and then wife, to the list of those in whom Zola mirrors part of his personality and outlook—as a perusal of the plot will show.

From the opening page of the novel, Claude reveals himself as a potential savior, as he rescues the terrified Christine from a lustful cabdriver as well as from thunder and lightning, by offering her shelter for the night. We should note, however, that while

Claude, the artist, is capable of intuitive discernment, it is to the girl that Zola grants a genuinely prophetic glimpse of the city's future: " ... elle venait de revoir la ville tragique dans un éclaboussement de sang" (4, p. 13) [She had just seen the tragic city again, spattered with blood]. It is almost as though, through her nightmarish intuitions, we are given a preview of the end of *La Débâcle*:

> C'était une trouée immense, les deux bouts de la rivière s'enfonçant à perte de vue, au milieu de braises rouges d'un incendie. (4, p. 13)

> [There was an immense gap, the two ends of the river disappearing into the far distance, amid the red embers of a great conflagration.]

To reinforce this apocalyptic impression, Zola makes Christine remember next morning (she has her eyes closed): "Elle revoyait la cité tragique, cette trouée de quais s'enfonçant dans des rougoîements de fournaise...." [And she saw again the tragic city, the gap where the quays plunged into the lurid, furnacelike glow] adding a few touches that evoke the prison-hulks and the gallows of la Commune:

> ... ce fossé profond de la rivière roulait des eaux de plomb, encombré de grands corps noirs, de chalands pareils à des baleines mortes, hérissé de grues immobiles, qui allongeaient des bras de potence. (4, p. 26)

> [... in the deep trench that was the river, the water flowed on, the color of lead, congested with large, dark shapes, barges like dead whales, bristling with motionless cranes that stretched out gibbetlike arms.]

Claude, too, however, has the eyes of a seer: having sketched the half-naked body of Christine while she slept, he decides to incorporate aspects of it in his riverside painting of Paris. Already, he discerns in her the living soul of the city, its complement of the life-force in human form.

To enlarge upon Claude's openness to the spirit of things, chapter 2 offers some flashbacks to Claude and his friends's youthful, adoring absorption in nature, which leads onto Claude's creed in chapter 3 of loving life as it is, experiencing and propagating it, as man's only title to divinity:

> Ah! la vie, la vie! la sentir et la rendre dans sa réalité, l'aimer pour elle, y voir la seule beauté vraie, éternelle et changeante, ne pas avoir

l'idée bête de l'anoblir en la châtrant, comprendre que les prétendues laideurs ne sont que les saillies des caractères, et faire vivre, et faire des hommes, la seule façon d'être Dieu! (4, p. 83)

[Ah, life, life! oh to feel and portray it as it really is, to love it for itself and see in it the one true beauty [that is] eternal yet ever-changing. It is stupid to try to ennoble life by castrating it; you need to realize that so-called ugly features are only projections of personality: causing life, making men is the only way of being God.]

So far, then, Claude is on the right track, although he goes through phases of discouragement when his creative will is paralyzed: he accepts his limits as an artist, respects Christine, his good companion and, through her, the life-force that he does not try to make subservient to his art. By chapter 4, however, there is a suggestion of trouble to come, as Christine regrets that her likeness is gradually disappearing from the painting that Claude destines for the exhibition. Maybe it is not only Christine that Claude is losing sight of!

At the critical stage, she well-meaningly makes the mistake of offering her nakedness, not for living communion with the man she loves, but for the sake of his art. Paradoxically, respite from error comes to Claude in the form of failure: when his painting is ridiculed at the Salon des Refusés, Christine comforts him by giving herself. In chapter 6, this act of love culminates in an idyll, as the couple roam along the Seine at Bennecourt—the paradise of *Le Voeu d'une morte* that turns into a scene of death in *Thérèse Raquin*—or go boating among the river-islands. In Claude, the man has taken over from the artist; passionate love, direct involvement in life, has replaced his aesthetic appreciation of womanly beauty.

Just as Christine has fallen pregnant and the artist in Claude is growing moody and restless, his literary friend, Sandoz, begins to call. The latter announces his wedding and then pours out his famous pantheistic hymn to the earth, nature, and the life-force—the kind of vision that could have saved Claude from an idolatrous perversion of his art: according to Zola's creed, as we have seen it emerge more consciously in *La Joie de vivre* and *Germinal*, the artist's role is to serve and celebrate the life-force, not to replace it by acts of rival creation.

Outwardly things go well for Claude, who is painting a little again and whose son, Jacques, seems to have grown into a healthy and robust two-and-a-half-year-old. As the charm of country-life palls, however, and Claude grows bored and depressed without

7: MESSIANIC MYTH IN CRISIS 143

his friends, Christine prevails on him to return to Paris and the world of art. Zola punctuates this by introducing a symbolic preview of future developments: Claude becomes guilty of an act of unfaithfulness to his love: he allows his friend, Jory, to take him to the artist's model and budding courtesan, Irma Bécot, who desires him and makes him talk about Christine.

This encounter with the perverted side of sexuality—a reminder of the world of *Nana*—is contrasted with Claude's experience of a Thursday evening at the home of Sandoz (fate seems determined to look after the hero's spiritual welfare). His writer-friend is planning a new cycle of novels, Claude learns, featuring

> la vaste nature, éternellement en création . . . et surtout l'acte sexuel, l'origine et l'achèvement continu du monde, tiré de la honte où on le cache, remis dans sa gloire sous le soleil. (4, p. 190)

> [Nature in her vastness, eternally creative . . . and, in particular, the sexual act, the world's perpetual beginning and conclusion, freed from the shame beneath which it is hidden and reinstated, in all its splendor, in the light of the sun.]

[If this celebration of "l'acte générateur divinisé" (the divinized act of procreation) is what Zola himself hoped to achieve in his next novel, *La Terre*, one can only comment that he first needed to work on his own unconscious attitude to sexuality that would not become wholesome, or at least less inhibited, until he was ready to write *Le Docteur Pascal*.)

Once again, Claude is unable to profit from Sandoz's higher vision (we read between the lines: the enlightened part of Zola is not getting through to his subconscious) and this is how, one evening, standing on a bridge over the Seine, he conceives the masterpiece that will estrange him from Christine and from life itself. Out of pity, he may go through the motions of marrying her but, in fact, he will increasingly neglect her, as he becomes absorbed in his sketch of Le Port Saint-Nicolas.

The dramatic scene of Mahoudeau's collapsing clay statue, La Baigneuse (The bather) (Claude's friend is too poor to be able to afford the supporting metal rods he needs) is no doubt intended as another omen or preview of Claude's destiny—maybe as an object lesson sent to him by fate. At the same time, Sandoz, uneasy about the resplendent nude Claude is painting in the middle of his contemporary river-view, complete with dockers, warns his friend: the naked figure may be a symbol of Paris, "la ville nue et passionnée" [the naked, passionate city], but it is too much involved with Claude's aesthetic fascination with sensuality. (Inasmuch as Claude prefers the artistic reproduction of woman to life in the raw—a phenomenon not uncommon among painters, inasmuch as he projects his repressed eroticism on to his canvas, rather than express it with Christine, he is going astray, he is no longer a faithful prophet of the life-force.)

Claude's spiritual apostasy is matched by his financial decline (he is living on his capital) and by the health problems of his son: little Jacques turns out to be retarded and hydrocephalic. The underlying reason for Claude's inability to finish any of his paintings is his constant overreaching of himself as an artist. Formulating the vague thoughts that flit through his character's consciousness, the author explains: ". . . il se brisait à cette besogne impossible de faire tenir toute la nature sur une toile. . . ." (4, p. 245) [. . . he was being broken by the impossible task of cramming the whole of nature into one canvas] The hero, in other words, has fallen into the error reflected in some of Zola's contemplated titles for the novel such as "La Vie universelle" [Universal life], "Faire un monde" [Making a world], and "Etre Dieu" [Being God].[23] Not content to be a prophet of the life-force, he tries to compete with it, with disastrous results.

On a purely physical level, Claude is seduced by Irma—another parallel situation to his espousing a perverted form of the life-force. On the level of art, his splendid decor of the port is ruined by the odd, hallucinatory female figure at its center: Claude's symbol of the living soul of Paris is turning into a grotesque idol. On the domestic level, too, he fails badly: little Jacques dies, hardly noticed by his preoccupied father. Claude may paint a masterful portrait of his dead son—yet another symbol of his failure, of his inability to collaborate with the life-force, but when the picture is poorly hung and totally ignored at the Salon, Sandoz can no longer console him by pointing to his role as a precursor for a whole school of painters.

Perhaps Zola should have ended his novel at the tomb of little Jacques, for at this point the author's depression prevails, as the plot takes on a perspective of unremitting gloom and doom. Significantly, Sandoz loses his mother (as Zola had in 1880) and several of Claude's artist friends fail utterly in their chosen calling. Mahoudeau's companion, Chaîne, gives up his painting to run a sideshow at a year-round fair. Claude's friend, Dubuch, fares disastrously in his architectural pursuits and retires to look after his sickly, degenerate children. When Claude and Sandoz make a pilgrimage to Bennecourt, all has changed for the worse. The extent of Zola's identification with both characters emerges clearly as Sandoz voices his doubts about posterity's doing justice to great art and as Claude gives free rein to his disillusionment:

> (Claude) Bah! qu'est-ce que ça fiche? Il n'y a rien. . . . Quand la terre craquera dans l'espace comme une noix sèche, nos oeuvres n'ajouteront pas un atome à sa poussière.
> —Ça, c'est bien vrai, conclut Sandoz, très pâle, A quoi bon vouloir combler le néant. . . . Et dire que nous le savons et que notre orgueil s'acharne! (4, p. 301)

> [Pooh! Who gives a damn? There is nothing. . . . When the earth cracks open in space like a dry walnut, our work won't add even an atom to its dust.
> —That's quite true, concluded Sandoz, turning very pale. What is the point of wanting to fill up the void. . . . And just to think that we know all that and our stubborn pride still hangs on!]

Sandoz may be constrained by his pride to carry on doggedly with his novels, but he too is shown to face failure of a sort: his cult of faithful friendship and mutually supportive fellowship founders, when the dinner he has arranged for his old companions is spoiled by a quarrelsome spirit and ends in some of the guests' regretting their former following of Claude's lead (shades of Zola and his disintegrating band of friends).

Afterward Claude feels drawn to the nocturnal scene of the Seine that has become for him a river of death. Placing himself in the mind of Claude, once again, Zola returns to Christine's early prophetc glimpses of Paris, adding the even more apocalyptic imagery of a threatening volcanic eruption:

> En haut, au-dessus de cet incendie (light reflected on the Seine), au-dessus des quais étoilés, il y avait dans le ciel sans astres une rouge nuée, l'exhalaison chaude et phosphorescente qui, chaque nuit, met au sommeil de la ville une crête de volcan. (4, p. 340)

> [High up above this fire [= light reflected on the river Seine], above the light-spangled quays, there floated in the starless sky a pall of red cloud—the hot, phosphorescent fumes which, each night, overshadowed the sleep of the city with a volcanic crest.]

Apprehensive Christine has followed her husband to the river, but can only stand by helpless, as he listens to the seductive whispers of the current. And so even Christine, this incarnation of the life-force, cannot help a man who has turned his worship of life into a form of pagan idolatry. This notion is elaborated further in the final chapter. The couple have gone home and have retired to bed, but soon Claude leaves his wife in order to work on the naked figure in his painting. Christine watches with jealous horror, as he turns her portrait more and more into a sacrilegious monstrosity, an idol dedicated to lust and omnipotent art:

> ... ces cuisses se doraient en colonnes de tabernacle, ce ventre devenait un astre, éclatant de jaune et de rouge purs, splendide et hors de la vie. Une si étrange nudité d'ostensoir, où des pierreries semblaient luire, pour quelque adoration religieuse, acheva de la fâcher. (4, p. 343)

> [... the thighs were gilded like the pillars of a tabernacle, the belly was becoming a star, an explosion of pure red and yellow, splendid and removed from life. Ultimately she was angered by such a bizarre, monstrance-like nudity, about which there seemed to be the gleam of precious stones, as though [set up] for some kind of religious adoration.]

In the end, Claude breaks free from his stupor and realizes the nature of his obsession:

> Qui donc venait de peindre cette idole d'une religion inconnue? qui l'avait faite de métaux, de marbres, de gemmes, épanouissant la rose mystique de son sexe, entre les colonnes précieuses des cuisses, sous la voûte sacrée du ventre? Etait-ce lui qui, sans le savoir, était l'ouvrier de ce symbole du désir insatiable, de cette image extraordinaire de la chair, devenu de l'or et du diamant entre ses doigts, dans son vain effort de faire de la vie? (4, p. 347)

> [Who then had just painted this idol from some unknown religion? Who had fashioned her from metal, marble, and precious stones, bringing to flower the mystic rose of her sex, between the golden columns of her legs, below the sacred vault of her belly? Had he unwittingly been the artisan of this symbol of insatiable desire, this extraordinary image of the flesh that had turned to gold and diamond in his hands, in his vain attempt at creating life?]

In order to take in the full implication of this quote, we need to keep in mind Nana's dream and the way in which Zola himself turned her into an infernal goddess of lust and corruption. In the light of that earlier scenario, we may well conclude that, in showing Claude's disarray in front of his painting, Zola is indirectly confessing his own aberration—his obsession that tends to turn his perennial vision of self-renewing life into a voyeuristic contemplation of sexual perversion. After writing the pantheistic conclusion of *Germinal* and showing the life-force (Pauline) in *La Joie de vivre* quietly triumphing over the fear of death, he must have sensed that there was something wrong with his earlier focus on corruption, decadence, and promiscuity.

Diagnosis of the problem, however, is only a first step toward healing. At the end of *L'Oeuvre*, the author is still projecting (onto Paris) his own need of purging: in his novel it is the pleasure-loving capital that sleeps on unconsciously, whereas, in fact, it is Zola himself who needs the experience of Apocalypse. Subsequent novels will show that the author is still troubled by the beast in man. True deliverance will not come until, like Dr. Pascal, he can fully acknowledge his own sexuality and then look beyond it.

In that respect, Claude is ahead of his literary creator: in this quote, he identifies the nature of his error, when he realizes that he has distorted his portrayal of the life-force with the caricature of his own insatiable desire. But he lacks the strength to turn back: even making love to Christine cannot reconcile him to reality. He slips out of bed and hangs himself in front of his picture.

Significantly the painting is destroyed by Sandoz—a promise of things to come in Zola's psyche. Christine ends up in a hospital with cerebral fever, while the novel closes pessimistically on Sandoz sharing with over-the-hill artist, Bongrand, both the essential frustration of the artist:

> Puisque nous ne pouvons rien créer, puisque nous ne sommes que des reproducteurs débiles, autant vaudrait-il nous casser la tête tout de suite. (4, p. 363)

> [Since we can't create anything and since we are only feeble reproducers, we might as well do ourselves in at once.]

and the paradoxical determination to battle on regardless: "Allons travailler" (4, p. 363) [Let's get back to work]. How then shall we fit *L'Oeuvre* into the evolution of Zola's messianic preoccupations? Like Etienne, in *Germinal*, Claude is no true messiah: rather than rescue Christine, he brings about her ruin. It might be more appropriate, in fact, to regard the heroine as Claude's chance of salvation (hence her messianic name)—a savior that he fails to appreciate as an envoy from the life-force. In spite of Sandoz's comforting words, he is not even a precursor, a St. John the Baptist, preparing the way for the coming messiah. Forgetting his human limitations, idolatrously substituting art (or his own repressed desire) for living reality (in Zola's eyes, the only divinity), he perverts his message. Unlike Philip Walker in his essay "Zola et la lutte avec l'Ange,"[24] the present writer cannot see any signs of Zola's emerging wounded from a struggle with the life-force and returning "a sadder and a wiser man," ready to be the father of a new nation. Zola may dream of this through a character like Etienne, stepping out into the dawn at the end of *Germinal*, but as yet we have only an expression of good intentions on the part of Sandoz, alias Zola (serving and glorifying nature as the dynamic force, esence, and purpose of his work). Unlike the coming hero of *Le Docteur Pascal*, however, Zola is not yet ready to step aside, to accept metaphoric death for himself, allowing the life-force to bring to birth the child who may be the world's new messiah.

At the risk of rewriting Stephen Leacock's famous chapter on "Snakes in Ireland": "There are no snakes in Ireland" (that is the whole chapter!) I will venture to pass in review some aspects of *La Terre* [The Land] that bear on the messianic theme, notably the unsatisfactory incarnation of the hero and related characters, Zola's "second look" at his theme of the life-force, and his growing preoccupation with the notion of Apocalypse.

La Terre is certainly the last novel anyone would put forward as a treatment of the messianic theme. Its hero, Jean Macquart, a brother of Gervaise's, is not even a failed or false messiah, but a nonmessiah. Having come into La Beauce as an outsider, he is unable to cope with the full force of the peasants' passion for the land or to compete with their somewhat crude and basic sexuality. Guy Robert puts down the intimate connection existing between the two drives featured in the novel to "l'une des intuitions les plus familières à Zola. . . .—l'unité des forces qui assurent partout la perpétuité de la vie"[25] [one of the intuitions with which Zola is most at home. . . .—the consistency of the forces that everywhere ensure that life is perpetuated].

As a newcomer from Provence, as a former joiner and cabinet-maker and, more lately, as a soldier fighting in foreign parts, Jean may have an emotional attachment to nature and to the passing seasons, he may dimly sense the poetry of "l'Eternel retour" (the Eternal return), but he cannot match the local passion for working, possessing, and accumulating the land. Just like Florent (*Le Ventre de Paris*) who was unable and unwilling to become part of the Parisian bourgeoisie, the hero of *La Terre* fails to be accepted into rural society. Restating this in terms more relevant to our study: Jean disqualifies himself as a savior or messiah because of his inadequate incarnation. Young Françoise, of peasant stock, responds to his kindness and gentleness but, when it comes to the point, she recoils from bearing a child to an outsider who strikes her as weak and ineffectual. Unconsciously attracted to the violently instinctive Buteau, the husband of her sister, Lise, she does not want the family land to go to a stranger: even after marrying Jean, she fails to write a will in his favor. And so, when she is violated by Buteau and then murdered by her own sister, Jean will lose any legal claim to the land and will see no alternative but to depart.

Into the wider plot, Zola has woven two characters who parallel the hero's incomplete integration. The first of these is the gentleman-farmer, Hourdequin, son of a bourgeois town-dweller, who loses his wife and daughter and whose son prefers the army to the land. With his intellectualized, rather sentimental love of the soil, and his less than successful experiments with agricultural machinery, he too remains an outsider: his de facto relationship with sluttish, promiscuous Jacqueline Cognet is no more satisfactory than his relationship to the land: he is cheated by both. Where Jean is virtually driven off the land, Hourdequin is murdered by a jealous lover of Jacqueline's. Both Jean and the farmer may be said to act out an allegory of Zola's estrangement from his physical and instinctive self (an estrangement that, in turn, is linked to what lingers in him of the Oedipal child's hopeless love for the mother—disguised as love for mother-earth—and his sense of being excluded from paradise).

Our views on this subject match Roger Ripoll's well-documented thesis that Zola's turning to detachment, realism, and objectivity is a form of defense against guilty desires and dreams.[26] In the process of solving one problem, of course, Zola creates another—his alienation from his own sexuality that is increasingly repressed and rejected as a monstrous aberration. As such, it becomes the bête noire, the rampant libido that haunts novels such as *Nana*, *Pot-Bouille*, *Germinal* and, especially, *La Terre*.

Reference has already been made to the well-known Jungian mechanism whereby we tend to malign our own shadow, the aspect of our psyche that we reject or censor as unacceptable.

Ousted from our conscious personality, no longer checked and balanced by other components of character, these aspects become more and more frightening and grotesque—much like the caricature of lust in Beauty and the Beast that is quickly tamed and even becomes beautiful and gentle, once it is loved and accepted. Emmanuel Le Roy Ladurie, in his preface to Zola's *La Terre*, is awake to the author's projection of his own negative attitude to his sexuality when he formulates the following question:

> Ce sang rural qui véhicule le chromosome du crime, renvoie-t-il à la réalité de nos campagnes, ou à la paranoïa des écrivains naturalistes?[27]

> [Does this country blood that transmits the chromosome for crime genuinely reflect what happens in our rural areas or, rather, the paranoia of naturalistic writers?]

(Implication: Zola's excessive, paranoid portrayal of peasant lust and violence is a projected vilification of his own repressed sexuality).

The third outsider in *La Terre* is l'abbé Godard, whom we could see as a projection of Zola's provisional rejection of any messianic role and as an expression of his continuing compassion for suffering humanity (l'abbé Pierre, in *Les Trois villes*, will be an elaboration of the same attitudes).

In the early stages of the novel, we see him rushing through mass, quarreling with the mayor about badly needed church repairs, fuming against the unchaste "filles de la Vierge" [daughters of Mary], and yet compassionate toward orphaned Palmyre and her retarded brother and ever generous to the poor whom he gives all he can out of his own pocket. Generally scorned, not taken seriously by his parishioners who treat him as a convenience, he finally gives up on his flock, preferring to be suspended by his bishop rather than continue to administer the sacraments to such a bestial community. Significantly, however, he will return to his duties in the end:

> Sûrement, le bon Dieu qu'on le forçait à rapporter, les enverrait tous rôtir en enfer, ces damnés de Rognes; seulement, quoi? ce n'était pas une raison pour les laisser trop souffrir dans cette vie. (4, p. 806)

> [Certainly the Good Lord, whom they were forcing him to bring back, would send all those damned people of Rogne to roast in hell. Well,

so what? That was no reason for letting them suffer too much in this life.]

—just as Zola himself will gradually be reconciled to his sexuality after 1888 and will eventually return to his prophetic and messianic vocation (as he sees it).

Even old Fouan, the martyrized father who finds it so difficult to renounce his lifelong passion for the land, may convey to us something of the predicament of Zola, the man who is not only estranged from his sensuality but who, now in his late forties, depressed and ailing, fears his vitality is abandoning him for good (actually the author is in for a great surprise, in the form of the linen-maid his wife will take on the next year, but he is not to know that in 1887).

Meanwhile Zola's troubled attitude to his instinctive self is reflected in the way in which he portrays man and nature in La Terre. On the one hand, there is the author's epic evocation of l'Eternel retour, "le poème vivant de la terre" [the earth's living poem],[28] the saga of man working the earth, the cycle of sowing, germination, harvesting, and death. As Guy Robert has shown so forcefully in La Terre d'Emile Zola:

> ... les générations humaines, dans leurs travaux, leurs passions, leurs revers se répètent les unes les autres et la Nature ramène inlassablement les fécondations et les morts.[29]
>
> [... the generations of man, with their work, their passions, their setbacks, repeat themselves and nature tirelessly goes on alternating insemination and death.]

On the other hand, the author exposes the base instincts, the immorality, and violence of his peasants (which he parallels with the unthinking cruelty of nature, for instance, in the episode of the destructive hailstorm)—or else he contrasts the frantic passions of his rustics with the supreme indifference of nature as she pursues her own unknown purposes. Zola acknowledges, in other words, that his exaltation of the life-force in his preceding novels has been somewhat one-sided although, there too, the ocean of life was shown to be capable of destructiveness. The point would seem to be that, as yet, he cannot wholeheartedly espouse the prophetic role of glorifying the life-force, because his perception of it is warped by confusion with his own repressed sexuality. This inability to accept fully the human manifestations of nature leads him to assert our loneliness, separateness, and otherness:

> La terre n'entre pas dans nos querelles d'insectes rageurs, elle ne s'occupe pas plus de nous que des fourmis, la grande travailleuse, éternellement à sa besogne. (4, p. 811)
>
> [The earth does not become involved in the quarrels that we carry on like angry insects. The great worker is eternally about her business and cares no more about us than about the ants.]

Zola, of course, has long been caught in the Oedipal dilemma of loving mother and needing to flee her, rejoicing initially in the delights of paradise and being exiled from it. Lately he has sublimated his old love into an exaltation of the life-force, but still does not know how to cope with its more animalistic manifestations—the instincts he gives such a bad press in creations like Nana or, in the present novel, in bestial, immoral, murderous Buteau. The latter not only chokes to death his own father, but, assisted by his wife, Lise, rapes Françoise and then allows his victim to be impaled upon the upturned blade of a scythe. The fatal weapon, a symbol both of death and of the phallus, lends itself to connotations of sadism.

Zola's interest in that subject will emerge more clearly in La Bête humaine. [The Beast in Man] Meanwhile, he reacts to his dilemma in the face of life and sexuality—a dilemma made more urgent by advancing years—in two main ways.

On the one hand, he wreaks vengeance on the religious and idealistic values that he holds responsible for his frustration by turning them inside out and upside down—the sort of thing Camus resorts to in his play Le Malentendu when he inverts the story of Christ raising Lazarus, by getting Martha to share in murdering the long-lost brother who could have saved the whole family from its dismal life-style. Jésus, the sad, disillusioned messiah of the tale "Le Sang" is replaced in La Terre by "un Christ soûlard, violeur de filles et détrousseur de grandes routes" (4, p. 380) [a sot of a Christ who violates girls, and plays the highwayman]. Zola may be forgiven for his farcical idea of turning Buteau's brother into a champion breaker of wind, but does not the author go beyond all reasonable limits when he stages a flatulent Jesus Christ who asks the village drummer to light his fart? What are we to make of the resulting incandescent "emission" rising to the heavens like a glorious sun? Is Zola parodying the Ascension or the Resurrection?

7: MESSIANIC MYTH IN CRISIS   153

In the same way, Zola's Chartres becomes the setting, not of a cathedral dedicated to the Virgin, but of a brothel that has fallen into decadent ways, but is going to be redeemed by the combined efforts of Nénesse Delhomme and the not-so-pious-after-all Elodie, brought up by the nuns, but finding her true vocation as a madame, to the delight of her churchgoing grandparents. There is no doubt a good deal of aggressiveness in Zola's demolition of his own ideals.

The author's alternative response to his dilemma is to vent his anger by reverting to his scenario of Apocalypse. It is true that he intended all along to introduce the theme of catastrophe in his *Rougon-Macquart*. Guy Robert quotes from Zola's "Note sur la marche générale de l'oeuvre" (Note on the general direction of the novel) to bring home this point:

> Je veux peindre au début d'un siècle de vérité et de liberté, une famille qui s'élance vers les biens prochains et qui roule détraquée par son élan lui-même, justement à cause des heures troubles du moment, des convulsions fatales de l'enfantement d'un monde.[30]

> [I want to depict, at the beginning of a century of truth and liberty, a family who rush after earthly goods and become derailed through their very momentum, simply because of the troubled times, the inevitable birth pangs of a new world.]

As we have seen in the course of this study, the theme of Apocalypse does not begin to emerge clearly until *Nana* and, particularly *Germinal*, but it is in *La Terre* that it manifests itself in many guises.

Just as, in *Germinal*, Zola frightens his readers with visions of barbaric hords on the rampage, he uses Jean's reading at a "veillée" [an evening social gathering of peasants] to a similar effect (the hero is quoting from "Le Malheur et le triomphe de Jacques Bonhomme" [The misfortunes and triumphs of Jack Goodfellow], a booklet of Bonapartist propaganda, which raises the possibility of the peasants' avenging themselves for their long-standing exploitation:)

> S'ils se fâchaient une fois de plus, eux qui sont le nombre, s'ils réclamaient enfin leur part de jouissance? Et la vision ancienne galope, de grands diables à demi-nus, en guenilles, fous de brutalité et de désirs, ruinant, exterminant, comme on les a ruinés et exterminés, violant à leur tour les femmes des autres. (4, p. 432)

[What if they were to rise up in anger one more time—they have the numbers—what if they were to claim their share of enjoyment? And the age-old vision comes galloping along—big, half-naked devils in rags, mad with savagery and lust, ravaging, exterminating, in the same way as they have been ravaged and exterminated, violating in their turn the wives of others.]

Jean's wife, Françoise, probably does not bear her name by chance. We may take it that she partly represents the country of France—close to the land, but tending, periodically, to fall prey to instincts of violence. Pursuing the allegory a little further, she is married to peace-loving Jean, half-artisan, half-peasant, but unconsciously attracted to Buteau and to his savage ways. Significantly her rape and death coincide with the young men of the region being called up for military service (through the "tirage au sort" or drawing of lots)—and that under the threat of war. As at the end of *Nana*, Zola is building up an atmosphere of crisis to prepare for the apocalyptic events portrayed in *La Débâcle*.

The death of Françoise is also set against prophecies of the imminent ruin of the French peasantry, with its problem of little, subdivided lots and its threatened submersion beneath floods of American wheat-imports. This specter of doom is raised by the schoolteacher Lequeu, during a quarrelsome evening at the pub. Actually, the radical "instituteur" [primary schoolteacher] reflects Zola's own fears that the only solution for the country may lie in a nihilistic upheaval. (Is a politically and scientifically created paradise still possible in France, the teacher wonders:)

> Est-ce que nous ne sommes pas trop pourris déjà? Il faudrait que des sauvages vinssent nous nettoyer d'abord, des Cosaques ou des Chinois. (4, p. 766)

> [Aren't we already too rotten? There would need to be an invasion of savages to purge us first—Cossacks or the Chinese.]

Mitterand demonstrates how close such sentiments come to Zola's own views at the time, by quoting the author's reaction to Jules Guesde's optimistic theories:

> Serait-ce possible dans notre vieille race pourrie de monarchisme? Ne faudrait-il point une race? La race nouvelle, les barbares, ce serait la race des travailleurs (la Chine si l'on attendait et si elle se jetait sur nous).[31]

[Would it be feasible in our old race, rotten as it is with monarchism? Wouldn't it take (another) race? The new race, the barbarians—it would be the workers' race (China, if we waited and if it were to fall upon us).]

Just before Jean returns home to find his wife has died from her wounds, the farmer Hourdequin sums up the whole apocalyptic tone of the chapter in question (part 5, chapter 4), by calling for the end of all things:

> ... Que tout craque, que nous crevions tous, que les ronces poussent partout, puisque la race est finie et la terre épuisée. (4, p. 772)

[May everything crack! May we all perish! May the brambles grow everywhere, because our race is finished and the earth exhausted.]

His despairing wish for Apocalypse now will come true—at least for him personally: he is about to be murdered and his farmhouse will be burned to the ground, with promiscuous Jacqueline running out, naked.

At that apocalyptic climax of the plot, however, Zola uses Jean's meditation on the state of affairs to toy with the idea that evil may be a necessary ingredient in life's progress (to complete the appalling picture, old Fouan has just been throttled and burned by Buteau and Lise:)

> Il y avait aussi la douleur, le sang, les larmes, tout ce qu'on souffre et tout ce qui révolte. Françoise tuée, Fouan tué, les coquins triomphants, la vermine sanguinaire et puante des villages déshonorant et rongeant la terre. Seulement, est-ce qu'on sait? De même que la gelée qui brûle les moissons, la grêle qui les hache, la foudre qui les verse, sont nécessaires, peut-être, il est possible qu'il faille du sang et des larmes pour que le monde marche. ... (4, p. 811)

[There were also pain, blood, tears—everything that people suffer and everything that is abhorrent: Françoise killed, Fouan killed, rogues triumphant, bloodthirsty, stinking vermin from the villages despoiling and gnawing away the land. Only, does anyone really know? Just as the frosts that burn the harvests, the hail that hashes them, the thunderstorms that drench them are necessary, it could perhaps be that it takes blood and tears to keep the world going.]

The same message had already been suggested symbolically at earlier deaths, for instance at Fouan's funeral, when Jean catches a last glimpse of the old man's coffin as it is lowered into the ground "comme une poignée de blé" (4, p. 805) (like a handful of corn).

And so Zola has staged the apocalyptic scenario he set himself in his Ebauche: "A la fin, il faut la débâcle de tout"[32] [In the end everything has to come tumbling down]. Having articulated all his misgivings about life's suffering, violence, and corruption, however, having faced once again the old temptation of regarding life as an empty dream, he tries to end on a more detached and philosophical note. Certainly, the life-force no longer receives the exalted treatment it did in La Joie de vivre or in Sandoz's pantheistic hymn to nature (L'Oeuvre), but at least the author grants it the potential of moving toward an unknown goal:

> ... Et la terre seule demeure, l'immortelle, la mère d'où nous sortons et où nous retournons, elle qu'on aime jusqu'au crime, qui refait continuellement de la vie pour son but ignoré, même avec nos abominations et nos misères. (4, p. 811)

> [... And the earth alone remains, the immortal mother from whom we all spring and to whom we all return, she whom we love to the point of [committing] crime, she who is forever remaking life for her unknown goal—even with [all] our abominations and wretchedness.]

Zola has not yet wholly emerged from his period of depression. The hero of La Terre has saved only himself, as he finally turns his back on the ploughed fields of Rognes that await the germination of spring. His priest has shown charity, but has not even tried to save anyone. We have been offered some symbolic prefigurations of an Apocalypse that may be the only hope of a new beginning—but that positive prospect is left very hypothetical. Yet the closing scene is not the threat of a nihilistic grand finale, but a faintly hopeful glimpse of l'Eternel retour: "Des morts, des semences et le pain pousse de la terre" (4, p. 811) [Deaths, seed—and bread grows from the earth.] Guy Robert is probably correct in claiming that, even in his blackest moments, the author cannot get away from the denouement of Germinal: "... le jeu grandiose de la vie sortant de la mort, des catastrophes engendrant l'espoir...."[33] [... the grandiose game of life emerging from death, of catastrophes giving rise to hope....]. At least, then, there is no doubt about Zola's deepest aspirations.

How did the author of La Terre come to write the pre-Raphaelite novel, Le Rêve (The Dream) (1888)—the idyllic fairy tale, almost medieval in its naïveté, of a poor foundling-girl,

Angélique, who is adopted by the devout Hubert family, who models herself on the young virgin-martyr, St. Agnes, and who is finally allowed to marry her wealthy Prince Charming, Félicien de Hautecoeur, son of the aristocratic local bishop? Was the work really a fantasy that the author had been planning for a long time, as he wrote to van Santen Kolff, on 14 November, 1887: " ... une fantaisie, une envolée que je médite depuis longtemps"?[34] [... a fantasy, a flight of the imagination that I have been thinking about for a long time]? If so, the novel was a well-kept secret, for it does not feature in any of Zola's lists, it was unknown to Paul Alexis, the most reliable recipient of Zola's plans and no allusion to it can be found prior to 1887.

Well then, is the author more forthright (or more honest with himself) when he writes in his Ebauche that he intends his next novel to express the new mood of the age, the modish thirst for spirituality?

> J'y mettrais aussi le moment, la réaction contre le naturalisme, l'impatience de l'au-delà, le besoin d'idéal, la convulsion de la foi.[35]

> [I would also include in it the present moment, with its reaction against naturalism, its eagerness for the Hereafter, its need for ideals, its convulsions of faith.]

This time we may believe him with fewer reservations, for his later novel, Le Docteur Pascal, confirms that exposing the current nostalgia for faith was a definite part of his preoccupations. Even that, however, is not the whole truth: in writing Le Rêve, Zola is not merely portraying what he sees as a troubling phenomenon of his day, but he is giving voice to a repressed part of himself—a part he had particularly "manhandled" in La Terre.

Accordingly, when he writes to his Dutch contact:

> On m'a souvent reproché de ne pas tenir compte de l'au-delà, et c'est pourquoi j'ai voulu faire la part du rêve dans la série du Rougon-Macquart....[36]

> [I have often been accused of ignoring the Hereafter and that is why I wanted do take dreaming into account in the Rougon-Macquart series.]

he is still rationalizing away his personal involvement. On the evidence of what we are about to analyze in Le Rêve, we may be led to conclude that Zola's deepest motivation in writing the work is more complex than he himself realizes or is prepared to admit.

Mitterand is one of those who discern in the novel much that is personal to Zola. Obviously finding it hard to stomach the author's unwonted recourse to sentimentality and implausible fantasy, he presents Le Rêve as a complement to La Terre, as the result of alternations in Zola's "rythme vital" [biorhythms],[37] his swings between a state of tension or depression, and periods of more dynamic optimism.

Auguste Dezalay develops a similar insight in his article "Zola et le Rêve." Quoting from the author's own preface to La Confession de Claude, which is critical of the hero:

> ... la manifestation maladive d'un tempérament particulier qui a l'âpre besoin du réel et les espérances menteuses et douces du rêve
>
> [... the morbid manifestation of a particular temperament that combines a keen need for what is real with the sweet, fallacious hopes of dreaming],

he finds elements of that possibly unconscious *self*-assessment in the three novels La Terre, Le Rêve, and La Bête humaine:

> C'est presque un triptyque qui montre, chez Zola, tout aussi bien l'opposition maintenue, dans la dualité de sa nature, entre "l'âpre besoin du réel et les espérances menteuses et douces du rêve", et le lien, peut-être, dans l'homme, entre l'ange et la bête.[38]
>
> [It's almost a triptych that shows the sustained dichotomy in Zola—in the duality of his nature—between his "keen need of what is real and the sweet, fallacious hopes of the dream," as well as the link in man between angel and beast.]

Dezalay's study of how Zola alternates gross realism with idyllic fantasy is in line with the Jungian theory that overinvestment in one polarity of an inner conflict will tend to provoke an assertion of its opposite. Could it be that, having somewhat extravagantly portrayed the basest instincts of man in La Terre, Zola subsequently cannot resist the urge to give expression to his old ideals of goodness, love, and purity even if, ultimately, he cannot believe that there is any future for those who pursue such values? Is that why disbelief in the messianic myth is temporarily suspended in Le Rêve?

There is ample evidence to support Mitterand's view that Le

Rêve incorporates much that is close to Zola's heart. Colette Becker points out that the heroine is "semblable à l'image gracieuse et blonde qui hantait ses rêves d'adolescent"[39] (similar to the graceful blond figure that haunted his adolescent dreams). It is fairly obvious, too, that the sorrows of the affectionate, but childless Hubert couple are modeled on the experiences of Emile and Alexandrine.

Like Flaubert's *Trois contes*, [Three Tales] the novel is essentially "une oeuvre de nostalgie" (a work inspired by nostalgia). In the midst of depression and despair about human perfectibility, the author allows himself some moments of respite, as he indulges in plain wishful thinking. As he puts it in his Ebauche, what he wants to contemplate at the moment is: "la vie telle qu'elle n'est pas, telle qu'on la rêve, toute une partie de rêve, l'inconnu, l'inconnaissable"[40] [life, not as it is, but as one dreams it to be, a whole excursion into dreaming, the unknown, the unknowable]. Zola's cultivation of nostalgia does not necessarily make for great literature, but it offers us insights into his fondest desires. Referring to our author's never-ending farewells to idealistic dreams, Henri Guillemin speaks of: "Le rêve du 'Si c'était vrai!' du côté de l'amour et du côté de Dieu"[41] [The dream of "If only it were true" with regard to God and love]. Elsewhere, the same critic comments on the cathedral setting of the novel in the folowing terms:

> ... une cathédrale de songe: C'est cela pour lui *Le Rêve*. La part submergée de lui-même. Submergée mais ne pas morte, et dont il ne veut pas qu'elle meure. Le meilleur de lui est là. Ce qui lui donne le courage de vivre.[42]
>
> [... a cathedral of dreams: that's what *Le Rêve* represents for him— a part of himself that is submerged but not dead, something that he does not want to die, the best part of himself that gives him the courage to go on living.]

Guillemin is perhaps inclined to overstate Zola's lingering attachment to Christian values, but his suggestion that the cathedral stands for the author's inner sanctuary, his subconscious refuge of idealism, rings true enough (Freudians may interpret the cathedral in terms of the womb—the maternal world that the author is loth to abandon).

Restating this in language more generally acceptable, it is hard not to believe, with Mitterand, that, in *Le Rêve*, Zola desires: "de retrouver, en ses personnages, les croyances simples, les prières, 'la vie sereine' de son enfance"[43] [to find again in his characters the simple beliefs, the prayers, the "untroubled life" of his childhood]. Could one find a more revealing confession than the following lines, taken from the Ebauche, where the author looks back on what he calls his "vie manquée" [failed life], faces the prospect of old age and declining vitality and, most poignantly of all, expresses his craving for love:

> Moi, le travail, la littérature qui a mangé ma vie, et le bouleversement, la crise, le besoin d'être aimé, tout cela à étudier profondément.[44]

[Myself, work, literature that has consumed my life, emotional upheaval, crisis, the need to be loved—all that to be studied in detail.]

It may be said, by way of summary, that *Le Rêve* embodies all the ideals Zola can no longer believe in. Yet these are the very ideals he most longs to see realized. Paradoxically, the shattering of the dream at the end of the novel—newly wed Angélique slips into death as she is about to step into the outside world of reality—is more than what the Germans call "Illusionszerstörung" [the ironic destruction of ideals]. As a narrative device, it may enable Zola to keep his self-respect as a naturalist but, at the same time, it allows him to keep intact the underlying metaphysical aspiration. In an arresting paragraph, Paul Pelckmans argues that, where individuals cultivate a "dream" (an actual dream or one translated into a real life quest), as a means of pursuing metaphysical goals, they often sabotage this dream just before fulfillment robs it of its otherworldly promise:

> Le désir, pour autant qu'il refuse de renoncer à ses illusions, en vient dès lors à cultiver l'échec—qui fonctionne à la fois comme une prophylaxie contre la déception et comme une preuve quasi tangible de ce que le but final dépasse, c'est-à-dire transcende, le sujet désirant.[45]

[Desire, inasmuch as it refuses to renounce its illusions, reaches the point of cultivating failure. The latter functions both as a prophylactic against disappointment and as an almost tangible proof of the fact that the final goal lies beyond, that is, transcends the party who desires.]

Does Zola then go through the motions of exploding his dream, so that he may unconsciously cling to the underlying ideals? Whatever we may think of that, it is clear that Angélique's demise is a neat way for Zola to postpone his elusive reconciliation of passion and purity—a pattern all too familiar to the reader of *Les Rougon-Macquart*.

We shall now pass in review aspects of the plot that are more directly pertinent to Zola's messianic aspirations—aspirations that cannot be quite as defunct as they appear to be at the end of *La Terre*.

A perspective of redemption is established from the opening scene: on a snowy, stormy Christmas eve, nine-year-old, runaway, Angélique, the abandoned, illegitimate daughter of shady, brutal Sidonie Rouget, neglected and ill-treated lately by an unsavory couple, finds a measure of shelter for the night against the cathedral door of Beaumont (a symbolic microcosm of Zola's tender years?). Early next morning, she is rescued from death from exposure by the kindly Huberts. Eventually they adopt her and teach her their trade of embroidering church hangings and vestments.

We soon learn that, for all their devoutness, purity, and mutual affection, the middle-aged foster-parents stand in need of redemption themselves. Hubertine, the daughter of a magistrate had eloped with Hubert against her mother's wishes. The latter had died cursing her daughter, whereupon the young girl had given birth to a stillborn child and had remained sterile ever since.

Just as the little waif finds shelter at the church-entrance and in her new home, just as the house itself nestles against the cathedral, young Angélique draws support from her devout milieu and absorbs the spirit of the saints' stories that become her daily meditation. For the first time, in Zola's novelistic world, milieu becomes a wholly effective redemptive factor. The author has planned, in his Ebauche, that the girl (who has inherited the Rougon pride and passion) is to be transformed in a manner consistent with the determinist dictates of naturalism:

L'éducation des Hubert, et le mileu qu'elle habite, la transforme [sic], et dès lors la lutte du respect et du devoir, contre l'orgueil et la passion. Tout le mouvement de la figure est là. . . . Toute l'hérédité, un rejet des Rougon-Macquart transplanté et cultivé, et dès lors sauvé. Tout l'effet du milieu.[46]

[Her upbringing by the Huberts, and the milieu she lives in, transform her, resulting in a conflict between respect and duty, on the one hand, and pride and passion, on the other. This constitutes the whole dynamics of my character. . . . The whole [business] of heredity—a scion of the Rougon-Macquart is transplanted and nurtured and saved in the process. The importance of milieu.]

Not only is Angélique saved, at first physically and then morally, by the cathedral and her adoptive parents, but the author manages to weave into his unfolding love-story a bishop and son whom he intends to be vaguely suggestive, respectively, of God the Father and God the Son. This time, it is no longer a matter of unconscious messianic symbolism, on the part of Zola. In his Dossier préparatoire, already, the author decides that young Félicien is to look rather like Jesus—"un peu l'air d'un Jésus," Zola tells himself[47] and soon after he opts for the complete "bride of Christ" scenario that often features large in the vocation of nuns:

> Le fils de l'évêque est comme le fils de Dieu le père, comme Jésus pour la jeune fille, c'est ce qu'il y a de plus haut ... épouser Jésus.[48]

[For the young girl, the bishop's son is like the Son of God the Father, like Jesus; to marry Jesus is the reach the highest ideal.]

Within the actual novel, the author is at first a little more subtle: the reader is left to draw his own conclusions from Angélique's impression when she casts her eyes on Félicien in full daylight:

> C'était lui, grand, mince, blond, avec sa barbe fine et ses cheveux bouclés de jeune dieu, aussi blanc de peau qu'elle l'avait vu sous la blancheur de la lune. (5, p. 875)

[It was he, tall, slim, and fair, with the light beard and the curling hair of a young god. His skin was as white as she had seen it in the pale moonlight.]

Subsequently there are a number of allusions to Angélique's seeing the bishop as God the Father, until the day she comes to plead with him in the St. Joseph chapel:

> Les jambes fléchissantes, anéantie de respect et d'effroi, Angélique était tombée sur les deux genoux. Il lui apparaissait comme Dieu le Père, terrible, maître absolu de sa destinée. . . . (4, pp. 944–45)

[Her legs giving way beneath her, overwhelmed with awe and dread, Angélique had fallen on her knees. He was like an appearance of God the Father—terrible and in complete control of her destiny.]

Why this deification of the bishop and his son? Principally, no doubt, so that Angélique may seem to fulfill her mystical dream of marrying Jesus (a way of solving the problem of sexuality that may possibly have crossed young Zola's mind, given his obvious literary interest in priests). Quite plausible in terms of the plot, this scenario suits the author while he is in the mood for a little holiday away from the world of stress where he has never managed to reconcile eros and idealism. We have already previewed the heroine's escape into death on her wedding-day. In an attempt to make this event seem more realistic, Zola has invented a whole Hautecoeur tradition of brides dying early (a phenomenon which, in itself, does not seem capable of a naturalistic explanation!), but the attentive reader of the *Rougon-Macquart* has long since noticed that Zola kills off young virgins like Miette in *La Fortune des Rougon*, allows chaste wives to die prematurely, like Caroline Hédouin in *Au Bonheur des dames*, and keeps some of his favorite heroines unmarried or mothers by proxy only, like Pauline in *La Joie de vivre*—all that simply because he cannot reconcile the spirit and the flesh.

While Zola is in dream-mode, so to speak—a state of mind in which all problems lend themselves to effortless solution—he tackles the Oedipal child's nightmare of a terrifying, hostile father-figure as well. In keeping with his stated intentions in his Premier plan [First plan], he will present the bishop as a godlike figure who will at first appear awesome in his majesty, but who will finally turn out to be the kindest of men, an understanding father and a savior to boot: "Il ne viendra, en bon père, que pour demander la jeune fille et la sauver" (Premier plan)[49] [As a good father, he will only come to ask for the young girl and to save her]. There are, of course, wider implications in this scenario than the wish-fulfillment-dreams of an Oedipal child. We have noted, in some of the early novels, that Zola's notion of God is very much caught up with his misconception of a cold, remote, vengeful father figure. We may well conclude from *Le Rêve* that his ideal world would be ruled by a compassionate father capable of relenting, a god who understands about passionate love and is willing to bless it in his creatures.

Accordingly, the central preoccupation of the novel is not so much "le renoncement à la chair pour l'amour divin, le renoncement au mariage, la vierge enfant qui renonce à la passion humaine et qui meurt par chasteté"[50] [the renunciation of the flesh for the sake of divine love, the renunciation of marriage, the child-virgin who renounces human passion and dies for the sake of chastity], as the wider theme of man coping with his sexuality. In the course of the novel, Angélique comes up against conventional parental objections to marriage partners on grounds of class and wealth, but even more against the hidden problem of parents who have misgivings about their passionate past and who fear to see their mistakes repeated by their children. As the bishop reacts to the fervent love he sees at work in pining, fading Angélique, he accomplishes an act of self-redemption. His unusual method of imparting healing—instead of the laying on of hands, he kisses the heroine on the mouth—suggests that, in him, the beauty of love has finally triumphed over guilt—a greater miracle, potentially, than his apparent raising of Angélique.

We have already discussed the heroine's death on the threshold of married life as Zola's way of allowing the girl to keep her virginity, and we have seen from his Dossier préparatoire how this matches his conscious intentions. But maybe more is involved: Zola does not articulate any causal connections but, in terms of plot sequence, Angélique's death seems to result in the redemptive miracle of Hubert and Hubertine's being released from their ancestral curse: the childless woman has at last fallen pregnant. On the surface, this looks like Angélique's having achieved the martyr's death she aspired to—a death with messianic implications. Decoding the symbolism, however, in as far as it may be applied to the author personally, we could read that, in allowing the dream of virginal purity to die, Zola is freeing himself for the role of fatherhood. Possibly the death of his own mother, in 1880, is at last beginning to have its releasing effect in his psyche.

Le Rêve has turned out to be a highly complex novel in which the original intention of creating a dream of purity and the eventual resolve of allowing that dream to die have had a salutary effect. There are many redemptive factors at work in the novel—the ecclesiastical milieu of serene piety; the charity and compassion of the Hubert couple; the bishop's acceptance, by proxy, of passionate love; the atoning death of the dreaming virgin. Repercussions in the author's life—or should we see them merely as parallels or echoes—will be almost instantaneous, but we shall have to wait for the last volume in the Rougon-Macquart before we can discover a clear literary counterpart.

And so the life-force that emerges as an ideal in La Joie de vivre and that seems to survive as a perspective of hope at the end of *Germinal* (in spite of failing messiahs in both novels) comes up, in *L'Oeuvre*, against the distorting idolatry of obsessive sexuality and the presumption of pursuing equality with the Creator: Claude turns out to be an unfaithful prophet, substituting his own warped, sensual visions for Sandoz's ode to Life. In *La Terre*, Zola rubs our noses in the problem of human bestiality—a problem from which there seems to be no redemption, apart from the regression to the past that is made to look so alluring in *Le Rêve*, but which, at best, can serve only as a temporary refuge, while a more realistic solution is looked for.

The next chapter will cover Zola's continuing quest for messianic hope—be it in diagnozing the full extent of the human predicament (*La Bête humaine*), in embracing the joy of life in spite of all our compromises (*L'Argent*), in the cleansing fire of apocalypse (*La Débâcle*) or, against all expectation or likelihood, in the belated acceptance of sexuality as a pure gift of self-giving (*Le Docteur Pascal*). In the light of that intoxicating experience, even death may become acceptable to the aging hero, alias Zola, who has now tasted the fulness of life and who may have played his part in engendering a future messiah.

8
From Death and Disaster to Messianic Hope

AT THE END OF THE PREVIOUS CHAPTER, WE SAW ZOLA TRYING TO stave off despair by regressing to the security of adolescent fantasy—as though it were only in a world of dream that his messianic myth of redemption had any hope of survival. On returning to reality, he must have remembered his original way of fighting hopelessness and depression. Was it not shortly after publishing his somber early novel, *Thérèse Raquin* (1867), that he wrote in *La Tribune*:

> Il est bon que la fange humaine soit parfois remuée devant la foule. Souvent on accuse les romanciers physiologistes de se plaire à l'étude des infamies du coeur et du corps; ils ne font cependant que ce que la justice fait en rendant publique la discussion des grands crimes: ils élargissent les plaies pour y enfoncer un fer rouge?[1]

> [It is right and proper that, from time to time, the mire of humanity should be stirred up for everyone to see. Often, physiologist novelists are accused of taking pleasure in studying the vile deeds of mind and body; all they are doing, however, is what the legal system does in making public the discussion of major crimes: they open up the wounds in order to insert a red-hot cauterizing-iron.]

While part of the rationale behind Zola's naturalism has always been to challenge social and individual ills by portraying them accurately, objectively, and honestly, it is reasonable to suspect that, in diagnosing the problems of society, the author has also been striving for self-knowledge and self-healing. That being so, *La Bête humaine* [The Beast in Man] is more than a variation upon a theme, more than just a restatement of human bestiality and depravity. When Zola tells himself in his Ebauche, or writes to van Santen Kolff, that he wants to illustrate what survives in modern, civilized man of the primitive savage, he may well be probing his own unresolved inner contradictions as well—the juxtaposition of "l'ange et la bête" [angel and beast]. It will be our thesis in this section that Zola removes a great obstacle to messianic aspirations when, through the symbolic screen of literary projection, he confesses his most troubling obsession: the repressed urge to inflict pain and death on the very people he loves most. Unconvinced readers should peruse the following examples, taken from the whole range of *Les Rougon-Macquart*, and ask themselves whether these do not recur too obsessively not to correspond to some temptation in the author himself.

In the opening volume of the series, already, we see the cruel Justin Rébufade torment young Miette and later exult over the execution of his rival, Silvère. Two volumes later, it is the beautiful Lisa Quenu who "brains" simpleminded Marjolin who is attracted to her and who tries to overpower her (cf. the similar scene in *La Terre* where old Fouan's sister, La Grande, kills Hilarion for much the same reason). In *Son Excellence Eugène Rougon*, strong-minded Clorinde Balbi handles her riding-whip very deftly to control her would-be lover. In *Germinal*, puny Jeanlin and his friends cruelly maim Savourine's white rabbit, symbol of warmth and fertility, while the hero, Etienne, has to kill Chaval before being able to make love to dying Catherine. Could not Bonnemort's senseless murder of Cécile, toward the end of the novel, be explained, in part, in terms of sadism, especially given the author's obvious fascination with the victim's white neck? We noted, in *La Terre*, how Buteau rapes his sister-in-law and then allows his wife to push her on to the upturned blade of a scythe. We shall turn later to Jules Lemaître's intervention, when he elaborates on the sadistic contents of *La Bête humaine* and then—God bless him!—releases Zola from his torment by pointing out that most people, civilized and God-fearing or otherwise, experience urges of a similar nature.

Probably in the strength of his new revelation of life and love, brought to him by Jeanne Rozerot, in December 1888, Zola at last gathers enough courage to face the darkest potentialities of human instincts, where even the love relationship between man and woman and the sexual drive that is meant to propagate life are shown to have hidden depths involved with aggression, violence, and death. (By comparing dates, Mitterand establishes that Zola actually left his first Ebauche of *La Bête humaine* for two months to devote himself to his intoxicating rebirth to happiness.)

It goes without saying that, in a tale dominated by murderers (eight of them, if we include the accomplice Séverine!), genuine messianic figures are conspicuous by their absence. On the surface, the wealthy president Grandmorin seems caring enough to bring up Séverine, the daughter of his late gardener, but actually he may well have intended from the start to abuse her sexually. Eventually he marries her off to unsuspecting "sous-chef de gare" [deputy stationmaster], Roubaud, and then becomes responsible for the death of another victim, Louisette Misard. He makes a further saving gesture when he rescues the outspoken Roubaud from dimissal, but this does not save Grandmorin himself, when Sévarine confesses her seduction by her former guardian and his continuing attentions: furious over being handed down what he considers a tainted woman, the station-master forces his wife to join him in trapping and murdering the aging pervert.

Jacques Lantier, the central character of the novel, the engine driver who cannot ultimately save his beloved locomotive, La Lison, from disaster, at first helps Séverine to escape from the hands of justice—a rather dubious act of redemption—and then initiates her into the bliss of satisfied passion. In turn, he cherishes the illusion that her tender love has redeemed him from his sadistic urge to kill the objects of his desire, but that hope proves ill-founded: he will finally stab the uncomprehending Séverine with the very knife that Roubaud used on Grandmorin. In fact, Séverine's greatest attraction, for Jacques, lay in her complicity in the slaying of her guardian, the fact, in other words, that she was an incarnation of his urge to kill.

At this stage we must take our turn, somewhat reluctantly, at trying to cast light on the mysterious association of love and violence, the generation of life and the infliction of pain and death. The theme of love and death is, of course, one of the constant preoccupations of art and literature. When Zola attempts to explain the phenomenon as a form of male vengeance for female offenses committed in the caves—a highly unlikely scenario, unless one were to invert the sexes—he may be simply indulging in the fantasy of the Oedipal child who has chanced upon his parents' lovemaking and has misinterpreted proceedings in terms of his father assaulting his mother. Alternatively, he may be projecting onto his father his own anger at seeing his mother interfered with—the mother being a figure whom the child would like to keep as his sole possession—or we might speculate that sadists symbolically express their resentment with a mother-figure to whom they were not the first to have access.

Of late, these Freudian scenarios have lost favor as explanations of sadism,[2] especially after the perhaps more plausible explanations offered by sociologists who argue that, in primitive societies, wives were often the prize after a fight, so that the acts of killing and mating may have become associated. Zola himself goes even further back in biologic history, when he refers to "la volupté douloureuse des bêtes qui s'éventrent pendant le rut" (4, p. 1105) [the painful pleasure of animals that disembowel each other during the rut]. On a later occasion, he postulates the egoism of the male who wants to make sure that he is the only possessor of a woman. Jacques is said to experience

... une nécessité de bataille pour conquérir la femelle et la dompter, le besoin perverti de la jeter morte sur son dos, ainsi qu'une proie qu'on arrache aux autres, à jamais. (4, p. 1044)

[... a compulsion to do battle in order to conquer the female and tame her, a perverse need to throw her dead body over his shoulder, like a prey that you snatch from the others—once and for all.]

The present writer favors the view that, on learning of Jeanne's pregnancy, the exulting Zola at last escapes from the thrall of immaculate virgins and is able to assume his proper role as a father—in line with the model of his own father, whose vision and enterprise he is about to glorify in *L'Argent*. This means, however, that Zola has to come to terms with the sadistic father-figure that has haunted his nightmarish plots—whether the scenes involving such a figure are simply a projection of his Oedipal frustration or the obsessive acting out of a troubling episode from early childhood (suppressed from the conscious memory). With the absurd logic of the uncomprehending child, Zola would have retained the notion, deep down in his psyche, that if ever he were to become a man like his father, he would have to assault a woman—something completely unacceptable to the author's conscious mind and therefore relegated to the realm of literary fantasy. When the resulting veiled expressions of sadism are correctly diagnosed by Jules Lemâitre and are given general human relevance, Zola can at last tell himself consciously that he is not a monster after all, but just a typical, unfortunate human being in whom idealism and checked savage instincts live side by side.

According to this thesis, both *La Terre* and *La Bête humaine* are literary "dreams" in which Zola is trying to confess his tormenting obsessions. In the light of that interpretation, we may understand more readily why the author should have been so grateful to Lemaître for his profound and eloquent article on *La Bête humaine*. It includes passages like the following:

> Nous-mêmes, chrétiens, civilisés, lettrés, artistes, nous avons des mouvements de haine ou d'amour, de concupiscence ou de colère, qui viennent pour ainsi dire de plus loin que nous; et nous ne savons pas toujours à quoi nous obéissons. Nos chétives et passagères personnes ne sont que les vagues infiniment petites d'un océan de forces impersonnelles, éternelles et aveugles; et sous ces vagues il y a toujours un gouffre. C'est, en somme, ce qu'exprime *La Bête humaine* avec une mélancolique et farouche majesté.[3]

> [We ourselves who are Christians, civilized folk, literary men, and artists have impulses of hatred or love, lust, or anger that come, so to speak, from beyond us; and we do not always know what we are obeying. Our puny and transient persons are merely the infinitely small waves of an ocean of blind, eternal, impersonal forces; and beneath those waves there is always an abyss. That, in short, is what *La Bête humaine* expresses with grim, melancholy majesty.]

Zola may owe his inner release to more than his exultation in love and paternity or the tactful diagnosis of his problems by an authoritative figure like Lemaître: Gilles Deleuze, in his introduction to *La Bête humaine*, formulates a theory that may be somewhat obscure to laymen, but is none the less worthy of consideration.

Elaborating on Zola's notion of the ancestral "fêlure" (crack) in particular heroes of *Les Rougon-Macquart*, he links it to Freud's "Todestrieb" (death wish or death-drive): for Freud, sadism is simply the Todestrieb, common to all, when it is directed at a person other than the self. Deleuze holds, in other words, that something like Jacques's "fêlure" is operative behind all instincts, either using them to pursue its own finalities or else becoming an organizing factor that gives the play of instincts its orientation, direction, and intensity. Accordingly, Zola's train becomes, for Deleuze, an epic representation of the death-drive, with the instincts swarming around and inside it. The essence of his view is that the joining up of an instinct and its object cannot give rise to a permanent feeling or relationship in Jacques (or man in general), because the meeting occurs across the gap or "fêlure," the inner emptiness that, Deleuze believes, yawns at the center of every individual. As in the case of Jacques, satisfied instincts may temporarily seem to cover up the gap. Bridging a void, however, they lack solidity and are little more than a passing illusion. They may even widen the crack and hasten the ultimate plunge of the personality into death:

> ... s'il est vrai que les instincts ne se forment et ne trouvent leur objet qu'au bord de la fêlure, la fêlure, inversement, ne poursuit son chemin, n'étend sa toile, ne change de direction, ne s'actualise en chaque corps qu'en rapport avec les instincts qui lui ouvrent la voie, tantôt la recollant un peu, tantôt l'allongeant ou la creusant, jusqu'au craquement final, là encore assuré par les instincts.[4]

> [... if it is true that instincts take shape and find their object only along the fault-line, inversely, the fault does not follow its course, extend its network, change direction, or become a reality in each body, except in conjunction with the instincts. The latter open up its way, sometimes gluing it together again a little, sometimes lengthening or deepening it, up to the final breaking point that is also ensured by the instincts.]

Evidently, any theory that sees human instinctive behavior as being centered around the death wish is not going to be very uplifting, nor will it meet with the approval of those whose beliefs do not allow for inner vacuums. While not questioning the fact that, ultimately, human instincts tend to death (humans are mortal, after all), the present writer holds that this does not stop those same instincts from first tending to life. It is only when their task has been accomplished, that they willingly take the descending path. Alternatively, it is particularly when their natural flow is frustrated (mental disease, impossible love, childless marriage, incompatible partners, broken expectation of happiness, etc.), that their striving becomes absurd, meaningless, which may result in their prematurely espousing death.

As for the death wish theory and for its relevance to Zola's emergence from the tangles of his psyche, Deleuze defends the author's approach by arguing that one can never go too far in the portrayal of social or individual decomposition "puisqu'il faut aller jusqu'à la fêlure"[5] [since it is necessary to go to the very edge of the fault]. Maybe, he speculates, by following it all the way, we shall come to a point where we can transcend it:

> Peut-être la fêlure a-t-elle de quoi se surpasser dans la direction qu'elle crée, elle qui n'est comblée qu'en apparence et pour un instant par les gros appétits. Et puisqu'elle absorbe tous les instincts, peut-

être aussi peut-elle opérer la transmutation des instincts en retournant la mort contre elle-même.[6]

[Perhaps, in the very direction that it creates, the fault offers us the means by which to transcend it—even though, for all that, it is a gap that even the great appetites can only appear to fill momentarily. And since it absorbs all instincts, perhaps it can also effect the transmutation of instincts, by turning death upon itself.]

Deleuze is not alone in believing that by draining the cup of its very last drop of poison (Rimbaud's famous "lettre du voyant") [letter of the seer/prophet], placing the fiery serpent on a stake for all to see (Moses in the Old Testament Book of Numbers), gathering all the sins of the world on the head of the crucified Christ, we may rob evil of its power and then await a resurrection. Is this what Zola hopes to achieve, personally and for the benefit of his readers, in *La Bête humaine?*

Meanwhile the author has not lost faith in the imminence of Apocalypse. Since we shall cover that topic at some length in our study of *La Débâcle*, it will be sufficient here to note briefly Zola's frequent hints in *La Bête humaine* (and his plain statements in his notes) that the train stands for human destiny, man's relentless progress toward the upheavals of the twentieth century and, more specifically, at the end of the novel, the destiny of France on the eve of war. We shall dispense with yet another detailed evocation of the apocalyptic train, coming to grief against Cabuche's cartload of masssive stone or, on the last page of the novel, of apocalyptic train-number-two thundering into the night, bereft of its driver and its stoker, carrying its complement of bawling, drunken soldiers.

Zola's next novel, *L'Argent* (1891) [Money], may feature some naive utopian dreamers, but no genuine messianic figure of any sort. Outgrowing his role as false messiah or false high-priest, as played in *La Curée,* Saccard gains the stature of a fully fledged Lucifer—an allegorical incarnation of the quest for absolute power, in defiance of God. We shall see, however, that, like Milton's Satan or Balzac's Vautrin—like the biblical Devil for that matter who, for all his rebellion, remains willy-nilly a servant of God—Zola's villain has his attractive side.

Thanks to the titanic battle between Saccard and the all-powerful Jewish banker, Gundermann (G for "God" and "undermann" as in "thunder-man"?), we may even gain a deeper understanding of Zola's antagonism toward the remote God of the Old

Testament who, apparently, has no time for passion and who wrathfully asserts his supremacy.

It is only to be expected that, as Zola approaches the end of his *Rougon-Macquart* cycle and is about to evoke the doom of the Second Empire, the theme of Apocalypse will again be stressed. We shall note in passing that the author's increasing wealth and his new situation as Jeanne Rozerot's lover will be reflected, in this novel, in some controversial reassessments of the roles of money and passion. Aspects of the messianic myth (or rather its inversion) just broached and some related themes will emerge more clearly as we consider relevant aspects of *L'Argent*'s plot, characterization, and mythical symbolism.

At the outset of the novel, Lucifer has just been cast down from Heaven: ostracized after some scandalous and disastrous land-deal and forced to leave his princely Monceau estate, Saccard can now only afford the *ground* floor of l'Hôtel d'Orviedo. In his humiliation, he is desperate to make a new attempt at glory and to venture all: "... il jouerait la suprême partie" (5, p. 48) [he would play the decisive game]. He has approached his brother, Eugène, for a helping hand, but scornfully rejects the minister's vague offer of a governorship in some remote French colony: with him, as with the Devil, it is a matter of all or nothing!

Immediately, however, Zola balances his picture of Saccard in a way for which the reader of *La Curée* is perhaps ill-prepared: seeing his aristocratic landlady, the princesse d'Orviedo, robbed royally by those on whom she depends for her charitable enterprises, the hero has offered his services and has become her *honest* administrator. He has even entertained the dream of becoming some kind of messiah—a king of charity! On being rejected as the princess's husband, however, he falls back on an alternative way of making his name: he must get even with the banker Gundermann, "le maître de la Bourse et du monde" [lord of the Exchange and the world], who controls the rise and fall of shares "comme Dieu fait le tonnerre" (5, p. 21) [just as God makes thunder]. The aging Jew, surrounded by his court that venerates him like a God, has mortally insulted the hero's pride by approving of his apparent exit from the business world.

In the opening pages of the novel, already, Zola discreetly introduces the theme of Apocalypse, as little Moser, a speculator at la Bourse, predicts the doom of the regime: "Je vous dis que le ver est dans le fruit. Tout crèvera" (5, p. 17) [I'm telling you, the worm is in the apple. Everything will die]. For the time being, the reader is allowed to take this disguised omen simply for an expression of Moser's perennial pessimism.

A little later, Saccard's latest dream of glory is given perspective by the lecture he receives from the Jew Sigismund Busch—an eloquent, passionate prophecy of the golden future of communism (not all of Zola's Jews in the novel are cold, hardfisted schemers and accumulators of gold!): unlike the ambitious Saccard, this noble-minded, if naive, disciple of Karl Marx does not wish to conquer the world, but confidently looks forward to its transformation. Unable to get away from the coexistence within himself of reforming zeal and ambition, Zola is reverting to his old juxtaposition of a frail idealist (Sigismund is a consumptive) and a more dynamic pragmatist (Saccard)—a pattern we have traced in some of his early novels.

Saccard's exposure to idealism continues as he grows more intimate with his upstairs neighbors, Georges and Caroline Hamelin. Had she been created a few years earlier (as a novelistic character, that is), charming, sensible, tolerant Caroline would no doubt have been a virgin, in the tradition of Pauline Quenu (*La Joie de vivre*) and Denise Baudu (*Au Bonheur des dames*). As matters stand, however, the author allows her a fleeting affair with Saccard, which neither lover deems an event of great consequence. Momentarily distraught after being let down by an inconstant suitor, Caroline soon regains her usual joyfulness, hope, and love of life. Seeing herself as a typical specimen of suffering humanity, the heroine, who will emerge as Zola's chief mouthpiece in the novel, exclaims:

> Je me suis crue finie, anéantie moi-même. Puis, pas du tout! voici que l'existence me reprend, je ris aujourd'hui, demain, j'espère, je voudrais vivre encore, vivre toujours. . . . Est-ce extraordinaire, de ne pas pouvoir être triste longtemps! (5, p. 73)

> [I thought I was done for and utterly ruined. Then, nothing of the sort! Now I'm caught up in life again; I'm laughing today; tomorrow I hope; I'd like to live some more and to go on living. Isn't it strange not to be able to be sad for long!]

Clearly, Caroline is no saint, but she matches Zola's growing conviction that, often, it is the life-force within us (linked to our capacity for hope) that has a redemptive power all of its own. Already discernible in Pauline and in the Christine of *L'Oeuvre*, this recurring motif suggests that Zola is moving toward a humanistic, or perhaps pantheistic equivalent of the more traditionally Christian messianism of his earlier writings.

Caroline's brother, Georges, is not short of plans and visions, but lacks the drive to realize them. Not so Saccard! Appropriating Georges's scheme for developing the Levant, intending to exploit his dream of setting up the pope in a restored kingdom of Palestine (solidly financed by Catholic funds), he resolves to launch his Banque Universelle. (The dynamic, visionary qualities of Saccard may well owe something to Zola's own father who was involved in the construction of the first Austrian railway line, tendered a proposal for enlarging the port of Marseille and got underway the large reservoir for which he is still honored by the people of Aix-en-Provence. On the debit side, biographers have pointed out that, rightly or wrongly, François Zola had to give up his army-commission in North Africa, after some scandal involving regimental funds.)

Without hesitation, Saccard begins to look for financial support. In spite of his better judgment, he finds himself back in the presence of the billionaire Gundermann. Even though he tends to see all Jews as hyperintelligent parasites, destined to gain control of the world in the name of their "Dieu de vol, de sang et de colère" [God of robbery, blood and wrath] (how Saccard bays at his own shadow!), his envy of him is colored by a sense of awe. The reader is left in no doubt that, Gundermann somehow reminds Saccard of God: "Et Saccard ... se sentait pris d'une sorte de sacrée terreur" (5, p. 96) [And Saccard ... felt himself gripped by a kind of holy dread]. When "God" is not interested in his schemes and predicts his collapse within three years, Saccard turns to the untrustworthy Christian speculator, Daigremont, and deceives him into backing him (he allows him to believe that he has Eugène's blessing). Princess d'Orviedo initially refuses her support, but falls for Saccard's religious masquerade: she cannot resist the prospect he paints of the pope's being restored to temporal power and enthroned in Jerusalem, thanks to a worldwide Catholic bank. Caroline is not blind to Saccard's devious devices and shady financial transactions, but she warms to his energy and vitality:

> Elle le regardait et, dans son amour de la vie, de tout ce qui était fort et actif, elle finissait par le trouver beau, séduisant de verve et de foi. (5, p. 116)

> [She watched him and, with her love of life and of everything strong and active, she eventually found him handsome and very attractive with his dynamism and faith.]

Be it through cunning, sham religion, or personal charisma, then, Saccard pursues his role as the great deceiver. Other subscribers, great or small, yield to the mystique of his Jerusalem-scheme, a man-made, ecclesiastical version of the kingdom Christians pray for. When Princess d'Orviedo makes her palace available as a home-base for the Banque Universelle, Saccard cleverly gives the building a religious decor and insists that his two hundred employees dress solemnly, speak quietly, and assume an air of clerical distinction. Zola's earlier satanic figures (Faujas in *La Conquête de Plassans*) and false prophets (Octave in *Au Bonheur des Dames*) were already past masters in the art of exploiting religious sentiments.

It is at this stage that Zola himself verges on becoming a false prophet as, through Saccard, he seems to defend speculation by comparing its role to that of lust or desire in procreating children (without the lure of easy riches, it is hard to mobilize funds). Some may agree with Saccard that speculation is like a dung or fertilizer that promotes growth, but does not Saccard's parallel, later taken up by Caroline, Zola's spokesperson, carry the unfortunate implication that sexual desire is evil in its nature, but good in its results? Does Zola hold the puritanical doctrine that the pursuit of sensual pleasure is justified only if it is accompanied by the intention to engender life?

The ambivalent nature of speculation and sexuality, as it emerges at the end of chapter 4, provides Zola with a good bridge to chapter 5, which relates how Caroline discovers some of Saccard's "passé inavouable" [unspeakable past] along with more evidence of his better side. She extricates his illegitimate son, Victor, from the hands of scheming, mean Mme Méchain and places him in the charitable institution founded by the princess. In the process, she learns to her horror that the twelve-year-old, precocious monster is already sexually active and even sleeps with the forty-year-old Mme Eulalie, whose vegetables he carries to the market. Nevertheless, her own frustrated maternal feelings prevail over her revulsion and even mysteriously lead her back into the arms of Saccard. While settling Victor into his new home, which the devilish child intends to exploit for all his worth, she learns from a visiting mother how Saccard busied himself selflessly to help the princess's model orphanage get off the ground.

True to the formula of many melodramas, Saccard wins his first skirmish with the great god of banking: using illegally obtained prior information on a peace-treaty between Italy and

Austria, he makes a small personal fortune buying up cheap shares—an operation in which his Jewish rival loses some eight million francs!

Zola had intended all along that the spectacular rise and fall of Saccard should parallel the fortunes of the Second Empire. Having just sketched out the faults and merits of his central character in his Dossier préparatoire, he had written: "Il faut qu'on entende dans tout le livre le craquement d'une société, le prochain effondrement"[7] [Throughout the book there must be heard the cracking up of a society, its imminent collapse]. Accordingly, we have noted the pessimistic prophecy of Moser in chapter 1, to which could be added the sinister hopes of the old crow, La Méchain, who is compared to the scavenger birds that follow an army headed for carnage. Now, at the end of chapter 6, the author ironically juxtaposes the ominous Prussian victory at Sadowa (the same Prussians were to be a problem to the French before long) with the culmination of Napoleon III's glory and prestige, and then inserts Saccard's vain meditation: " . . . n'était-il pas, lui aussi, le vainqueur inattendu, celui qui s'élevait au milieu des désastres?" (5, p. 199) [wasn't he himself too the unexpected victor, rising up in the midst of disaster?]. The Saccard-Second Empire parallel remains at the back of our minds, as we read in chapter 7 that the hero's bank continues to expand, partly thanks to more illegal operations. Caroline is well aware of Saccard's fraudulent schemes, but is more troubled by his sexual misdemeanors. Not only is he betraying her with Baroness Sandorff (who hopes to glean financial tips from her lover), but echoes have reached her from the past. She has learned from Saccard's son, Maxime, that his father tacitly consented to his incest with Renée for the sake of financial advantage. After that Caroline can have little doubt about the primacy in Saccard's world of money as a source of pleasure and power and she is horrified at this revelation of his "diabolique grandeur" (5, p. 220) [diabolic stature]. Just as she is nostalgic for the simple faith of her youth and is preparing to run away to her devout brother in the Near East, the latter sends her a glowing account of prosperity and fertility spreading in Lebanon thanks to the funds mustered by Saccard, whereupon Zola makes his heroine adopt Saccard's earlier defense of speculation:

> Alors Mme Caroline eut la brusque conviction que l'argent était le fumier dans lequel poussait cette humanité de demain; . . . sans la

spéculation, il n'y avait pas de grandes entreprises vivantes et fécondes, pas plus qu'il n'y avait d'enfants sans luxure. . . . (5, p. 224)

[Then Mme Caroline suddenly had the conviction that money was the manure in which tomorrow's humanity could grow ... there were no great, flourishing, fruitful enterprises without speculation, anymore than there were children without [prior] sexual pleasure.]

For good measure, Zola throws in his own commentary at the end of the chapter, probably not realizing, that he is engaged in whitewashing his own extramarital relations, on the pretext that they generate new life:

C'était l'amour triomphant, ce Saccard, ce bandit du trottoir financier, aimé si absolument par cette adorable femme, parce qu'elle le voyait actif et brave, créer un monde, faire de la vie. (5, p. 228)

[It was love triumphant; Saccard, that highwayman of the financial world, loved so absolutely by this adorable woman, because she saw him as dynamic, creating a world, making life.]

Chapter 8 uses the Exposition Universelle (1867) as a symbol to correspond both to the glory of the regime and to that of Saccard: he is opening up a new, sumptuous temple for his Banque Universelle. Prior to a fresh isssue of shares, the hero has a meeting with Caroline and Georges that shows them to be torn between admiration for Saccard's financial "poetry" and remorse over their complicity in something dishonest. Zola juxtaposes their repressed sense of "complicité salissante" [sullying complicity] with one of those visionary evocations of decadence and debauchery that sound vaguely biblical, but that are really the product of the author's inimitable imagination:

... la débauche veillait jusqu'à l'aube. La joie avait gagné de maison à maison, les rues étaient une ivresse, un nuage de vapeurs fauves, la fumée des festins, la sueur des accouplements s'en allait à l'horizon, roulait au-dessus des toits la nuit des Sodome, des Babylone et des Ninive. (5, pp. 253–54)

[... the debauchery lasted till dawn. The merriment spread from house to house. The streets were a drunken ecstasy, a steamy haze of musky emanations; the smoke from the banquets, the sweat of the couplings extended as far as the eye could see, unfurling above the rooftops the night of [every] Sodom, Babylon, and Nineveh.]

8: FROM DEATH AND DISASTER TO MESSIANIC HOPE 179

The apocalyptic implications of the cities mentioned will not be lost on anyone who is even vaguely familiar with the Old Testament. It was no doubt such a scene Zola had in mind when, in his Dossier préparatoire, he foresaw the social and political background of his novel as follows:

> C'est la dernière flambée de l'empire, une fin d'empire, une danse sur le volcan classique, la guerre de 70 est là, et on se rue une dernière fois à la jouissance, à la satisfaction de tous les appétits.[8]

> [It is the Empire's final flare up, the end of an empire, a dance on the rim of the classic volcano. The 1870 war is there and there is a last mad scramble for enjoyment and the satisfaction of every appetite.]

After that typical instance of "perspective bending," Zola makes a point of alluding to Napoleon III's Mexican disaster and then, in the same breath, reports Saccard's growing audacity: not only does the latter start using the newspapers he controls in order to openly attack his brother, Eugène, but he intends to take on the major Jewish bank, headed by Gundermann, as well. The author then closes his chapter on another choice specimen of prophetic allegory, as Saccard proudly shows off the courtesan, Mme de Jeumont, at the Foreign Affairs ball (he has bought her services for the modest sum of two hundred thousand francs). Bismarck himself watches the couple from a corner "en bon géant goguenard" (5, p. 258) (in the role of a good-natured, slightly mocking giant).

Chapter 9 brings premonitory rumbles of disaster to come. The Hamelins progressively sell their shares (virtue and faith are giving up on the hero); Saccard makes an enemy out of Sigismund Busch's ignoble elder brother and the rumor spreads that Gundermann is setting aside three hundred million to ruin his rival. When the Banque Universelle shares reach the preposterously inflated price of three thousand francs, Saccard becomes king for a day. At his exulting headquarters, he may be given a literal red-carpet treatment, but he already senses his imminent fall. Note the effective manner in which the author hollows out the ground beneath his hero's feet before proclaiming him king in the shortest of main clauses:

> Et à cette minute suprême, où Saccard, au sommet, sentait trembler la terre, dans l'angoisse inavouée de la chute, il fut roi. (5, p. 295)

[And in that supreme moment, when Saccard, at the pinnacle (of his career), felt the earth tremble [beneath his feet], in his unavowed terror at the thought of falling, he was king.]

The battle of Saccard and Gundermann in chapter 10 takes on mythical proportions. The whole of Paris is reported as watching with bated breath "ce corps à corps des deux monstres légendaires ... menaçant de s'étrangler l'un l'autre, sur le monceau de ruines qu'ils entassaient" (5, p. 315) (this hand to hand combat between two legendary monsters ... threatening to strangle each other atop the pile of ruins they were amassing). The hero's scheme of humbling Gunderman—"le chef tout-puissant", "l'invincible force," "le premier du monde" (5, p. 313) [the all-powerful head, the invincible force, the ruler of the world]— along with all his "créatures inconnues" [unknown creatures], falters. In the attempt to defend the value of his shares, Saccard has drained all his liquid assets, but Gundermann does not know this and is himself thinking of pulling out of the contest. At the critical moment, Zola gives an interesting twist to the plot: what seals the hero's doom is not his lack of reserves, but his sexual libertinage. During his moments of relaxation and "solace" with Baroness Sandorff, the lady goes through his pockets in order to pass on vital information to the enemy. There is poetic justice in this, but it is also possible to suspect that the episode amounts to a covert confession of the chink in Zola's own armor. Just as the hero of *La Confession de Claude,* alias young Zola, betrayed his messianic ideals by falling into sordid sensuality, middle-aged Zola, with his mission of morally purging French society, has blotted his copybook by his liaison with Jeanne Rozerot. It is clear that, with his conscious mind, Zola has long since lost faith in the God of Christianity, but could his subconscious still be haunted by the myth that it is arrogant to fight the Almighty and hazardous for a would-be reformer to indulge in the pleasures of illicit love?

However that may be, this climactic scene is followed immediately by a close-up on Saccard that is suggestive of Satan at his moment of final defeat:

.... il s'était raidi pour mourir debout. Un froid de glace montait du sol à son crâne, il avait la sensation de l'irréparable, c'était sa défaite à jamais.... (5, p. 330)

[... he had braced himself to die on his feet. An icy coldness was rising from the ground to his head; he felt as if something irreparable had occurred: this was his defeat forever.]

This mythically charged scene leads on to some interesting speculations on Saccard's irrational acts of self-destruction (Georges has returned to Paris and asks himself]:

> ... quelle puissance mystérieuse venait de pousser Saccard à s'acharner ainsi contre l'édifice colossal qu'il avait élevé, à le détruire, pierre à pierre d'un côté, tandis qu'il prétendait l'achever de l'autre? (5, p. 335)

> [... what mysterious power had just now impelled Saccard to turn like this against the colossal edifice he had raised, and destroy it stone by stone while, at the same time, claiming that he was adding the finishing touches?]

Given the fact that, on completing his monumental *Rougon-Macquart*, Zola himself will set about systematically to undermine, in his last six novels, the literary renown he has so painstakingly built up, given the fact that he will be quite ready to risk his national reputation, late in life, to come to the defense of an obscure Jew, we had better take Georges's question seriously. Do we answer, with Freud, in terms of man's inbuilt deathwish? Do we believe with J. R. R. Tolkien in *The Lord of the Rings* that the emblem of power must be destroyed if we are to find peace of mind? Do we hold, with several world religions, that even the greatest human achievements are ultimately but a barrier between us and the infinite? Or do we fall back on the earlier quoted insight of Paul Pelckman (apropos of the denouement of *Le Rêve*) that those who pursue symbolic goals (unconsciously), may want to destroy them in the end, in order to keep intact the underlying dream or ideal?

Zola himself does not immediately answer this question. (Saccard's move to Holland, at the end of the novel and his becoming involved in some vast scheme to reclaim land from the sea, suggests that, for him, "the game is more important than the marbles," that he simply enjoys the exercise of his dynamic creativity, that he likes to pit his strength against powerful opponents, regardless of the outcome.) By the end of the chapter, however, Caroline, who has been made to witness many of the human tragedies Saccard has brought about, asks herself a question very similar to that put by her brother:

> Quelle force mystérieuse, après avoir édifié si rapidement cette tour d'or, venait donc ainsi de la détruire? Les mêmes mains qui l'avaient

construite, semblaient s'être acharnées, prises de folie, à ne pas en laisser une pierre debout. (5, p. 359)

[What mysterious force, after erecting the golden tower so rapidly, had just destroyed it in this way? It was as if the very hands that had constructed it, had been gripped by madness and had been [hell-]bent on leaving not a stone standing.]

The end of the quotation, in particular, takes on an apocalyptic tone and suggests that the same demonic force that is predicted to provoke a cosmic Apocalypse at the end of time, the same power that drove Napoleon Bonaparte into Russia and led Hitler to follow his example, has been at work in Saccard. This demonic perspective, in keeping with our thesis in this section, is borne out by the chapter's closing decor: Caroline walks out into the night and sees la Bourse outlined against a lurid sky (we are back to something like the river Seine decor at the end of *L'Oeuvre*):

Le crépuscule tombait, le ciel d'hiver, chargé de brume, mettait derrière le monument comme une fumée d'incendie, une nuée d'un rouge sombre, qu'on aurait crue faite des flammes et des poussières d'une ville prise d'assaut ... derrière cette fumée rousse de l'horizon, dans les lointains troubles de la ville, il y avait un grand craquement sourd, la fin prochaine d'un monde. (5, pp. 360–61)

[Twilight was falling; behind the monument, the winter sky, heavy with mist, formed a backdrop of dark red cloud, like smoke from a large conflagration. One might well have taken it for the flames and dust of a city taken by storm ... behind this reddish-brown smoke on the horizon, in the distant confusion of the town, there was a great, dull cracking sound, the imminent demise of a world.]

The double prophetic allusion to Paris burning during the Commune and to the end of the world neatly rounds off Zola's apocalyptic theme in the novel.

At the end of chapter 11, Caroline reacts to the suicide of one of Saccard's victims by cursing her former lover: "Ah! que Saccard ne trouvât pas de pardon ... et qu'il mourût seul un jour dans le mépris!" (5, p. 360) [Ah, that Saccard might find no pardon and that he might die one day, alone and in the midst of contempt]. However, having come to this point in his tale, Zola does not want to end on a note of Apocalypse and the final condemnation of Lucifer. Yet this may well have been his original purpose: in an interview given to M. Fenouil and published in

Le Gil Blas 4 August 1890, he had previewed his hero's destiny as follows:

> ... une de ces montées brusques, soudaines, vers des hauteurs prodigieuses, suivie d'une dégringolade subite, d'un anéantissement complet ...
>
> [... one of those abrupt and sudden ascents to prodigious heights, followed by an unexpected tumble and total annihilation. ...]

although it is equally true that, almost from the outset, he intended to show that his villainous hero was capable of generosity, of disinterested activity and kindness as well. Accordingly, chapter 12 reconsiders subjects such as the role of money, speculation, and human passion, as part of a reassessment of Saccard. Caroline, as Zola's chief spokesperson, is given the task of conducting this final review.

The power of money—even money devoted to charity—the heroine decides, is limited. In Princess d'Orviedo's model institution, she comes across some innocent young girls praying that Saccard may be rewarded for all his kindness to them. The same orphanage, however, Caroline finds, has done nothing for Victor, Saccard's delinquent son: at last reports, he has raped the aristocratic virgin, Alice de Bourvilliers (already deprived of her dowry by the crash of l'Universelle), and he has escaped into the night to spread the Rougon virus of evil wherever he goes. In Caroline's eyes, he is like a mad dog on the loose:

> ... le monstre était lâché par le monde, à l'avenir, à l'inconnu, ainsi qu'une bête écumante du virus héréditaire, qui devait élargir le mal à chacun de ses coups de dents. (5, p. 395)
>
> [... the monster had been let loose into the world, into the future, into the unknown, like a beast foaming at the mouth with the hereditary virus that was to spread the evil with every bite inflicted.]

So far, then, we have a plus and a big minus on Saccard's account, but Caroline's provisional judgment is tolerant and merciful: "... il n'y a pas d'homme condamnable, qui, au milieu de tout le mal qu'il a pu faire, n'ait encore fait beaucoup de bien" (5, p. 377) [... there is no man worthy of condemnation who, amid all the evil he may have done, has not also done a lot of good]. When the heroine visits Saccard in prison, she at first finds him unrepentant (the crash was brought about by government plots, he claims!). In a moment of truth, however, he confesses that his excessively passionate nature is to blame and he formulates the whole myth of passion which, by its very nature, must expire at its moment of triumph:

> Moi, je suis trop passionné, c'est évident. La raison de ma défaite n'est pas ailleurs. . . . Et il faut ajouter que, si ma passion me tue, c'est aussi ma passion qui me fait vivre. Oui, elle m'emporte, elle me grandit, me pousse très haut, et puis elle m'abat, elle détruit d'un coup tout son oeuvre. (5, p. 384)

> [I'm too passionate; that's obvious. The reason for my defeat is to be found nowhere else. . . . And I must add that, if my passion kills me, it also keeps me alive. Yes, it carries me along, builds me up, compels me to climb very high and then it knocks me down, and with one blow destroys everything it has created.]

—profound words, no doubt, words that do not apply only to Napoleon Bonaparte, to whom Saccard likes to compare himself (Zola has learned a few things about himself and about passion of late). We should note, in passing, that, through his central character, Zola has come up with his own answer to Georges and Caroline's earlier question: self-destructive acts are not necessarily demonic in inspiration, but may be the natural outworking of human passion.

Saccard is less impressive when he shrugs off all the sufferings he has caused: "Est-ce que la vie s'inquiète de ça? Chaque pas que l'on fait écrase des milliers d'existences" (5, p. 383) [Does life worry about that? Each step that you take wipes out thousands of lives] or when he slings off at Gundermann (and the likes of him): ". . . un sale juif, qui triomphe parce qu'il est sans désirs" (5, p. 384) [. . . a filthy Jew who comes out on top, because he is without desires]. Once again it is Caroline who draws up the balance-sheet: over against Saccard's passion and his lack of scruple, she sets his "force débordante" [overflowing strength] his hope, and his radiant vitality. Like her brother, who has already forgiven Saccard, she can no longer feel angry with him.

Next we find her standing at Sigismund's bedside as the noble dreamer expires, his eyes still glowing with the distant vision of the blessed city. Caroline herself has no illusions left: "Certes, aucune illusion ne lui restait. La vie était décidément injuste et ignoble, comme la nature" (5, p. 397) (Certainly, she had no illusions left. Like nature, life was positively unjust and ignoble] but she cannot help loving life all the same, in spite of all its horrors:

Ah! La joie d'être, est-ce que au fond il en existe une autre? La vie telle qu'elle est, dans sa force, si abominable qu'elle soit, avec son éternel espoir. (5, p. 397)

[Ah! The joy of existence! Is there basically any other [to compare it to]? Life just as it is, in its dynamism, however abominable it might be, with its eternal hope.]

Caroline may be thinking in terms of generalities, but her philosophical musings amount, nonetheless, to an absolving of Saccard, who simply incarnates the ambiguous life-force in its destructive and its creative aspects. As part of the means, the machinery of the life-force, Mammon too is rehabilitated—a view that holds some difficulties for modern readers who are familiar with the dubious activities of currency and stock-market speculators and who may be less than enthusiastic about the activities of multinationals in the Third World.

Now that immaculate virgins are out of favor and money rules the scene, Zola's attempt, earlier in the novel, to trivialize passing love affairs and his later tendency to glamorize financial entrepreneurs, threaten, for a season, to make him bow down to idols he used to scorn. Jewish readers, in particular, who wince at the way some of Zola's characters speak rather too freely of "la sale juiverie" [filthy Jewry], will agree that L'Argent is not one of his most idealistic novels.

As for the very negative picture of Gundermann and, by implication (conscious or unconscious) the Old Testament Jehovah that he represents in part, it could be pointed out that individuals trying to cope with sexual guilt are sometimes tempted to adopt an unattractive view of the God who formulated the sixth commandment. It will be remembered that, in novels like *Les Mystères de Marseille* and *Madeleine Férat*, already, we encountered evidence of Zola's Oedipal guilt projecting itself on to remote and cruel father figures and a God who does not pardon ("Dieu le Père n'aurait pas pardonné!") [God the Father would not have forgiven!]. A related state of mind in the mature Zola could explain why the author of *L'Argent* interferes with the Lucifer myth he has so carefully built up in the first eleven chapters, only to modify it, somewhat controversially, in the last. If we remember that novelists are often said to "dream on paper," there may be food for thought in the following note on "dream-making": psychiatrists are well acquainted with the phenomenon whereby patients, about to awaken from a dream whose message is too revealing for comfort, hastily adapt the ending of the dream or else modify their subsequent recollection of sensitive details. Is that what Zola has done in L'Argent?

In terms of the evolution of Zola's messianic myth, the most positive element to come out of the novel is the author's conviction that the life-force has a redemptive value all of its own and that it may be operative both in the virtuous and in rogues like Saccard. If our symbolic reading of the novel is correct, the most negative element to emerge is the author's utter denigration of Gundermann, alias God. In the final novel of his cycle, Zola will modify that stance as, through his mature and charitable hero, Dr. Pascal, he adopts a greater degree of tolerance for the mystery of "l'au-delà" [the beyond]. It should be noted, finally that, just as Saccard is in no way improved or redeemed by his trials, there is no suggestion as yet that the impending national Apocalypse will bring about a moral regeneration of French society.

Zola's La Débâcle (1892) marks the end of an era in more than one way—for the Second Empire, which has been the normal setting of the Rougon-Macquart cycle but, in a certain sense, for the author himself as well. It is in this novel that, maybe for the first time, one senses that the author's desire to communicate a message begins to interfere with his ability to mount a genuine human drama. Didacticism, in other words, competes with that mysterious creative gift of Zola's which, at its best, can project a world as gripping and convincing as the real one.

Admittedly, the overall epic canvas of the war is still captivating, the episodic appearances of the emperor are most effective, the evolving relationship of Corporal Jean Macquart and the more educated Maurice has its poignant moments, but even the two friends, not to mention the host of secondary characters, have lost some of the weight, the density, the three-dimensional reality that characterizes the cast of, for instance, L'Assommoir, Germinal, or even La Bête humaine.

The plot of La Débâcle has been described as overburdened with material—which no doubt is a fair criticism. Even the more "homely" scenes, moreover, are crowded with characters but, in that respect, the novel is no worse than War and Peace: no author can be expected to write a clear, straightforward account of a chaotic complex of events. The real problem is Zola's growing stress on imparting ideas, the heavy-handed symbolism, the pure "functionality" of many of the characters who are no longer allowed to act or to react in terms of their own nature, but who are forced to perform the role, to formulate the message, or provide the information that the author requires of them.

Given the fact that, for each of his novels, Zola has selected a subject, conceived characters, arranged a plausible sequence of events, imposed an orderly structure, why should the absence of creative freedom start to show in *La Débâcle*? One answer could be that, in the past, his mode of literary creation owed as much to unconscious myth as it did to planned scenarios: his writing was marked by a dialectic tension: Zola the naturalist was aided by Zola the visionary poet. Now he is reaching a stage in his maturity where his unconscious myths are surfacing in his conscious mind, so that they can be controlled and manipulated rationally. And the result becomes noticeable: where, previously, plots were moved along and characters were animated not only by the conscious will of the author, but also by the more mysterious archetypes or blueprints of myth, we now witness the gradual fading of a whole dimension. Where, in the past, we followed characters that evolved "organically," from within, through the complex interplay of determinism and free will, we now begin to meet puppets controlled, however ingeniously, by visible strings.

Actually, the changeover does not occur overnight: there are still unconscious myths at work both in *La Débâcle* and in *Le Docteur Pascal* that cast their spell, draw us in, and so impart a sense of life and reality, but their diminution is already more obvious in *Lourdes* and becomes critical in *Les Quatre evangiles*. We shall need to assess, in due time, how the drying up of Zola's "artesian" stock of myths affects his messianic outlook. For the time being we must ascertain how the author's preoccupations in *La Débâcle*—conscious or unconscious—fit into his eschatology—his prophetic framework involving catastrophe and renewal, true and false messiahs, and the "end of the age."

We gather from Zola's dossiers that he had long wished to write a military novel, as part of his panorama of mid-nineteenth-century France and that the fall of Napoleon III had provided him with a timely bonus—an ideal way of epitomizing the materialistic, decadent, pleasure-driven society he had chosen to portray. Even at the time of writing *La Débâcle*, his chief purpose remains to complete his historical saga. As he writes to van Santen Kolff, his title has more than a military connotation: "Ce n'est pas la guerre seulement, c'est l'écroulement d'une dynastie, c'est l'effondrement d'une époque"[9] [It's not just the war; it's the downfall of a dynasty, the collapse of an epoch]. We shall argue later that the aspects of the novel Zola refers to above have a prophetic bearing on world society in the "latter days."

Mitterand and others have elaborated on Zola's stated intention to use his hero, Jean Macquart and his Parisian friend to juxtapose positive and negative aspects of French society under the Second Empire (with the sensible, moderate, dutiful, and persevering side eventually eliminating the more neurotic, unstable, volatile, and easily discouraged side). What could be added, perhaps, is that, in the process, the author inverts his old recipe of weak hero and robust friend (presented in four out of the five early novels) and that the new scenario, besides being an intentional allegory of France, dramatizes his own evolution from neurosis to mental health between 1880 (his mother's death) and 1890.

Within the same context, it is worth noting that it is in his moments of greatest depression and despair, that Maurice is irresistibly drawn to a setting of Apocalypse (La Commune) and eventually calls for a scenario of destruction and rebirth:

> Que Paris s'effondrât, qu'il brûlât comme un immense bûcher d'holocauste, plutôt que d'être rendu à ses vices et à ses misères, à cette vieille société gâtée d'abominable injustice. (5, p. 875)
>
> [Let Paris come tumbling down; let it burn like a gigantic sacrificial fire, rather than return to its vices and miseries, to that old society tainted by abominable injustice.]

and again: "L'heure avait sonné que la ville entière flambât donc comme un bûcher immense, que le feu purifiât le monde" (5, p. 883) [The hour had struck, then, for the whole city to burn like an immense bonfire and for the world to be cleansed by fire] (note that the burning of Paris merges into that of the whole world). Jean's protest to Maurice: "Non, non! il ne fallait pas vouloir le mal! Si c'était la destruction de tout, eux-mêmes allaient donc périr?" (5, p. 894) [No, no! You shouldn't desire evil. If there were total destruction, then weren't they themselves going to perish?] and his outrage with the Communard retreat-and-burn policy suggest that Zola has seen through his own fascination with apocalypse and that he symbolically dismisses it along with his former neurotic self (in the novel Jean unwittingly bayonets his former soul mate). Through staging a scenario of Apocalypse in three successive novels and finally centering it around two characters that contain a good deal of himself, Zola has released another myth from his unconscious (it was Zola, all along, who needed the purging and rebirth). Now that he has exposed this myth to the clear light of day, he will be in a position to assess it soberly and rationally.

It is not only Corporal Jean and his friend that reflect Zola's changing attitude to himself and to the world. Napoleon III, formerly his bête noire par excellence, will retain his planned role in La Débâcle of representing the end of an age, the collapse of a regime that is rotting from within, but the author's attitude to him will be colored by a new pity and understanding—a change that cannot be explained purely in terms of greater familiarity with the facts of history.

Why, up to 1892, did Zola detest the emperor so cordially? If we can accept the Jungian insight that we hate most in others what we disapprove of in ourselves, we may find merit in the suggestion that, in Napoleon III, Zola dimly perceived shades of his own sensuality, immense ambition, desire for display, and tendency to indulge in utopian dreams. As long as the author failed to realize that he was projecting his own shadow onto the villains of his fiction, he could make the most of the emperor's many failings—the messianic alibi spun around the coup of 1851; the scandals of his regime; his indulgence in sensuality, vanity and empty show; his extravagant spending on public works; his adventurism abroad; his ill-considered declaration of war in 1870—all of which constitutes a very one-sided panorama of his reign. Readers not versed in nineteenth-century French history who have taken Zola's portrayal of Napoleon at face value, are in for a surprise when they come upon a more objective appraisal of the Second Empire.

Zola's episodic presentation of Napoleon III before La Débâcle is indeed far from balanced. In La Fortune des Rougon, we see him only through the eyes of those who frequent Félicité's "salon jaune" (yellow drawing room), but we gain the impression that Eugène Rougon and his father, Pierre, have their own selfish reasons for passing him off as a messiah, a savior from chaos and disaster.

Commentators have no trouble in discerning Zola's very negative picture in various volumes of Les Rougon-Macquart. Auguste Dezalay, in his article "Zola et Le Rêve," reminds us of Napoleon the sensualist who wants to add Renée to his list of conquests (La Curée), Napoleon the vague utopian dreamer whom Eugène imagines brooding on land reform or on the extinction of poverty (during his cabinet sessions), or Napoleon the mystical dreamer given to premonitions (*Son Excellence Eugène Rougon*), before leaving us with a vision of Napoleon the powerless leader, paralyzed by sickness in the moment of crisis (*La Débâcle*.)[10] Maurice Descotes offers us a fine study of Zola's Napoleon as a prisoner of high finance and sectional interests as well as of his own sensuality and addiction to dreams, as the man who was incapable of a heroic destiny because he lacked the indispensable element of the charismatic or supernatural.[11] Raoul Girardet uses his introduction to *La Débâcle* to insert Zola's portrait of the emperor into the study of decadence that occupied many minds in the closing decades of the last century.[12] Emile Faguet points out perceptively that Zola uses the well-orchestrated appearances of Napoleon in *La Débâcle* to punctuate his account of the war up to Sedan and to periodically bring back our minds to his general theme of the empire's collapse.[13] All of these assessments are valid, but we need to be alert to a subtle shift in perspective that Zola introduces in the novel that completes his coverage of the Second Empire: we propose to show that the author's use of satire and irony there is attenuated by a quasi-tragic tone involving an element of compassion.

Early in *La Débâcle*, Maurice dwells on the ironic situation of the emperor as, stripped of military rank and authority, disowned by his wife who does not want him back in the capital, he continues to surround himself with a vast and pointless retinue—a picture Maurice contrasts with his schoolboy recollections of Saint Joan and "toute la glorieuse vieille France" (5, p. 446) [all the splendors of the old France]. Note, however, how he qualifies his often-quoted opinion of the emperor ("C'était le conspirateur, le rêveur à qui l'énergie manque au moment de l'action") [He was the conspirator, the dreamer bereft of energy when the moment for action came]:

> On le disait très bon, très capable d'une grande et généreuse pensée, très tenace d'ailleurs en son vouloir d'homme silencieux, et il était aussi très brave, méprisant le danger en fataliste prêt toujours à subir le destin. (5, p. 458, 459)

> [He was said to be very kind, very capable, a man of great and generous thoughts, very tenacious, moreover, with that willpower of his [that one may encounter in] a silent man; he was also very courageous, in his stance of a fatalist always ready to submit to destiny.]

8: FROM DEATH AND DISASTER TO MESSIANIC HOPE

In part 1, chapter 5, Zola features more irony in the form of the elaborate culinary activity that is required for the emperor's table, but that perspective suddenly fades as we catch a glimpse of a virtual martyr—sick, pale, and unable to eat his food. That piteous evocation culminates in part 2, chapter 3 when, at Sedan, the emperor loses his makeup and cuts a very sorry figure:

> ... le fard s'en était allé des joues, les moustaches cirées s'étaient amollies, pendantes, la face terreuse avait pris l'hébètement douloureux d'une agonie. (5, p. 621)

> [... the makeup had gone from his cheeks, his waxed moustaches had become limp and drooping, his ashen face had taken on the suffering, dazed expression of some one in his death throes.]

The casual reader might interpret this description as more satire on the part of an unsympathetic author, but that is not at all the effect intended by Zola. Even before publishing the novel in weekly installments, he had written an article for *Le Figaro* (9 January 1891) in which he expressed his pity for Napoleon III:

> Ah! ce misérable empereur, dans toute cette marche, quelle figure tragique et lamentable! Il a pu être le grand coupable, mais une pitié irrésistible monte du coeur, quand on le voit, malade, déchu, emporté à l'ignominie dans le torrent débordé....[14]

> [Oh, that wretched emperor, in this whole course of events! What a tragic and pitiful figure! He may have been the great villain [of the piece], but one feels an irresistible surge of pity that comes from the heart, at the sight of him—sick, fallen from power, swept away into ignominy by the raging torrent....]

and when later readers of his novel take him to task for turning the emperor into a cheap play-actor who uses makeup, he protests in no uncertain terms and actually comes to expressing his admiration for Napoleon as a sublime figure, worthy of Shakespeare's great tragic heroes. (Had Zola reduced the emperor to "un rôle louche d'histrion) (the role of a shifty play-actor)?

> Mais, pas du tout! ... Moi je trouve superbe, ce fard, digne d'un des grands héros de Shakespeare, haussant la figure de Napoléon III à une mélancolie tragique d'une infinie grandeur.[15]

> [Not at all! ... I, personally, find that makeup superb and worthy of one of Shakespeare's great heroes. It raises the figure of Napoleon III to a level of tragic melancholy and infinite greatness.]

In fact, Zola falls far short of such eulogies in the actual novel, where he restricts himself to a sober exposition of the facts. The final glimpses we have of the emperor when, after the unconditional surrender, he spends a restless night in a small room at the post office:

> ... il n'eut que la distraction de regarder contre le mur, aux deux côtés de la cheminée, des gravures qui se trouvaient là, l'un représentant Rouget de Lisle chantant la Marseillaise, l'autre le Jugement dernier. ... (5, p. 727)

> [... his only distraction was to look at the engravings that were hanging on the wall on either side of the chimney; one depicted Rouget de Lisle singing the Marseillaise, the other the Last Judgment.]

or when he shamefully journeys back into France through apocalyptic battlefields, leave little doubt about the grim harvest he leaves behind. This quotation not only contrasts Napoleon's fate with the heroic days of the Marseillaise, but suggests that the emperor is facing divine judgment for the death and desolation he has caused: Zola alludes to the "charnier des batailles montant témoigner devant Dieu" [charnel house of battles, rising up to testify before God] featured in the second picture.

What has inspired the author to attenuate his negative picture of Napoleon III? Is the happy father more ready to pardon? Has Zola mellowed with age or has a greater awareness of his own shortcomings taught him that Napoleon III was not the only self-styled savior to have failed?

The seed of Apocalypse is already present in Zola's work before the *Rougon-Macquart:* we see it germinating, for instance, in individual destinies in the closing pages of *Thérèse Raquin* and *Madeleine Férat*. Back in 1870, Zola told the readers of *Le Siècle* that, artistically speaking, he needed the downfall of Napoleon III and that recent events had provided him with "le dénouement terrible et nécessaire" [terrible and inevitable resolution] of his vast project.[16]

In the course of analyzing successive volumes of Zola's cycle, we have seen the theme emerge clearly in *Nana* and *Germinal*, with the open ending of the second novel holding out some vague promise that Apocalypse may lead to a new future. After reading the prophetic denouement of *L'Oeuvre*, Jules Lemaître predicts that Zola may finish up writing "des livres d'un naturalisme apocalyptique, qui pourront, d'ailleurs, être fort bons"[17] [books (characterized by a perspective of) apocalyptic naturalism that may well turn out to be very good]. Having elaborated on the myth of l'Eternel retour [Eternal return] in his study of *La Terre*, Guy Robert is ready to see the connection between Zola's recurring vision of death and fertility and the theme of catastrophe leading to hope:

> *La Débâcle* enfin précipite l'avènement de la Catastrophe finale qu'on pressentait de plus en plus inévitablement, mais qui peut préparer la voie à un avenir déjà tout prêt à s'installer.[18]

> [*La Débâcle*, in short, precipitates the onset of the final disaster—something sensed as ever more inevitable, but that may prepare the way for a future that, even now, is ready to move in.]

Without that redemptive perspective, one is likely to misread the Commune appendix at the end of the novel as a variation on "Babylone en flammes" [Babylon in flames] or on the lake of fire reserved for the Beast in the Book of Revelation.[19]

Like Guy Robert, Roger Ripoll draws attention to the change that occurs in Zola's presentation of Apocalypse, notably in the related "mythe de calvaire" [Calvary myth]: *La Débâcle*, he shows, no longer enacts a myth of death and failed redemption, but rather introduces a scenario of expiation. The novel points beyond Apocalypse to a future of resurrection and reconstruction.[20]

Ripoll's observations certainly are in keeping with Zola's conscious intentions; witness the following notes for *La Débâcle* to be found in his Deuxième Plan [Second Plan] and in his Plan Détaillé [Detailed Plan] respectively:

> (1) La leçon terrible, mais l'espoir jaillissant du sang et des larmes, la France renouvelée et grandie. (M.S.10286 Fo 135)

> [The dreadful lesson, but hope springing up from the blood and tears; France renewed and made greater.]

> (2) "L'immense espoir au-dessus des flammes" (ibid, Fo 136)

> [The immense hope beyond the flames.]

The same ideas are presented in greater detail in Zola's article for *Le Figaro*, dated 9 January 1891, when he describes the French defeat as a salutary blow to unwarranted pride[21] and especially in "Retour de voyage" [Returning from a voyage], where he adds the surprising rider that national sins should not only be atoned for, but should be confessed if there is to be any salvation:

> Nous avons besoin que la faute soit avouée et payée, que la confession soit faite, pour sauver de la catastrophe notre fierté et notre espoir dans la victoire future.[22]

> [It is necessary for us that the sin be admitted and paid for, the confession be made, in order to salvage from the carastrophe our pride and our hope of future victory.]

It is not very difficult to guess how Zola arrived at these (for him) novel views. The man who argues in the press that a nation that has survived the disaster of Sedan is invincible, has himself come through ten years of darkness and trouble and has only recently experienced a rebirth to life and joy. Having diagnosed the spirit of death and depression in *La Joie de vivre* and exorcised the demons of repressed lust and sadism in *L'Oeuvre* and in *La Bête humaine*, respectively, having exposed, through the figure of Maurice in *La Débâcle* , that, often, indulgence in apocalyptic dreams is a last resort of the desperate, Zola is in a sound position to proclaim that confession is good for the soul.

Within the actual novel, the myth of Apocalypse and atonement follows its own logic that corresponds, in broad outline, to the author's evolving attitude over the years. For a scenario of catastrophe to have its optimal impact, of course, it is advisable not to sound the trumpets of hope too early.

The heavy, brooding decor on which the novel opens no more suggests a happy outcome than do the first ten novels of the *Rougon-Macquart* cycle: "Une grasse fumée, noire et lente, montait dans l'air du soir, d'une infinie tristesse" (5, p. 401) [Thick black smoke rose slowly into the evening air, infinitely sad].— an impression strengthened at the end of the chapter by the ominous bird-cry that gives the lie to Lieutenant Rochas's celebration of the past glories of the French forces:

> Sous le ciel sombre, à ce moment, un grand cri douloureux passa. Etait-ce la plainte d'un oiseau de nuit? Etait-ce une voix de mystère, venue de loin, chargée de larmes? (5, p. 415)

> [Under the dark, lowering sky, at that instant, there came a great cry of pain. Was it the plaint of some night-bird? Was it a mysterious voice come from afar, full of tears?]

8: FROM DEATH AND DISASTER TO MESSIANIC HOPE

By the end of chapter 3, the theme of expiation has become explicit but, as yet, there is no suggestion of redemption: the march into death of the Châlons army is presented merely as an attempt to appease an angry fate, as a blood-offering to pay for the sins of all:

> ... c'était l'armée de la désespérance, le troupeau expiatoire qu'on envoyait au sacrifice, pour tenter de fléchir la colère du destin. Elle allait monter son calvaire jusqu'au bout, payant les fautes de tous du flot rouge de son sang. (5, p. 460)

> [... it was the army of despair, the expiatory flock sent to the sacrifice, in an attempt to avert the anger of destiny. It would climb its Calvary to the very end, paying for everyone's sins with the red tide of its blood.]

The concluding lines of chapter 5 make the whole exercise seem futile: the army is being sacrificed for the survival of a dynasty that is not worth saving; the perspective that prevails seems to be one of absolute doom, that of the ride into the abyss:

> Ah! cette armée de la désespérance, cette armée en perdition qu'on envoyait à un écrasement certain, pour le salut d'une dynastie! Marche, marche, sans regarder en arrière, sous la pluie. dans la boue, à l'extermination! (5, p. 503)

> [Ah! that army of despair, that army of the doomed, sent to certain destruction—to save a dynasty. March on, march on without looking back, through rain and mud, march on to your extermination!]

In the same way, Maurice may hold forth, from time to time, on the necessary role of war that ensures that only the fittest survive and that causes new life to spring from the fields of death, but most of part 2 of the novel suggests the unmitigated triumph of the forces of destruction. No comforting dawn of hope transforms the desolate battlefields of Sedan, the cartloads of corpses, the devastated forests, and the cavalcades of starving horses. The reader is made to traverse the same dark night that characterizes Zola's novels from *La Joie de vivre* to *La Bête humaine*.

Even after that, there is no respite, as the author focuses on the drawn-out martyrdom of the defeated army, especially as it faces starvation in the infamous POW camps of the Iges peninsula:

> L'armée de la désespérance, le troupeau expiatoire, envoyé en holocauste, avait payé la faute de tous du flot rouge de son sang, à chacune de ses stations. Et maintenant, égorgée sans gloire, couverte de crachats, elle tombait au martyre, sous ce châtiment qu'elle n'avait pas mérité si rude. (5, p. 774)

> [The army of despair, the expiatory flock sent out as a sacrifice, had atoned for everyone's sins with the red tide of its blood at each of its stations; slaughtered without glory, covered with spit, it now came under torture with this new punishment that was far harsher than it had deserved.]

It should be noted that Zola now refers to the army's "holocauste" and that, through the use of terms such as "crachats" [spit] and "stations," he implicitly compares the suffering of the soldiers to the experiences of Christ as he carries his Cross through the streets of Jerusalem.

We have already touched elsewhere on the climactic events of the Commune, where the whole world seems to be on fire and the flames reach so high that they even put out the stars, but it remains for us to draw up a balance-sheet of Zola's vision of Apocalypse at the end of the novel. It is clear that the author has little sympathy for the hard and cold Protestant mentality, voiced in the novel by Otto Gunther, according to which the German army was "envoyé par le Dieu des armées pour châtier un peuple pervers" (5, p. 887) [sent by the God of battle to chasten a wayward people]. There is no room in Zola's worldview for a traditional religious interpretation of history à la Bossuet. As we have noted before, however, neither does he approve of Maurice's nihilistic dream of destruction, be it for its own sake or in the vague hope of a better world to come:

> Détruire pour détruire, ensevelir la vieille humanité pourrie sous les cendres d'un monde, dans l'espoir qu'une société nouvelle repousserait heureuse et candide, en plein paradis terrestre des primitives légendes. (5, p. 902)

> [Destroy for the sake of destroying, bury the old, decaying human race beneath the ashes of a world, in the hope that a new society will grow again—joyous and without guile in the midst of the kind of earthly paradise that is the stuff of primitive legends.]

Zola's use of the expression "primitives légendes" and, a little later, in the same context, of "idylle" conveys his skepticism toward such dark dreams. He seems to take a dim view of

> ... cette grandiose et monstrueuse conception de la vieille société détruite, de Paris brûlé, du champ retourné et purifié, pour qu'il poussât l'idylle d'un nouvel âge d'or. (5, p. 911)
>
> [... this grandiose and monstrous idea [that sees] the old society being destroyed, the field turned over and purged, so that the idyll of a new golden age might burgeon.]

Nevertheless, while he rejects the active pursuit of Apocalypse, he does not deny that the actual baptism of fire constitutes a form of expiation and gives birth to hope. Accordingly, the end of the novel takes us into the mind of Jean, who is fully aware of the surrounding sea of flames, but is able to raise his eyes to a higher reality beyond the immediate scene:

> Et pourtant, par delà la fournaise, hurlante encore, la vivace espérance renaissait, au fond du grand ciel calme, d'une limpidité souveraine. C'était le rajeunissement certain de l'éternelle nature.... (5, p. 912)
>
> [And yet, beyond the fiery furnace that still roared, lively hope was being reborn in the supremely limpid depths of the great, calm sky. It was eternal nature's unfailing renewal of youth.]

Waxing as poetical as Zola at his best moments, the hero muses on the tree that produces a powerful new shoot, after a rotten limb has been cut off, whereupon the author decides it is time to take over in his own name: he expands the tree metaphor into a pastoral scene that has been visited by disaster, but that leaves the future open to the "grande et rude besogne" (momentous and heavy task) of reconstruction: "... toute une France à refaire" (5, p. 912) [... the whole of France to rebuild]. Significantly, that task is confided, not to some all-conquering messiah, but to a simple soldier—Jean, the most humble and sorrowful of men. While we must not lose sight of Zola's purely secular perspective, those closing words "le plus humble et le plus douloureux" [the humblest and saddest], are not unrelated to the "man of sorrows and acquainted with grief" described by Isaiah—the same prophet who provides the closing image of Zola's next novel, when he proclaims: "A Virgin will conceive and bear a son...."

Having allowed national and personal Apocalypse to clear the scene, the author is about to set the stage for a purely human messiah who is open both to the need of his brethren and to the ever-new energies of the life-force. Whether that pure humanity includes an element of the divine is another matter.

Zola's letter to van Santen Kolff, dated 25 January 1893, makes it clear that he intended Le Docteur Pascal (1893) to serve as a general conclusion to the Rougon-Macquart. The novel was meant to provide "une sorte de résumé, où l'idée scientifique et l'idée philosophique de l'ensemble seraient nettement indiqués"[23] [a kind of summary in which the scientific and philosophical ideas behind the whole series would be clearly indicated]. Even Mitterand, however, a scholar little given to psychoanalytical speculation, observes that, in the final volume of the cycle, author and hero "se rejoignent et se confondent"[24] [meet and meld]. One could even claim that, like Georges Raymond, the young scientist in Le Voeu d'une morte, Pascal corresponds to Zola's ideal self, albeit an ideal self of greater maturity, wisdom, and insight: the author has come a long way since his youthful conversion to science and to the theories of determinism.

One is surprised, on the other hand that, in spite of a long series of failing or false saviors, featured in earlier volumes of the series, Pascal is allowed to take up young Zola's messianic dream, now referred to as "l'espoir noble et fou de régénérer l'humanité" (5, p. 947) [the mad and lofty hope of regenerating humanity]. Back in the 1860s, the author saved himself from despair by adopting scientific objectivity as a way of viewing reality and he dramatized this in his fiction by killing off his dreamy idealist (Daniel) and by granting success to his sturdy scientist. Now, however, Zola is on the verge of a new synthesis. He still sees science as man's only hope, but he has also acquired a profound faith in the life-force—a faith that his conscious mind would like to pass off as purely positivistic, materialistic, and secular, but that strikes many commentators, including Colette Becker, as being tinged with mysticism.

We are faced with the same amalgam of science and faith in Zola's Doctor Pascal: the page, which refers to the hero's mad hope, goes on to define his faith in the following terms:

> En somme, le docteur Pascal n'avait qu'une croyance, la croyance à la vie. La vie était l'unique manifestation divine. La vie, c'était Dieu, le grand moteur, l'âme de l'univers. (5, p. 947)

> [In short, Doctor Pascal had only one belief, belief in life. Life was the only manifestation of the divine. Life was God, the great moving power, the soul of the universe.]

So far, the doctor has avoided having to abandon either pole of his dialectic—faith or science—by finding a synthesis: he has promoted heredity from being just another scientific theory to the rank of tool [outil] of the life-force (p. 947). Like the genetic engineers of our day, he hopes that a more perfect understanding of hereditary principles will one day enable science to reshape human destiny and bring in a form of Utopia. The long-awaited messiah may turn out to be a scientist!

A document like Zola's *Lettre à la jeunesse* (1879) and passing allusions, in novels such as *La Joie de vivre* and *L'Oeuvre*, show that, for some years prior to writing *Le Docteur Pascal*, Zola had been concerned about a resurgence of religion, brought about, he thought, by society's impatience with the slow progress of science. (One half suspects that the author's holiday visit to Lourdes in 1891 was inspired by more than documentary interest, in view of a future novel.) After all, Jeanne Rozerot, Zola's daily preoccupation, was a believer and his subsequent profound compassion for the figure of Bernadette Soubirous may reflect a certain nostalgia, on his own part, for the lost faith of his youth. His choice of a priest as the central character for his next series of novels (*Les Trois villes*), Pierre's painful quest for faith, his ardent attempt to reform Catholicism, and his eventual agonizing decision to abandon his priestly calling could be construed as reflections of conscious or unconscious impulses in Zola himself). Pascal, as Zola's ideal self, is supposed to be immune to that temptation, but the same cannot be said of the doctor's young niece, Clotilde. Thanks to her growing admiration and love for the old master, she will eventually stop practicing her faith, but she will always reserve a corner of her heart for the mystery of the beyond.

In his Ebauche, somewhat erroneously, Zola makes a point of contrasting niece and uncle (we are quoting Mitterand's summary of the Bodmer Library manuscript):

A la différence de Pascal, elle éprouve le "besoin de l'au-delà", "de connaître l'inaccessible, le futur", "le pourquoi". Il y a en elle une tendance au "mysticisme". Elle accepte enfin le "positivisme", "mais avec la réserve des forces inconnues"....

[Unlike Pascal, she experiences a "need of the beyond," "to know the inaccessible, the future," "the why." She has "mystical" tendencies. She finally accepts "positivism," "but makes allowances for (the existence of) unknown forces."][25]

In the novel, however, she is in many ways a double of her uncle. In the same way that Pascal defends science, but upholds the supremacy of the life-force, she is capable of patiently copying a hollyhock for scientific purposes and then sketching some dream-flower, for the sheer beauty of it or to satisfy her need of the "au-delà" [beyond]. We shall see later that Zola tacitly juxtaposes her oblation, or offering, of herself and Pascal's renunciation of marital bliss, messianic ambitions, and life itself, as though to suggest that their respective self-sacrifices make possible the birth of a future messiah.

The theme of renunciation is not a late development in the novel: humility and self-abnegation color the whole of Pascal's approach to life. In a thoughtful and well-researched article, Claudie Bernard demonstrates that, unlike ambitious Eugène Rougon, described by Pascal as "presque empereur" (5, p. 927) [almost an emperor], unlike Saccard, compared by him to Napoleon Bonaparte (5, p. 1010), unlike Octave Mouret, "le conquérant audacieux" (5, p. 1010) [the audacious conqueror], the hero is content to be a quiet researcher and an obscure country-doctor who devotes himself to the poor. The same critic shows how Zola brings out the futility of all those family ambitions by focusing on little Charles, Maxime Rougon's illegitimate son:

> Mais la vacuité de toutes ses prétentions apparaît bien avec le petit bâtard imbécile, Charles, à la "pâleur de lis" (975), "pareil à un de ces petits rois exsangues qui finissent une race" (965).[26]

> [But the emptiness of all his pretensions becomes obvious in the little illegitimate idiot, Charles, "white as a lily," looking "like one of those little anemic kings who mark the end of a family line".]

Pascal's royalty is of a different sort, won, as it is, not by personal ambition, but by selfless devotion to science and to his compassion for suffering humanity. Endowed with such virtues, he does not only represent Zola's ideal self, but also approximates the messianic ideal of the Shepherd-King proclaimed by Old Testament prophets, thus rendering himself worthy of the truly royal gift with which Clotilde will grace his life.

Like all doctors featured in Les Rougon-Macquart, Pascal is both a rationalist and an agnostic. What makes him exceptional, however, is that his desire to heal takes on messianic proportions. Working initially toward what he calls "l'alchimie du vingtième siècle" (5, p. 949) [twentieth-century alchemy], he places high hopes on the purified animal nerve-extract with which he injects his patients. When the doctor holds out to the light the small phial of distillate "comme s'il avait tenu le sang régénérateur et sauveur du monde" (5, p. 950) [as though he had been holding the blood that would regenerate and save the world], there can be little doubt about Zola's intentions (he is suggesting that Pascal strives for salvation through scientific research rather than through the blood of Christ). Pascal's faith in his panacea seems to be justified by some early success: when two consumptives respond well to injections or to a change of environment, the doctor is hailed by the locals as "sauveur" (savior) and as "messie attendu" (long-awaited messiah): "Il pouvait donc tout, il était donc le bon Dieu, qu'il ressuscitait les morts!" (5, p. 956) [He could do anything, then, he must be God, seeing that he could raise the dead!]. There is likely to be some link between the desire of Pascal, Zola's ideal hero, to be a healer and the author's own need, at various stages of his life, to overcome his neuroses. Jean Borie makes a comment along those lines in his seminal work, Zola et les mythes (1971), when he claims:

> Et le personnage du médecin, à la fois témoin et guérisseur, indique la présence en Zola d'une problématique de l'action et de l'adaptation, d'un sentiment d'exclusion caché sous le désir de faire du bien, et d'un besoin de se guérir caché sous le besoin de guérir les autres.[27]

> [And the figure of the doctor [doctors in general], at once a witness and a healer, indicates, in Zola, the presence of a problem area with regard to action and adaptation, a feeling of being excluded hidden behind the desire to do good, and a need to heal oneself hidden behind the need to heal others.]

As any psychiatrist knows, that kind of "symbolic problem solving" (e.g., tidying up one's desk or cupboard when one feels confused mentally) works only when the underlying need is faced and met. In the case of Pascal, this comes to pass in two stages. When one of his patients dies as a result of an injection with impure nerve-extract, the doctor has a virtual breakdown, from which he emerges only thanks to Clotilde's tender care and her (no doubt symbolic) suggestion that he inject himself with his own medicine. (Could Zola's subconscious be hinting that, if healing society is not possible, he could always try healing himself?) More effective still is her profound love for him and for the royal gift she makes of her young body—something he experiences as an unmerited boon of pure grace.

The two lovers find divinity in each other ("elle apparaissait divine" (5, p. 1059) [she appeared divine] and in the ecstasy of passion

> ... le lieu, le temps, les âges avaient disparu. Il ne restait que l'immortelle nature, la passion qui possède et crée, le bonheur qui veut être.... Pascal et Clotilde restèrent aux bras l'un de l'autre, noyés d'une extase, divinement joyeux et triomphants. (5, p. 1061)
>
> [... time, place, the [very] ages had disappeared. There remained only immortal nature, passion that possesses and creates, happiness that wants to be.... Pascal and Clotilde remained in each other's arms, bathed in ecstasy, divinely joyful and triumphant.]

And it is after being initiated into the intoxicating play of the life-force or, as David Baguley puts it, after discovering his "participation cosmobiologique à la création universelle"[28] [cosmobiologic participation in universal creation], after knowing in the depth of his being that he is no longer just an outsider, excluded and persecuted by his family, that Pascal is able to renounce his need to be a healing messiah. Accordingly, he confesses to Clotilde his doubts about his "alchimie du vingtième siècle" [twentieth-century alchemy] and his preference for letting nature have its way. From now on, he will simply inject his patients with pure water, for life is its own savior:

> Tant que je ne t'avais pas, je cherchais la vérité ailleurs, je me débattais, dans l'idée fixe de sauver le monde. Tu es venue, et la vie est pleine, le monde se sauve à chaque heure par l'amour, par le travail immense et incessant de tout ce qui vit et se reproduit, à travers l'espace.... La vie impeccable, la vie toute-puissante, la vie immortelle! (5, p. 1085)
>
> [As long as I did not have you, I sought truth elsewhere; I floundered about, obsessed with the idea of saving the world. You have come, and [now] life is full and the world is saved every hour by love, by the immeasurable, incessant work of everything that lives and reproduces, throughout space.... Immaculate, omnipotent, immortal life!]

The relevance of all this to Zola himself should be plain enough to anyone familiar with the author's personal history from December 1888 onward. In any case, Zola gives the show away rather poignantly when he writes in his dossier préparatoire:

Tant que (Pascal) ne se sent pas aimé, qu'il ne la possède pas, il ... garde son idée fixe de guérir tous les maux; et il ne s'élève au doute philosophique, à son respect de la nature, au point de ne pas la changer, que lorsqu'il aime et est aimé. L'analyse de cela n'est pas encore bien claire, mais évidemment c'est là qu'il faut chercher. ....[29]

[As long as [Pascal] is not aware of [Clotilde's] love for him and he has not possessed her, he holds onto his idée fixe of healing every ill; and he does not attain his position of philosophical doubt, or his respect for nature, to the point of not changing it, until after he loves and is loved in return. The analysis of that is not altogether clear as yet, but obviously that's the area to investigate.]

The comment that closes the quote, in particular, reveals a Zola who has himself been through an overwhelming experience and is still sorting out its repercussions in his life. In one of his early tales, "Aventures du grand Sidoine et du petit Médéric," the unsuccessful messiah-queen, Primevère, found consolation in the arms of Médéric. Now, at long last, Zola has found in his own life that those who experience true love no longer need to indulge in morale-boosting messianic dreams. He is therefore free to start looking for salvation outside of himself.

Many critics have commented on the change that comes over Pascal, alias Zola. The doctor is wiser than the painter Claude in L'Oeuvre, claims Roger Ripoll, when, rather than try to rival with God in the act of creation, he trusts in the impulse "de se laisser fondre dans le cours de la nature"[30] (of allowing himself to merge with the flow of nature). The corresponding change in Zola himself amounts to a thorough reinterpretation of sexuality: previously seen as a source of guilt and anguish, it is reassessed as participation in the creative life-force. David Baguley holds that, in surrendering to nature, through his union with Clotilde, Pascal reverses the Genesis myth of the Fall by preferring the tree of life to the tree of knowledge.[31] Philip D. Walker, in keeping with his usual approach, sees the change in Pascal/Zola in biblical terms as one from would-be messiah to forefather or humble herald: Dans l'attente du nouveau Messie, il se résigne à n'être qu'un patriarche, un précurseur"[32] [While awaiting the new Messiah, he is resigned to being merely a patriarch, a forerunner.] We shall leave aside the less fortunate aspects of Pascal's patriarchal dream (mythical identification with Abraham, Boaz, and the aging king David, elaborated by Zola, no doubt, to lend respectability to his own liaison with a young girl) in order to concentrate on his final, seemingly irrational acts of self-renunciation.

Having scorned fame and fortune throughout his life, having spent his dwindling funds extravagantly to express his adoration for Clotilde, having given up his dream of saving humanity, he climaxes his self-immolation by urging his love to leave, supposedly for her benefit, and by serenely facing death. Critics have commented, quite correctly, how little sense this makes in terms of the lovers' physical, emotional, and spiritual intimacy. Yet Zola did not stumble into this surprising finale unawares. Near the end of his Ebauche, we see him searching for some plausible reason to justify Clotilde's departure as though, through her, he is acting out some mysterious impulse that he cannot understand or put into words. By way of explanation, one is tempted to quote the biblical Nunc Dimittis: "Lord, now lettest thou thy servant depart in peace according to thy word: For mine eyes have seen thy salvation . . . (the Christ-child) (Luke 2:29–30) but that text can be more fittingly applied to Zola overcoming his fear of death after fatherhood than to Doctor Pascal giving up Clotilde: the doctor does not learn of Clotilde's pregnancy till well after her departure.

The simplest explanation is no doubt that Zola wanted a half-tragic conclusion to lend dramatic interest to his rather thin plot. Freudians might well comment in terms of the death wish: having carried out his biologic duty by fathering two children, they might say, Zola begins to sense the impulse to bow out in order to make way for the rising generation and, for the time being, he acts this out through his hero's irrational act of abnegation.

Clotilde's oblation of herself, in love and virginal purity, matches Pascal's noble humility and provides a useful contrast with the fateful heritage left by old Adélaïde and by the perennial, grasping ambition of Félicité (respectively, Pascal's grandmother and mother). Claudie Bernard draws attention to phrases the heroine addresses to Pascal such as: "Je suis ta servante, ton oeuvre et ton bien" (5, p. 1061) [I am your handmaid, your creation, and your possession] and: "Que ta volonté soit faite" (5, p. 1154) [Thy will be done] which cast her into a Marian role. The critic has this in mind when she refers to former Adélaïde Fouque as "l'Eve primitive" [the First Eve] and to Clotilde as "l'Eve régénérée"[33] [regenerated Eve] (the latter expression is reserved by Catholics for the Madonna). It could be added, perhaps, that Zola, nostalgic for his old myth of virginal purity and not at all indifferent to the story of Bernadette Soubirous, expresses this indirectly by giving vaguely Marian touches to the beloved of Pascal, his alter ego. Possibly it is for that reason, too, that the author leaves her alone on the stage, at the end of the novel, to nurse her newborn son, who may be the world's new messiah.

Before that final scene of hope, Zola stages the burning of Pascal's family dossiers and unpublished volumes of research, at the hands of Félicité and the doctor's misguided maidservant, Martine. The imaginative, highly colored language used to describe the women's rifling of Pascal's wardrobe and the burning of the papers portrays them as witches lighting a "bûcher diabolique" [diabolic bonfire]. In fact, the whole scene lends Pascal's death the perspective of "le martyr d'un saint" (5, p. 1200) [a saint's martyrdom]. In Clotilde's eyes, Félicité has virtually burned her own son.

Yet most of the sting has been taken out of this drama by an earlier scene: when, not long before his death, Pascal learns that he is going to be a father, he formulates in his mind the superior value of a living child to that of all his scientific work:

> Ah! C'était l'oeuvre vraie, la seule bonne, la seule vivante, celle qui le comblait de bonheur et d'orgueil. Ses travaux, ses craintes de l'hérédité avaient disparu. . . . (5, p. 1168)

> [Ah, that was his real work, the only work that was good and alive, the work that filled him pride and joy! His [scientific] labors, his fears concerning heredity had disappeared. . . .]

In the light of that joyful conviction, the subsequent destruction of the manuscripts seems less devastating. One could even conclude that the burning scene and later references to the wardrobe that will now house an envelope (containing Pascal's family-tree and scarred remnants of the manuscripts) as well as the baby's layette, constitute a kind of self-inventory on the part of Zola, as he looks back over his past, his theories, and his literary achievements.

Such a conclusion would be supported by a declaration Zola made to an assembly of students, three days after completing the serial publication of the novel:

> A cette heure, je puis même confesser que, personnellement, j'ai été un sectaire, en essayant de transporter dans le domaine des lettres la rigide méthode du savant.[34]

> [At this point, I can even confess that, personally, I have been a sectarian in trying to transpose into the domain of literature the rigid, scientific approach.]

That sounds as though, now consciously and publicly, Zola is turning his back on the excesses of naturalism. It is no accident, of course, that Pascal's tracing of heredity, as it affects five generations of his family, covers the same ground as Zola's *Rougon-Macquart*. And so the ashes left on the floor and the empty wardrobe, soon to be used for a new purpose, may well reflect how the author rates his literary assets when he compares them to his new patrimony—two children who fill him with hope for the future. Zola's work, for all the author knows, may perish, but not the self-propagating virtue of life, now manifested in his personal experience.

Once again conscious symbolism and unconscious myth combine to make a scene pregnant with meaning: at a deeper level, Félicité's burning of the papers becomes a polyvalent myth. It renders not only the Oedipal's child's sense of being persecuted by a mother who sabotages his calling in life, but also the positive notion that it is the mother (or life-giver) in Zola's psyche that disposes of arid theory in order to make way for the nurturing of life. This, in fact, will be an important part of Zola's new mission: to devote himself to the defeat of dogma and to the triumph of life.

Given the fact that *Le Docteur Pascal* features a hero who abandons messianic endeavor, why does the author lend Clotilde's baby a messianic aura? Simply to reflect the changeover in Zola from personal messianic ambitions to a messianism outside of himself? A further letter to van Santen Kolff reveals that the advent of the baby is meant to celebrate the divinity of life, "le recommencement éternel de la vie" [life's eternal rebirth], hope in the future, and confidence in unceasing human effort toward some mysterious, unknown goal.[35]

What a surprising way to complete a cycle of novels constructed around the theme of heredity: having imagined a hero and a heroine who have nothing in common with their Rougon ancestors, he finishes up with a baby whom his mother imagines to be the future messiah: Et c'était le rêve de toutes les mères, la certitude d'être accouchée du messie attendu" (5, p. 1218) [This was the dream of every mother, the certainty of having given birth to the long-awaited messiah]. Zola's messianic hopes here try to hide behind the unconvincing alibi of what all mothers are supposed to expect, as though it were not only Jewish mothers who harbor such dreams! Of course, the baby may also turn out to be Antichrist:

8: FROM DEATH AND DISASTER TO MESSIANIC HOPE

> A moins qu'il ne fût l'Antéchrist, le démon dévastateur, la bête annoncée qui purgerait la terre de l'impureté devenue trop vaste, et la vie continuerait malgré tout.... (5, p. 1219)

> [Unless he were the Antichrist, the ravaging demon, the beast foretold [in the Bible] that would purge the earth of its vast excess of impurity; and life would go on in spite of everything.]

The reader will not have missed Zola's passing allusion to some possible future Apocalypse (the nihilistic dreams of anarchists still trouble the society of his day) and his apparent indifference as to whether the child will be messiah or Antichrist (Zola now knows that each has his role to play in the scheme of things).

At the end of *La Débâcle*, the burning of Paris set the stage for a rebirth of France. In the last novel of the series, the burning of Pascal's life-work could be seen as a personal or mini-Apocalypse, a symbol of a dead past that is reduced to ashes in favor of a new beginning.

Before closing this section, we need to consider the metaphysical implications, if any, of Clotilde's infant-messiah. Zola himself does not want the mother-child symbolism to be interpreted along religious lines. In the same letter to his Dutch correspondent in which he elaborates on "le recommencement éternel de la vie" [eternal rebirth of life], he declares:

> Enfin, il est encore très vrai que le livre finira par une mère allaitant son enfant. Il n'y a seulement rien là d'idéaliste. C'est au contraire, selon moi, tout à fait réaliste.

> [Finally, it is true enough that the novel will finish with a mother suckling her baby. Only, there's nothing idealistic/metaphysical about that. On the contrary, in my opinion it's completely realistic.]

And then he quotes a line from the final page of his novel (as yet unpublished): Une mère qui allaite, n'est-ce pas l'image du monde continué et sauvé?[36] [Isn't a nursing mother the image of a world that continues and has been saved?] As happens frequently in his novels, Zola asserts one thing with his rational mind—in all sincerity—while another part of him uses mythical allusions to suggest something more metaphysical. It is doubtful, in any case, whether even a mere faith in the "divinity of life" does not constitute some form of mysticism. In the course of this chapter, we have witnessed the usual parade of false and genuine messianic figures and we have passed through the fire of Apocalypse to marvel at the advent of a newborn child (Clotilde is daydreaming):

> L'enfant était venu, le rédempteur peut-être. Les cloches avaient sonné, les rois mages s'étaient mis en route, suivis des populations, de toute la nation en fête, souriant au petit dans les langes. (5, p. 1218)
>
> [The child had come, the redeemer, perhaps. The bells had rung, the three magi had set out followed by (whole) populations, by the entire nation in festive mood, smiling at the child wrapped in swaddling clothes.]

At least Zola has not made his heroine give birth in a stable to the singing of the herald angels!

What is undeniable, in spite of Zola's protestations to the contrary, is that much of the *Rougon-Macquart* is characterized by a dialectic tension between materialism and idealism, Vanity fair and Utopia, Apocalypse, and rebirth, the abstract powers of Mammon, and the more personalized activities of messiahs, devils, and antichrists. The essential conflict between light and darkness is not about to disappear from Zola's work, but his increasing awareness of the mythical forces that operate within him will tend to replace unconscious dynamics by conscious manipulation—a phenomenon that will increasingly rob his writing of much of its impact and power.

9
The Impossible Quest

EVEN BEFORE CONCLUDING HIS *ROUGON-MACQUART* CYCLE, ZOLA HAD been deeply affected, in September 1891, by the sorrowful spectacle of Lourdes. A letter he wrote at the time shows that he meditated at length on "le besoin de surnaturel persistant chez l'homme"[1] (man's persistent need of the supernatural): those who suffer intently and without respite, he concluded, need the illusion of hope to help them face another day. There will be an echo of that view in the early pages of the novel, as the author follows the train on its way to Lourdes:

> Ils roulaient, ils roulaient encore, ils roulaient sans fin, charriant la misère de ce monde, en route pour la divine illusion.... (O.C. 7, p. 35)[2]
>
> [They rolled on and still they rolled on; they rolled on endlessly, carrying the misery of this world, en route for the divine illusion.]

René Ternois links the author's theme with "la religion de la souffrance humaine" (the religion of human suffering), a concept made fashionable by de Vogüé in his *Roman russe*[3]—a valid observation—but we should also keep in mind that the 1880s had been a dark period for Zola and that he may therefore well have used his experience of Lourdes as a mirror, in which to take stock of his own attitude toward suffering, religion, and his tendency to be torn between science and persistent messianic ideals.

In any case, the impact of Lourdes was strong enough to make him record in the Ebauche for his new novel: "Je veux au centre la souffrance humaine, tout un groupe de malades emportés dans l'éternelle illusion"[4] [In the center I want human suffering, a whole group of sick folk carried away into eternal illusion] and again later: "... étudier et peindre ce duel intéressant entre la science et le besoin surnaturel"[5] [... study and portray that interesting duel between science and the need for things supernatural]. There are two other factors involved in Zola's fascination with Lourdes—his long-standing interest in the priestly calling and his tender pity for the figure of Bernadette— or was it more than that? Pierre Ouvrard has devoted a whole study to Zola's attraction to (and antagonism toward) religious vocation.[6] Clearly, the man who hangs the entrance-hall of his Parisian residence with twenty-six paintings featuring New Testament scenes and who clutters his desk with ecclesiastical paraphernalia, such as a chalice and a ciborium (container in which the sacramental "host" is kept), is acting out some kind of fantasy when he writes in his notes: "me mettre moi-même sous une incarnation"[7] [put myself [into the novel] in some incarnation] only to settle on a priest who has lost his faith and is making a last-stand effort to retrieve it in the Grotto of Lourdes. Surely, the man who sends Alexis, his intimate friend and disciple, some Lourdes water, for the sake of his eyes, is at least toying with the idea that there may be something in that "extraordinaire histoire de Bernadette Soubirous"[8] (that extraordinary tale of Bernadette Soubirous)! "Le naïf Zola ne pouvait pas rester insensible au culte de Marie et de la petite sainte pyrénéenne. . . ." [Naive Zola could not remain indifferent to the cult of Mary and the little Pyranean saint. . . .] claims Armand Lanoux, in his *Zola vivant,*[9] and then goes on to point out that Bernadette corresponds to Zola's youthful myth of virginal innocence. Henri Guillemin, in his preface to *Lourdes*, quotes Zola's confession to the editor of *Le Gaulois*: "Je me passionne (pour Bernadette) à mesure que je l'étudie"[10] [The more I study [Bernadette], the more enthusiastic I feel about her] adding the plausible suggestion that the love Dr. Chassaigne expresses, in the novel ("C'est vrai, je l'aime, et plus j'ai songé à elle, plus je l'ai aimée") [It's true, I love her and the more I think about her, the more I have come to love her], is a transposition of Zola's own. After all, Zola had informed the editor in the same context that Bernadette would be the real heroine of his work. The narrator's observation, early in the novel, that the scientist-father whom Pierre admired so much had kept a dossier on Bernadette's visions and had been "infiniment séduit par la figure droite et pure de la voyante" (O.C. 7, p. 39) [immensely charmed by the pure and upright figure of the visionary] contains more food for thought.

One might speculate further that the mysterious rose scent, picked up by Pierre and his childhood sweetheart, Marie, during the evening of the torchlight procession at Lourdes, corresponds to something as intangible as Zola's romantic idealization of a pure and saintly girl: it is as though the author responds to the sweet dream surrounding Bernadette (and Marie), but prefers not to pinpoint its precise nature.

While Bernadette is the intended heroine, the character we follow throughout the novel is Pierre. In some ways, he is another projection of Zola's ideal self: in his dossier préparatoire, the author says of him: "un saint. Il a maté sa chair. . . . Il est pauvre, il donne tout"[11] [a saint. He has mastered his flesh. . . . He is poor; he gives away everything.] Catholic readers may beg to differ on Zola's use of the term *saint*. In the novel, the author's attempts to motivate Pierre's decision to stay a priest, in spite of his loss of faith, make little sense—unless we apply the arguments involved to Zola himself and to his indelible sense of vocation. Like his hero, the author has long since lost his faith but, like Pierre witnessing the commercial exploitation at Lourdes, he has always felt the urge, in a manner of speaking, to drive the merchants and money changers out of the temple. Early in the novel, Zola's self-identification with Pierre becomes evident when the priest, having described his devout mother and his agnostic father (deceased), relates his loss of faith and his continuing need of some higher mission:

Parfois, seulement, il avait l'amer regret de n'être pas utile, de ne pas s'employer à quelque grande oeuvre, à la pacification de la terre, au salut et au bonheur des peuples, comme l'enflammé besoin l'en tourmentait. (O.C. 7, p. 43)

[Only at times he bitterly regretted that he was not useful, that he was not engaged in some great task—in bringing peace on earth, bringing salvation and happiness to humanity, tormented as he was with a burning need (to do such things).]

The most one can say of Pierre, however, is that he suffers from frustrated messianic aspirations. In *Lourdes* he does not save anyone himself and he becomes simply the author's device for passing in review a number of failing or false messiahs.

The first of these is brother Isidore, a young missionary-priest Pierre meets on the train to Lourdes, who is dying of a liver infection he contracted in Senegal. His capacity for love and self-giving is beyond question, but his messianic status is that of the vainly dying Jesus Zola portrayed in his adolescent tale "Le Sang":

> Seuls ses yeux vivaient encore, des yeux d'amour inextinguible, dont la flamme éclairait son visage expirant de Christ en croix. (O.C., 7, p. 39)
>
> [Only his eyes remained alive, eyes (filled with) an unquenchable love; their fire lit up his dying face of Christ crucified.]

He will pass away eventually, his peasant face transformed, through suffering, into a picture of sublimity and passionate devotion, his eyes fixed on a statue of the Virgin (O.C. 7, p. 268).

Another minor character, Father Pyramale, Bernadette's original parish priest, who wants to honor his former catechist by building an impressive church, but is frustrated and persecuted by the "pères de la Grotte" [the Grotto fathers], becomes a pathetic martyr figure. He serves mainly to show up the grasping ambition of the religious order Zola believes to be cashing in on the success of Lourdes. For the author, the monks typify the false, apostate church, hungry for power and money, of which he will have more to say in his next novel, *Rome*.

In the course of *Lourdes*, Zola will expose other flawed clerics—the hysterical father Massias, for example (note his messianic name), who sweeps his listeners into delerium, the fanatic father Fourcade who fails in his attempt to raise a dead body by having it dipped in the pool of the Grotto or the wordly, sensuous abbé des Hermoises, who carries on with society women and the local girls, helping to turn the once devout village into a den of iniquity. Zola dares to use the formula "changeant en Gomorrhe et en Sodome, le Bethléem de Bernadette" (O.C. 7, p. 241) [changing Bernadette's Bethlehem into Sodom and Gomorrah]— a phrase that did not win him many friends in religious circles.

While the author presents a whole gallery of ecclesiastical rogues, he does not allow us to forget that his main grievance is with a church that encourages superstition. As Guy Robert puts it in his *Emile Zola*:

> [Pierre] a vu le catholicisme tenter de séduire l'âme humaine, au mépris des exigences élémentaires de la raison et de la science.[12]
>
> [Pierre has seen Catholicism trying to seduce the human spirit, in contempt of the basic demands of reason and science.]

When it comes to the "real heroine" of the novel, we find a Zola who has a gentle touch, a Zola who tries hard not to be negative, critical, or scathing. And that is quite understandable:

9: THE IMPOSSIBLE QUEST

it is through Pierre's emotional involvement with Bernadette that the novelist acts out the unresolved dichotomy in his own psyche between idealism and science, dream and reality. Bernadette incarnates for the author that "divine illusion" he craves, but cannot believe in, and it is precisely this inner polarity that lends the novel its dynamic tension, neutralizes some of its many faults, and stops it from becoming a pure "roman à thèse."

As we follow Pierre's evolving assessment of the girl, we sense that Zola's own attitude wavers between fascination and skepticism, between an unspoken love or veneration and a final, tragic renunciation of a transcendental ideal for which there seems to be no match in this world. Without realizing it, perhaps, Zola has been digging up the romantic ideals of his youth and hesistates before discarding them for good.

In the first of the novel's five "Journées" [Days], we learn that Pierre has read his father's dossier on Bernadette. Like the scientist, he is quite sensitive to the charm and mystery that surround her person. As Pierre reads a naive, clichéd publication about the saint to his fellow-travelers to Lourdes, he weaves in some of his own findings. This "double" narrative creates a quaint perspective: without losing anything of the freshness and appeal of the heroine, Zola manages to portray her as the product of her simple, pure, devout environment, the unwitting victim of superstitious tales, the victim, too, of her own poor health that leaves her open to hysteria and hallucination. In the same way that, earlier on, Pierre suffered intensely from his loss of faith: "... il était éperdu de la tristesse de ne plus croire" (O.C. 8, p. 42) [... he was distraught with his grief at not believing anymore] he now hates his rational mind that excludes him from the hopes of his fellow-pilgrims: "Pierre frémissait de tout le mystère évoqué, éperdu, et ... finissait par détester sa raison" (O.C. 8, p. 94) [Pierre trembled at the evocation of all that mystery: [he felt] overcome and eventually came to detest his reason]. After this, Bernadette fades from view, as Zola surveys the wider Lourdes scene. On the evening of the second day, when Pierre resumes his improvised saint's story in front of a whole ward of sick folk, there is a change of perspective. In his Ebauche, already, Zola had focused on the "suffering servant" aspect of his heroine: "Elle a été la victime, la sacrifiée, l'oubliée"[13] [She has been the victim, the one who has been sacrificed and forgotten]. Now he concentrates on a Bernadette who is harassed by the authorities, even though she is exalted as messiah by those who believe in her. In keeping with his theme of "la divine illusion," Zola comments:

> C'était le Messie, l'éternel Messie que les peuples attendent, dont le besoin renaît sans cesse à travers les générations. (O.C. 7, p. 161)
>
> [It was the Messiah, the eternal Messiah for whom the nations wait: the need for him is reborn constantly from generation to generation.]

As Pierre relates how the girl's visions are challenged, first by the "commissaire de police" (police superintendent) and then by a local tribunal, Zola, through his narrator, slips in his own observations: Bernadette is not guilty of deliberate falsehood, but simply lacks the strength to snap out of her initial hallucination. For all that, the author maintains his double perspective: he refers to the girl as "l'élue et la martyre" (O.C. 7, p. 162) [the chosen one and the martyr]. Faced with irrefutable evidence of past healings, Pierre formulates a purely human explanation that once again confirms the author's thesis:

> Le désir de guérir guérissait, la soif du miracle faisait le miracle. Un Dieu de pitié et d'espoir sortait de la souffrance de l'homme, de ce besoin d'illusion consolatrice. (O.C. 7, p. 169)
>
> [The desire to heal healed, the thirst for miracles created miracles. A God of pity and hope arose out of the suffering of humanity, out of this need for comforting illusions.]

The Deuxième and the Troisième Journées [Second and Third Days] offer us only passing glimpses of Bernadette. During an early morning walk, Pierre learns from Dr. Chassaigne, who has actually met the girl, about her departure from Lourdes: troubled by the "adorations bruyantes" [noisy adulation] of wealthy visitors, she had retired to the convent of Saint-Gildard at Nevers.

In the course of Day Four, Zola relates the climactic healing of Marie (whom Pierre had accompanied to Lourdes), at the passing of the host. After covering the saintly death of Isidore, he evokes the dismal, neglected state of Bernadette's former home and the sad spectacle of Father Pyramale's half-finished church, before leaving us with a deglamorized vision of the heroine. For Pierre, she has become merely "une soeur humaine, chargée de toutes les douleurs" (O.C. 7, p. 314) [a human sister burdened with every form of suffering]. Zola uses the Cinquième Journée (Fifth Day) to formulate his familiar philosophy of the all-powerfull life-force: "Il n'y avait sûrement de divin que la possession, la vie qui se complète et qui enfante" (O.C. 7, p. 377) [Surely, the only divine [thing to exist] was [physical] possession—life completing itself and giving birth] but he reports, nevertheless, that, before leaving Lourdes, Pierre buys a simple portrait of Bernadette. That symbolic gesture conveys, no doubt, that, while Zola must turn away from the phenomenon of Lourdes, the dreamer in him treasures the ideal that Bernadette stands for.

The concluding chapter takes us back to the "train blanc" [white train], in which the pilgrims are returning to Paris. Pierre enlarges on a third reading about Bernadette in which the human and the metaphysical aspects of the girl are given equal exposure. Even at the convent of Saint-Gildard, she suffers from being on exhibit, especially as her health deteriorates. Yet Zola makes a point of reporting that a paralytic child is healed as she carries it inside. We see her again as a martyr: she will die in agony from the combined effects of consumption, asthma, and degeneration of the bones. However the double perspective—human and religious—is sustained by the author. On the one hand Bernadette is presented as a poor wretch, suffering from hallucinations: after receiving the last rites for the third time, she thinks the Devil is after her. On the other hand the author shows her to be identifying herself with the dying Christ: "Et cette idée de sa passion la poursuivait, l'attachait plus étroitement sur la croix avec son divin Maître" (O.C. 7, p. 392) [And this idea of her passion obsessed her, bound her more closely to the Cross with her divine Master] and he captures this in a poignant image that betrays both his own compassion and his sense of tragic waste: "Elle s'était fait donner un grand crucifix, elle le pressait violemment sur sa triste poitrine de vierge" (O.C. 7, p. 392) [She had them give her a large crucifix, which she clasped violently to her sad virgin's breast]. Her death remains ambiguous: her last words echo those of Christ—"Mon Dieu!" [My God!] and "J'ai soif" (O.C. 7, p. 393) [I thirst], but fall short of those reported in the Gospels suggesting a sense of achievement ("It is finished!") and trust in God ("Father, into thy hands I commit my spirit."). At least in its religious perspective, Zola's messianic vision has not progressed beyond the dismal scene depicted in "Le Sang."

Probably Zola would have been wiser to dispense with the concluding pages where, through Pierre, he preaches on a number of themes, among them that of tolerance: " . . . il fallait tolérer Lourdes, ainsi qu'on tolère le mensonge qui aide à vivre" (O.C. 7, p. 395) [. . . one must tolerate Lourdes, in much the same way as one tolerates the lie that helps one go on living]. By way of a bridge to his next novel, he has his mouthpiece speculate on the possibility of bringing in a catholic democracy, whereupon he brings home mercilessly the plight of those who fall victim to a dream of virginal purity. The work ends with a postmortem on Bernadette, an eloquent object lesson for those who embrace ideals that are contrary to life:

> Là-bas, Bernadette, le nouveau Messie de la souffrance, si touchante dans sa réalité humaine, est la leçon terrible, l'holocauste retranché du monde, la victime condamnée à l'abandon, à la solitude et à la mort, frappée de la déchéance de n'avoir pas été femme, ni épouse ni mère, parce qu'elle avait vu la sainte Vierge. (O.C. 7, p. 400)

> [There, Bernadette, the new Messiah of suffering, so touching in her human reality, offers a terrible object lesson: the sacrificial offering cut off from the world, the victim condemned to abandonment, loneliness, and death, struck with the degeneration of not having been a woman, spouse, or mother, because she had seen the Virgin Mary.]

The delivery of sermonettes is not Zola's only shortcoming in *Lourdes* but, at least in the first of his *Trois villes*, we may choose to forgive him in the light of the work's deep human compassion, its impressive evocations of sites and crowds, and the homage it pays to a pure, fresh, and touching dream, as haunting for Zola as it is for the reader.

While *Lourdes* still offers grand spectacle and some genuine human drama, that novel already suffers from a surfeit of documentary detail. Not only does Zola find it difficult to integrate such an abundance of material into a coherent human story, but he has landed himself with a central character, Pierre, who is too static, who evolves too slowly to warrant his presence on every page.

The defects involved only grow more blatant in *Rome* (1896), the second of Zola's *Trois villes* [Three Cities]. This time round, the author is taken up more than ever with emptying his various dossiers—topographical, historical, economic, social, political, cultural, and ecclesisastical—into his novel. He is so busy sending Pierre from pillar to post—supposedly to obtain an audience with the Pope, but actually to explore all the aspects of Rome the author wants covered—that he leaves himself neither the leisure nor the freedom to create convincing, lifelike characters. Such drama as remains is cliché-ed (the poisoned figs sequence) or yields to extravagant fancy (the much-discussed love-death of Dario and Benedetta). *Rome*, then, is overextended in its scope and it is not exempt from lurid melodrama. Worst of all, it turns unashamedly into a roman à thèse: the message outweighs all other considerations; the strings of the plot show at every turn. As Jacques Noiray remarks pithily in a recent article, *Rome* is a novel

> où l'idéologie fait irruption dans le romanesque, où les personnages ne sont plus que l'incarnation d'une idée, où le texte se fait discours.[14]

> [where ideology breaks into the story to be told, where the characters are no more than the incarnation of an idea and the text turns into a discourse.]

Zola's original idea for the novel was simple enough. About a year after his first visit to Lourdes, he confided to G. Stiegler, a journalist for *L'Echo de Paris*:

> Ce serait bien curieux de tracer le portrait d'un pape socialiste renonçant au pouvoir temporel. Savez-vous que celui-là serait capable de ressaisir sa puissance et de fonder une nouvelle religion?[15]

> [It would be very curious to trace the portrait of a socialist pope who renounced temporal power. Do you know that he would be capable of regaining his power and founding a new religion?]

Actually, Zola's notion of a socialist pope can be traced right back to his *Germinal* (1885). Pierre Ouvrard reminds us, in his *Zola et le prêtre*,[16] of l'abbé Ranvier's dream of a church on the side of the poor, of a pope who would bring justice to the workers:

> Il disait que l'Eglise était avec les pauvres, qu'elle ferait un jour triompher la justice.... Quelle force aurait le pape ... lorsqu'il commanderait à la foule innombrable de travailleurs!" (Pléiade 3, pp. 1772–73)

> [He said that the church was on the side of the poor and that one day it would make justice triumph. What power the pope would wield when he was in command of the multitudinous crowd of workers!]

In any case, the ideas underlying *Rome* had already come to Zola when, in 1894, he read the French translation of F. S. Nitti's

Socialismo cattolico. He summarized the work and made it his chief source of inspiration on matters pertaining to his principal theme.

This time there is no need to speculate whether, like the story of Bernadette, the notion of catholic socialism struck a chord in Zola's own heart, for we read in his Dossier préparatoire for *Rome:*

> Peut-on faire le rêve d'un christianisme dépouillé de merveilleux, en ne prenant dans l'évangile que la morale du Christ? . . . On imaginerait alors une vaste communauté humaine, le royaume de Dieu sur terre.[17]

> [Is it possible to envisage a Christianity stripped of the miraculous, by taking from the Gospel only Christ's moral teachings? . . . If such were the case, one could imagine a vast community of human beings, the kingdom of God on earth.]

Whether such a meditation reflects a quest for religious conversion is another matter. Even Henri Guillemin is a little skeptical about Zola's sincerity, when he quotes from the author's letter to Pope Leon XIII, requesting an audience: "Si je ne puis *malheureusement* pas encore apporter à Sa Sainteté la rétraction d'un croyant. . . ."[18] (italics added by A. J. E.) [If, unfortunately, I am not yet able offer Your Holiness a believer's recantation. . . .]. The exposition of *Rome* returns us to a Pierre who is still an unbeliever. In the three years since Lourdes, he has realized the futility of charity and has even come to sympathize with the nihilist approach to world renewal—"l'ouragan dévastateur et purificateur, la terre régénérée par le fer et le feu" (O.C. 7, p. 523) [the hurricane that devastates and purifies, the earth regenerated by fire and the sword]. Mild and selfless Abbé Rose has calmed him down, advocating a return to the simplicity of the early church. Further influenced by a French cardinal and by a viscount active in Catholic workers' associations, Pierre has written *La Rome nouvelle* [The New Rome], which provides the Pope with a blueprint for returning to primitive Christianity, adopting socialist principles, and coming to the defense of the exploited workers.

Pierre, it would seem, no longer entertains messianic dreams for himself, but has decided to act by proxy: he has made himself the prophet or spokesperson for a new messianism involving the Pope and a renewed church:

Mais cette main secourable de l'auguste vicaire du Christ, tendu publiquement aux humbles, et aux pauvres, n'était-ce pas le signe certain d'une nouvelle alliance, l'annonce d'un nouveau règne de Jésus sur la terre? (O.C. 7, p. 537)

[But was not the august vicar of Christ's helping hand, held out publicly to the humble and needy, the sure sign of a new covenant, the proclamation of a new kingdom of Jesus on earth?]

When Pierre learns that his book is about to be placed on the index, he heads for Rome to defend himself and, if possible, persuade the Pope. Lodging in the home of Cardinal Boccanera, the young priest has his first taste of Rome's attachment to blind faith and unchanging dogma, its mind-set of burying itself in a sterile defense of the past. Significantly, the cardinal and his relations live in a crumbling palace and the family itself is threatened with extinction. During a walk along the Appian Way, lined with the tombs of the past, Pierre catches a glimpse of the aged prelate, a fairly obvious symbol of a moribund church:

Rien que la silhouette du cardinal Boccanera, debout parmi les tombeaux, et qui se détachait, grandie, sur la pourpre dernière du soleil. (O.C. 7, p. 643)

[Nothing but the silhouette of Cardinal Boccanera, standing among the tombs, looming, larger than life, against the last purple splendor of the sun.]

In the same way, Zola will focus, from time to time, on the closed, heavy bronze door of the Vatican and he will link it with a painting in the Boccanera residence, showing a forlorn lover sitting on the threshold of a palace from which she is forever excluded: the Vatican does not seem to be a place that is open to those in distress.

There is little point in retracing Pierre's endless movements in and around Rome, as he meets a profusion of working people and aristocrats, paupers and socialites, politicians and religious authorities (most of the latter are singularly unhelpful). The novel becomes more relevant to our present study when Zola begins to concentrate on Leon XIII. In order to prepare the reader, the author has Pierre meditate on what the Pope means to Catholics—the presence of God in human form, Zola decides, "une ouverture sur l'au-delà" (O.C. 7, p. 691) [an opening on the next world]. Watching the near-ecstatic crowd that adulates the Holy

Father, at the receipt of his "St. Peter's pence," our shocked hero can only murmur: Quelle idôlatrie! (O.C. 7, p. 693) [What idolatry!]. He is further saddened to learn from his acquaintance, Narcisse, a walking guidebook on Rome, that His Holiness speculates on real estate and invests his money with Jewish bankers.

Reacting to the triumphalism he senses at St. Peter's Basilica, the "idolatry" that surrounds the Pope, and the Vatican's involvement with money and power, Pierre spells out his contrasting vision to Fornaro, a theologian at the Gregorian University:

> ... le catholicisme retournant à la primitive Eglise, puisant un sang régénéré dans le christianisme fraternel de Jésus, le pape libéré de toute royauté terrestre, régnant sur toute l'humanité par la charité et l'amour, sauvant le monde de l'effroyable crise sociale qui le menace, pour le conduire au vrai royaume de Dieu, à la communauté chrétienne de tous les peuples unis en un seul peuple. (O.C. 7, p. 795)

> [... Catholicism returning to the primitive church, drawing revitalized blood from the fraternal Christianity of Jesus; the Pope, freed from any secular sovereignty, ruling all humanity in charity and love, saving the world from the dreadful social crisis that threatens it, in order to lead it into the true kingdom of God, the Christian community of all peoples united as one.]

In Pierre's allusion to the "effroyable crise sociale" [dreadful social crisis] that threatens the world, we may discern Zola's continuing preoccupation with Apocalypse—a state of mind he also attributes to old Boccanera:

> Peut-être, en effet, s'écria le cardinal, la fin des temps est-elle proche et allons-nous assister à cet écroulement du vieux monde dont on nous menace. (O.C. 7, p. 972)

> [Perhaps, exclaimed the cardinal, the end of time is really at hand and we are going to witness the collapse of the old world that people are threatening us with.]

Faced with the extinction of his clan, the cardinal makes a messianic gesture: as he administers the last rites to his poisoned cousin, Dario, he offers God his own life in exchange and ardently prays for a miracle, but only to see the naked Benedetta, the bride to be, expire of heart failure, in the arms of the corpse.

It is shortly after witnessing Boccanera's failed bid to be a savior, that the hero is admitted into the august presence of Leon XIII—an old and frail octogenarian, dressed in a tobacco-stained soutane. The confrontation that follows constitutes no doubt the most effective scene in the novel. Pierre immediately senses the will to power of the old Pope but, in his state of nervous excitement, he continues to see him as

> le messie attendu, le sauveur envoyé pour conjurer l'effroyable désastre social où sombrait la vieille société pourrie (O.C. 7, p. 927)
>
> [(the long-awaited messiah, the savior sent to ward off the dreadful social disaster in which (our) old, rotten society was foundering].

(It should be noted in passing that, after being ascribed to the nihilists and then to old Boccanera, the vision of Apocalypse is now projected into the mind of Zola's chief spokesperson in the novel.)

The Pope listens quietly to Pierre's impassioned pleas for church involvement in social reform and is moved by his tears, but then he makes his position quite clear: (1) he has no intention of renouncing claims to worldly power; (2) the church cannot sacrifice dogma for the sake of unity or compromise; (3) the Vatican is interested in social reform, but not under the banner of a form of socialism that denies God; and (4) Pierre's notion of a "religion nouvelle" [new religion] is anathema, because it would give rise to schism.

After that Pierre has no option but to abandon his dream of being a prophet or messiah by proxy. Given the close nexus between author and hero, Pierre's decision raises an interesting question: through his central character, is Zola simply restating a position he had come to in the dim past or do we catch, in the following passage, something of his own sentiments after his first visit to Lourdes, his exposure to the ideals of Catholic socialism, and the subsequent rejection of his ideas?

> C'est vrai, j'avais perdu la foi, mais je croyais l'avoir retrouvée, dans la pitié que la misère du monde m'avait mise au coeur. Vous étiez mon dernier espoir, le Père, le sauveur attendu. Et voilà que c'est un rêve encore, vous ne pouvez de nouveau être Jésus, pacifier les hommes, à la veille de l'affreuse guerre fratricide qui se prépare. . . . (O.C. 7, p. 936)
>
> [It's true, I had lost my faith, but I thought I had found it again in the pity that the world had kindled in my heart. You were my last hope, the Father, the long-awaited savior. And once again it is just a dream; you cannot be Jesus all over again and bring peace to humanity, on the eve of the dreadful, fratricidal war that is brewing. . . .]

The bronze doors of the Vatican finally close behind our hero and he sadly returns to the palace of Boccanera, who is prepared to face the end of the world and to assume the role of "le fossoyeur auguste" (the august gravedigger) of God's "sainte religion" (holy religion) (i.e., to be the next Pope), "le pontife de la destruction, de la mort du monde" (the pontiff of destruction, of the death of the world) (O.C. 7, p. 973).

A young anarchist is allowed once again to sound the nihilist warcry: " ... oui, la raser (=Rome), n'en pas laisser une seule pierre! mais la détruire pour la reconstruire" (O.C. 7, p. 984) [Yes, raze it (Rome) to the ground; don't leave a stone of it standing! But destroy it in order to rebuild it] and the picture of the rejected lover, on Pierre's bedroom wall, now strikes him as a symbol of man, unable to force the gates of Truth and the Unknown—an interpretation confirmed by the art-lover, Narcisse, who has been a veritable fund of information throughout the novel:

> L'artiste (Botticelli) avait prévu tout notre siècle douloureux, nos inquiétudes devant l'invisible, notre détresse de ne pas pouvoir franchir la porte du mystère, à jamais close. (O.C. 7, p. 991)

> [The artist (Botticelli) had foreseen our whole sorrowful century, our anxieties in the face of the invisible, our anguish at not being able to pass through the door to the mystery, forever closed to us.]

If it is true that, after meeting Jeanne Rozerot and seeing his life renewed, Zola felt tempted to take another look at revealed religion, his endeavors were not crowned with success (living in adultery is seldom conducive to conversion, especially to Catholicism). And so any "second thought" served only to confirm his skepticism about religious messiahs. In any case, such was the experience of Pierre: in the closing chapter of the novel, Zola sketches a philosophical portrait of his hero that ends as follows: " ... il avait renoncé à son rêve de sauver des peuples" (O.C. 7, p. 1004) [he had renounced his dream of saving the nations]. And yet those final fifteen pages of the work show us a Pierre pondering about the feasibility of an "anti-pape" [antipope], who is nothing but a messiah in disguise. To Pierre's mind, the notion of a Pope with purely spiritual powers seems to favor "l'avènement d'un anti-pape" [the advent of an antipope], possibly in the Americas, whereupon our "prêtre sans croyance" [priest without faith], alias Zola, dreams away:

Etre ce prêtre, ce grand réformateur, ce sauveur des sociétés modernes, quel rêve énorme, quel rôle de messie espéré, appelé par les peuples en détresse! (O.C. 7, p. 998)

[Oh, to be that priest! that great reformer, that savior of modern society! What a stupendous dream! What a role (for him to play) that of the hoped for messiah summoned by the nations in distress.]

Evidently our author is quite incorrigible: his later *Evangiles* will bear this out.

Paris (1898), the third and last of Zola's *Trois villes*, takes up Pierre Froment's story after a further break of three years. In essence, he is still the same person who was born from Zola's wish to portray himself "sous une incarnation"[19] [in (the form of) an incarnation], except that, in the course of the novel, he will finally be moved to abandon his priestly robes. As Armand Lanoux puts it, rather laconically, in his *Zola vivant*: "C'est toujours Zola métamorphosé en prêtre sans soutane"[20] [He is still Zola, transformed into a priest without a cassock]. Pierre's crucial decision to leave the priesthood may well correspond to Zola's own resolve to turn away from a religious messianism that he has found wanting. We shall see, in the final chapter of this study, that the author will orientate himself more and more toward purely human saviors, even if he will find it difficult to shed biblical imagery and scenarios. The via dolorosa Zola himself will have to tread in 1897 and 1898 (he became involved in the Dreyfus affair just after completing *Paris*) will ensure, however, that he will not deviate too far from the messianic ideals he set himself from his youth onward.

Meanwhile, Zola is quite convinced in his own mind that the social ideal Pierre has been searching for is most likely to be realized by science. In the early stages of planning *Rome*, already, he had glimpsed the substance of *Paris* in the following terms: "Le besoin religieux et sa satisfaction par la science, ce sera *Paris*"[21] [The need for religion and how it is satisfied through science will be [the subject of] *Paris*]. The finished novel will involve a rather more complex scenario, aptly summed up by René Ternois in his *Zola et son temps: Lourdes, Rome, Paris* (1964):

Une femme l'a sauvé (Pierre). Il comprend qu'on trouve 'la force et la joie de vivre' dans l'acceptation du travail, dans l'amour de la femme, dans la paternité, dans la science et "dans l'espoir de la justice".[22]

[A woman has saved him (Pierre). He understands that "strength and the joy of living" are to be found in the acceptance of work, in the love of woman, in fatherhood, in science, and in "hope for justice."]

Paris is not just the novel where Pierre changes into secular attire. The whole work marks, for Zola, a moment of changeover or transition: starting from a Parisian scene set in historical reality, it will take wing in the final pages to embrace a vision of Utopia. As early as in his Dossier préparatoire, Zola tells himself that, one day, "la vieille société s'écroulera" [the old society will collapse] and that the future will bring "un monde de justice et de paix"[23] [a world of justice and peace]. The plot of *Paris* will suggest that this is to be achieved, not through the violence of anarchism, but through the ordered, peaceful pursuit of work, fertility, truth, and justice.

In the opening pages of the novel, Pierre is still assisting the mild, selfless priest who incarnates the failed messianic ideal Zola regretfully dismissed in the days of "Le Sang" (*Contes à Ninon*). L'abbé Rose is in trouble over his unthinking charity and his habit of giving asylum to all and sundry (implication: his superiors do not approve of those who practice the social virtues preached by Jesus). Pierre himself is quite disillusioned with Christian charity (ironically, his Neuilly parishioners see him as a saintly, miracle-working figure) and he lives under the shadow of impending Apocalypse—"la guerre fratricide des classes qui emportera le vieux monde condamné à disparaître sous l'amas de ses crimes" (O.C. 7, p. 1181) [the fratricidal class war that will sweep away the old world, condemned to disappear under the accumulation of its crimes].

As he carries out an errand of mercy that takes him all over Paris, he has repeated glimpses of sullen, dark Salvat. The latter has turned anarchist out of bitterness and despair and is about to make a bomb attack on the corrupt "jouisseur" [sensualist], baron Duvillard. Instead of blowing up the carriage that brings home the baron's envious, spiteful daughter, Camille (she is out to snare her mother's lover) and his decadent, androgynous son, Hyacinthe, Salvat succeeds only in killing the innocent "modiste" [milliner] who is delivering a hat for the baroness.

Significantly, the explosion is witnessed by Pierre who has just been deciding that Christianity is derelict and that the world needs a new savior: without that, he thinks, society faces catastrophe as the inevitable outcome of the poverty and wretchedness, the moral, financial, and political corruption he has been encountering all around. The way the author concludes the Livre Premier (First Book) of his novel leaves little doubt about the vision of Apocalypse that still seems to be haunting his imagination:

> Et, au-dessus Paris grondant, la nuit noire s'était faite, une nuit sans pardon où les étoiles sombraient, sous la brume de crimes et de colère montée des toitures. Le grand cri de justice passait, dans le bruit d'ailes terrifiant que Sodome et Gomorrhe avaient entendu venir, de toutes les ténèbres de l'horizon. (O.C. 7, p. 1254)

> [And above the rumbling city of Paris the night had set in, a night without pardon in which the stars were drowning in the miasma of crime and anger that rose from the roofs. The great cry for justice rang out, amid the terrifying sound of wings that Sodom and Gomorrah had heard approaching from all around the dark horizon.]

The same terrorist-attack that prefigures Apocalypse brings Pierre back into contact with his estranged elder brother, Guillaume. The latter is Zola's secular alternative to l'abbé Rose, the by now familiar projection of the author's ideal self that combines dedication to science with lofty, quasi-messianic aspirations. The noble scientist is in touch with anarchist circles and has even invented the powerful explosive used by Salvat but, at this stage, he merely intends to make it available to the French government (to pursue its civilizing role in the world). He lives up to Zola's new, humanist brand of messiahship when he risks his own security by offering refuge to seventy-four-year-old Barthès, the eternal martyr of freedom, who is once again running from the authorities.

Pierre is soon filled with respect for the rebellious brother he once distrusted. He is even more deeply affected by Marie, the cheerful, sensible, unbelieving girl Guillaume has received into his household and whom he now hopes to marry the following spring. Pierre is susceptible to the wholesome, tranquil grace of the lass, while the quiet dignity of Guillaume's three sons and the ordered, harmonious home environment, centered upon scientific research and constructive or creative activity, gives him his first intimation of the redemptive role of work:

> Et pour la première fois ... la nécessité du travail lui apparaissait, une fatalité qui se révélait aussi comme une santé et une force. Là, il découvrait enfin un terrain solide, l'effort qui entretient et qui sauve. Etait-ce donc la première lueur d'une foi nouvelle? (O.C. 7, p. 1297)

[And for the first time . . . the necessity of work dawned upon him—an inevitability that was also revealed as [a source of] health and strength. There at last he found solid ground, the exertion that keeps things going and saves. Was this the first glimmer of a new faith, then?]

Not long after this revelation, two of Pierre's nephews take him to see the sculptor Jahan and his inspiring statue called *Fécondité* (Fertility):

. . . avec ses fortes hanches, son ventre d'où devait naître un nouveau monde, sa gorge d'épouse et de mère gonflée du lait nourrisseur et rédempteur. (O.C. 7, p. 1308)

[. . . with her solid hips, her belly from which a new world was destined to be born, her wife and mother's bosom, swollen with nourishing, redemptive milk.]

Zola's new "gospels" are clearly beginning to fall into place and the reader is not surpised, in the very next chapter, to hear one of Guillaume's many visitors expatiate on Charles Fourier, the visionary Socialist economist, as "le Messie des temps modernes" (the modern-day Messiah) (O.C. 7, p. 1315). For the sake of perspective, Zola chooses that moment to have Pierre formulate his doubts about the anarchist scenario that might simply relaunch the familiar, disastrous cycle of history. In his opinion, anarchism is simply a secular, modern-day equivalent of the messianic hopes that took shape at the decline of paganism.

Book Three returns us to the corrupt society of Paris, where Baron Duvillard and his associates are playing their usual financial and political games, where Camille is still torturing her mother, Eve, and where perverse Silviane, the baron's mistress, acts out her fascination with "l'immonde" [decadent, obscene sexuality]. The latter, Zola's incarnation of evil, is determined to play Corneille's noble heroine, Pauline, at the Comédie Française! Ironically, the wicked prosper and it is the bitter idealist, Salvat, who is tracked down by the authorities and the courageous freedom-fighter, Barthès, who once again has to run for cover.

Book Four brings on a crisis for three of the novel's principal characters. Pierre, unconsciously in love with Marie, now bewails his condition that excludes him from normal life and work. No longer believing in his self-imposed mission of serving the human need for "l'illusion divine" [divine illusion], he is increasingly distressed by his false position: " ... il n'était plus que blessé par ce rôle d'apostolat mensonger" (O.C. 7, p. 1427) [... now he was only hurt by this role of lying apostleship].

His soul-searching culminates in his pulling on an ordinary pair of trousers and in his joining Guillaume's mechanic son in the family workshop. Still not aware of his love for Marie, he calls on l'abbé Rose and airs his grievances against Christianity, notably its failure to redeem society:

> Voici près de deux mille ans que l'Evangile avorte. Jésus n'a rien racheté, la souffrance de l'humanité est restée aussi grande, aussi injuste.... (O.C. 7, p. 1442)

> [That makes almost two thousand years now that the Gospel has been miscarrying ... Jesus has not redeemed anything; humanity's suffering has remained just as great, as unjust as ever.]

In the process, Zola closes in on his most fundamental objection to the faith, the very principle that threatened to annihilate his youthful dream of nature, love, and fertility and forced him to escape into the arms of science: "(Jésus) a nié la femme et la terre, l'éternelle nature, l'éternelle fécondité des choses et des êtres" (O.C. 7, p. 1442) [(Jesus) denied woman and earth, eternal nature, the eternal fertility of things and beings]. Pierre goes on to explain how the doctrine of original sin sets man at war with himself, his basic instincts, and the world of nature and he then comes out with a line that may throw much light on the darkness and violence of Zola's fictional world from *Thérèse Raquin* to *La Débâcle*: "Dès lors, la terre n'est plus qu'un péché, un enfer de tentations et de souffrances...." (O.C. 7, p. 1443) [From then on, the earth has been no more than a transgression, a hell of temptation and suffering]. For all that, Zola and his hero have not given up their dream of the infinite, of paradise, or Utopia, even if, now, it can be pursued only unconsciously, for instance, in the thrill of riding a bicycle downhill (Zola has been out cycling, by himself and with Jeanne, and Pierre is made to repeat the experience in the company of Marie:)

> ... la brise souffle en tempête, on est parti pour l'horizon, pour l'infini là-bas qui toujours se recule. C'est l'espoir sans fin, la délivrance des liens trop lourds, à travers l'espace. Et rien n'est d'une exaltation meilleure, les coeurs bondissent en plein ciel. (O.C. 7, p. 1448)

[. . . the breeze becomes a storm-wind, you have set out for the horizon, for that far-off infinity that always retreats from you. This is unbounded hope, deliverance from the fetters that weigh too heavily upon you, flight through space. And nothing could be more exhilarating; your heart soars right up into the sky.]

Salvat, the terrorist with a messianic name, has his greatest moment when he faces the judge who has just condemned him to death with his anarchist credo: "Que tous aient mon courage, et demain votre société pourrie sera balayée, et le bonheur enfin naîtra" (O.C. 7, p. 1463) [If everyone had my courage, your rotten society would be swept away tomorrow and happiness would at last be born]. Guillaume Fromentin, who is approaching his fifties, has realized that Marie is in love with his younger brother and makes a heroic gesture of renunciation. Zola's notes show that, originally, he had planned to cast Pierre into that self-sacrificing role. Just as he had already done in *Le Docteur Pascal*, however, the author inverts the scenario of *Le Voeu d'une morte* (it will be remembered that, in the early novel, idealistic Daniel effaces himself for the sake of his scientist-friend, Raimond). One may speculate that, in this way, Zola avoids a scenario of saintly renunciation on the part of Pierre, whose emancipation can be more satisfactorily demonstrated if he is allowed to marry and have children.

In Book Five, Zola repeatedly uses irony to express his moral indignation with a corrupt society. After witnessing Salvat's gruesome execution, we are treated to the edifying spectacle of a fine social wedding, officiated over by Msgr Martha, a Parisian counterpart of the sinister prelate (Nani) who seemed to be orchestrating Pierre's movements in Rome. Wicked vixen, Camille, can now publicly gloat over the lover she has snatched from her own mother out of pure spite.

Depraved Silviane has her coveted entry into the Comédie Française and is able to give her role of Pauline a saintly, mystical interpretation. The sculptor Jahan, obviously a projection of Zola's plans for the future, holds forth on the demise of religion and is shown at work on a naked, female statue of Justice, whose arms reach out in welcome to all humanity.

The only detail that is strictly relevant to our study of the messianic myth is Guillaume's dreadful resolve to blow up the Basilique du Sacré Coeur, pilgrims and all, as a fitting enactment of a society that destroys the innocent. Pierre realizes that his brother's mad dream has been triggered off by Salvat's unjust execution and, perhaps, by the loss of his intended bride. He manages to stop the planned holocaust at the last moment—a scene that prompts Jacques Noiray to call *Paris* "le grand roman de la catastrophe évitée" [the great novel of averted catastrophe].[24] In the same context that critic makes some very pertinent remarks on Zola's rejection of the anarchist recipe for transforming society: he shows how Zola's hitherto dynamic vision of history, where change was brought on by crisis, catastrophe, and threat of revolution, capitulates to a utopian dream of appeasement, with the former metaphoric rivers of blood and fire turning into an endless "fleuve de lait" [river of milk].

The conclusion of the novel juxtaposes the birth of Pierre's son with the death of l'abbé Rose: the broken, disillusioned priest is not unhappy to leave behind a hopeless world. Guillaume will turn his explosive into a fuel for industry and science for, as René Ternois points out ironically: " .. c'est la science qui transformera le monde, c'est la science qui y fera régner la justice"[25] [It's science that will transform the world; science will ensure that justice prevails]. And so all ends well: now that he has become a father, Pierre has given up his religious vocation and his messianic dreams—an allegory one is tempted to apply to Zola himself; Guillaume has thought the better of playing Antichrist and the novel can conclude with some consoling previews of Zola's new gospels: work, fertility, and justice. In the final scene Marie holds up her baby and dedicates him to the harvest field of Paris that stretches out at her feet: "Du blé, du blé partout, une infinité de blé dont la houle d'or roulait d'un bout de l'horizon à l'autre" (O.C. 7, p. 1567) [Corn, corn everywhere, an infinity of corn surging in a golden tide from horizon to horizon].

What has become of Zola's messianic myth after the completion of his *Rougon-Macquart*? *Lourdes* stages a failed attempt at reviving the old Christian ideal: Bernadette is shown to have no answer to the problem of human suffering. Pierre, alias Zola, cannot retrieve a faith forever lost.

Rome turns the author's gaze upon an apostate church that has been unfaithful to its Founder—an institution that is more interested in maintaining wealth, power, and influence than in taking the side of the suffering workers (Zola, in other words, has found an ecclesiastical counterpart to the Great Whore he exposed in Nana's Paris). Pierre is not cut out to be a John the Baptist, calling men to repentance as he prepares the way of the Lord, as he heralds the promised Messiah.

Paris surveys a world that continues on its merry course of evil and corruption, in spite of would-be messiahs and antichrists. It is in this work that our weary novelist turns his back on a depressing reality, blurring the whole picture with a vision of paradise-to-come. Our final chapter will examine how successful Zola is in evoking Utopia and in conceiving a set of purely human heroes that may worthily shape and realize his persistent messianic ideal.

10
Toward a Humanist Messiah

BY THE TIME ZOLA IS ABLE TO TURN HIS ATTENTION TO *FÉCONDITÉ* [Fertility] (1899), the first of his *Evangiles*, he is battle-scarred and weary. His role in the Dreyfus Affair, heroic and even messianic as we may see it now, has put him through a year of turmoil, conflict and, finally, public disgrace. On 18 July 1898 the Versailles Court of Assizes has condemned him to a year's emprisonment. Zola has been advised to flee to England and there he has just learned that he has been struck from the order of the Légion d'Honneur. The stress of all this must have exacted its toll.

It is hardly surprising, then, that the fifty-eight-year-old author, once reunited with his dossiers through the services of a friend, should have looked for refuge in the fertility myth and in the messianic aspirations of his youth. Advancing years and the strain of battle help to explain why he should have revived the very dreams he tended to scorn in the more dynamic years of his prime. Was it not His Excellency Eugène Rougon, incarnating the author's ambition and will to power, who was made to muse disparagingly on Napoleon III's ineffectual rêveries in the following terms:

> Peut-être, maintenant, l'empereur songeait-il au défrichement d'un coin des Landes, à la fondation d'une ville ouvrière, où l'extinction du paupérisme serait tentée en grand? . . . (Pléïade, 2, p. 176)

> [Perhaps now, the emperor was thinking about reclaiming an area of the Landes (coastal marshes to the southwest of Bordeaux), founding a city for workers where there would be a large-scale attempt at putting an end to pauperism.]

And yet such are the very projects that are about to be realized in novels such as *Fécondité* and *Travail*.

We have already come across hints of Zola's new approach in *Le Docteur Pascal* and *Les Trois villes*, but what used to be a vague tendency now becomes a conscious policy. In the following passage, quoted by René Ternois, the author records his intentions in 1898 and virtually congratulates himself on what amounts to an escape into fantasy:

> Je puis contenter mon lyrisme, me jeter dans la fantaisie . . . dans le rêve et l'espoir. . . . C'est la conclusion naturelle de toute mon oeuvre. Après la longue constatation de la réalité . . . je suis content de pouvoir me livrer à tout mon lyrisme et à toute mon imagination.[1]

> [I can satisfy my lyrical bent, immerse myself in fantasy, dreams, and hopes. It is the natural conclusion of all my work. After documenting reality for so long, I am pleased to be able to give free rein to all my lyricism and imagination.]

It is fairly obvious that what the author tries to pass off as a matter of continuity and natural evolution is, in fact, a yielding to regression.

Zola's revival of messianism not only has its roots in the fertility myth of his youth, but is also connected with his experience of paternity and his defeatist impulse to retreat to Utopia. A preliminary survey of these three components will help us to assess the perils to which he is about to expose his literary reputation. Is his pursuit of the messianic myth—first in the defense of Dreyfus and then in the cultivation of Utopia—a disguised expression of the death wish, the desire to break free from material reality, acquired fame, and past conquests?

The fertility myth or dream of paradise is harmless enough as a background scenario, as long as the plot includes more realistic and more dramatic elements such as passion and conflict, human failings, or the ironies of fate. *La Faute de l'abbé Mouret* may suffer from an orgy of descriptive detail on the author's part, but it remains, on the whole, a viable novel. In the same way, Zola's discovery of the joys of fatherhood, when transposed into his novels, may raise the odd ironic smile from the reader, but seems, at first, to allow for a positive extension of the author's scope, an enrichment of his world. As we peruse the closing volume of the *Rougon-Macquart*, we gain the impression that paternity has confirmed the author's confidence in the life-force and that it has even granted him a humbler perspective on life: Pascal (and no doubt his literary creator as well) no longer needs to be a messiah, but can serenely accept his place as a simple link in a continuing chain of life. In the early 1890s, it seems enough for Zola and his ideal hero to be a precursor or patriarch, in the purely genealogical sense of the word. Philip D. Walker touches on that positive aspect of the paternity myth in his article "Zola et la lutte contre l'Ange."[2]

At the stage of launching his *Evangiles*, however, Zola has become so taken up with the mystique of fatherhood that he becomes trapped in a narcissistic desire to reproduce himself ad infinitum in his heroes and their offspring. David Baguley, with some justification, deplores this degradation of the paternity myth:

> La puissance de la volonté et de la voix du pater familias est telle que, dans chaque roman, la société entière est transformée en une vaste famille émanant de son être et centrée sur lui. Un sujet unique se dédouble infiniment en un ensemble totalitaire de sujets créés à son image.[3]

> [The authority of the paterfamilias' will and voice is such that, in each novel, the whole of society is turned into an enormous family, emanating from his person and centered upon him. A single subject splits into two an infinite number of times, forming a totalitarian ensemble created in the image of the first one.]

In *Fécondité* he points out that the hero and his expanding family tend to be rather self-centered. Baguley further echoes the Socialist criticism, formulated at the turn of the century, that both Mathieu, the hero of *Fécondité*, and Luc, his counterpart in *Travail*, are overpaternalistic toward the people they engender or save from wretchedness and exploitation. The plot of all three gospels, he complains, is distressingly predictable as a given hero encounters a form of social evil, makes up his mind to tackle it, passes through a crisis of doubt and suffering, and then triumphs and is granted a virtual apotheosis.[4] We shall see later how this repetitive paternalistic or messianic scenario casts the hero into the incongruous role of being a mortal who rises to quasi-divine perfection.

The paternity myth, then, holds some traps for the unwary, but these are nothing compared to the snares concealed along the flowery paths of Utopia. At its best, utopian writing is a literary genre cultivated by philosophers like Plato or serious thinkers like Sir Thomas More. Their purpose is to formulate a pattern for an ideal society or, maybe, to impy criticism of the contemporary scene. On a less reputable level, utopianism becomes a form of wishful thinking for the disillusioned and the world-weary. A "perfect" world is constructed, but at the cost of a gross misrepresentation of reality. The writers in question confuse social reform with personal dreams of compensation or self-aggrandizement. They escape from the ravages of time by turning to a world of fancy where all conflicts are resolved or simply denied: life and death, summer and winter, day and night—all merge into harmony; the individual is no longer at odds with self, neighbor, society, or state; the sexes relate perfectly, the wolf lies down with the lamb, and all needs are met. What one might call the "decadent utopian" disregards the facts of nature; cheats against the most basic social, political, or economic realities; and refuses to allow for human fallibility.

Just like the paternity myth, utopianism may have literary implications: it is clear that a writer cannot step out of time and conflict and still be able to conceive a plot that lends itself to drama. Since a perfect society does not need to evolve and, in fact, has nothing to gain from change, utopian narrative favors static tableaux, or the evocation of ritual celebration. Voltaire knows this full well, for he allows his Candide a restful interlude in Eldorado—for the sake of perspective—but then smartly plunges him back into the rush of time. The novelist who lingers overlong in Utopia will realize, sooner or later, that he has completely suspended his plot.

Zola will not stumble into all of these traps, but he does go astray in a number of ways. He sins against the reality he once championed, when he begins to paint everything in black and white, when he divides his characters into two camps, with the wicked invariably coming to grief and the virtuous being rewarded with prosperity and long life—not to mention a host of descendants! As long as he concentrates on Utopia in the making, he can still evoke convincing scenes or stage arresting conflicts. In the final section of each novel, however, when the forces of evil have been defeated or have simply petered out, the plot invariably grinds to a halt: the reader soon wearies of watching crowds of rejoicing citizens or feasting, grateful descendants, seated at tables lining the road, all paying tribute to their smiling patriarch.

Zola himself must have realized the unsatisfactory nature of such denouements. At least in *Vérité*, [Truth] the last gospel he completed, he comes up with an unresolved family conflict at the last moment. Nevertheless, that afterthought smacks too much of a token gesture—a way of confessing, somewhat belatedly, that Utopia is not a very likely eventuality and that the vagaries of human nature will always remain a source of discord and strife.

10: TOWARD A HUMANIST MESSIAH

Zola's original idea for *Fécondité* (1899) was neither to write an "évangile nataliste" (gospel supporting a rising birthrate) nor to entone a joyful hymn to fertility. An article he composed for *Le Figaro* (some twenty-six months before he started work on *Les Evangiles*) shows him preoccupied with birth control, abortion, and the high mortality rate among the newborn. For the author, depopulation not only places France at a disadvantage, compared to Germany—a widespread concern at the time—but it jeapardizes the nation's ability to play its civilizing role in the world at large. The key-line of the article contains the title Zola had in mind for a future novel: ". . . je voudrais que *le déchet* de la vie cessât" (italics added by A. J. E.)[5] [I should like the *wastage* of life to cease]. In his Dossier préparatoire of 1898, the author recalls the projected work, but then expresses his intention to expand the subject and to use a more warmhearted approach than he has so far:

> Dans le premier (évangile), *Fécondité*, je traite le sujet qui m'a hanté sous le titre *Le Déchet*. Mais j'attendris le sujet et je l'élargis, en en faisant un chant à la fécondité. Rendre esthétique la femme féconde avec Jean (later changed to Mathieu), fils de Pierre et de Marie, la femme qui nourrit, qui a beaucoup d'enfants. Contre la virginité, la religion de la mort, et pour l'expansion de tous les germes.[6]

> [In the first (gospel), *Fertility*, I deal with the subject with which I have been preoccupied under the title of *Le Déchet* [*Waste*]. But I make the subject more moving and extend it, turning it into a hymn in praise of fecundity. To show the aesthetic beauty of the fertile woman with Jean (later changed to Mathieu), Pierre and Marie's son, the breast-feeding woman, the woman who has lots of children. Against virginity, the religion of death and in favor of broadcasting all the germs of life.]

Zola carried out his program to the letter. Oddly, French birth statistics around the turn of the century do not suggest that his idea of giving pregnant women a more aesthetic image proved efficacious!

In view of the novel's prevailing message, one understands Edmond Pelletier's satiric reference to Zola's "lapinisme" (rabbitism) and his wry résumé of the novel as "l'expression des rêveries optimistes d'un écrivain fort satisfait de sa récente paternité"[7] [the expression of the optimistic reveries of a writer who is very pleased with his recent fatherhood].

Zola's policy of putting more tender feeling and emotion into his writing does not impress Jacques Noiray, who complains:

> Nous sommes passés de la grandeur d'un univers tragique, dominé par le mal, à la candeur d'une idylle sentimentale et moralisatrice.[8]

> [We have moved fom the grandeur of a tragic universe, dominated by evil, into the ingenuousness of a sentimental, moralizing idyll.]

One can but concur. Yet Zola convinced himself that he had acted for the best of motives. Was not a poet entitled to engage in speculation or to devote himself to imagining a better future? As he wrote to Paul Brulat (15 October 1899), just after *L'Aurore* had printed the concluding episode of *Fécondité*: "L'hypothèse, l'utopie est un des droits du poète"[9] [Hypothesis, wishful thinking is one of the poet's rights]. And was it not the quasi-messianic role of poets and visionaries to formulate new gospels, in order to redeem the souls of men?

> Ce n'est pas seulement un nouvel évangile que le monde attend, ce sont aussi des croyants, des poètes, des héros, qui referont une âme à la vieille humanité.[10]

> [It's not just a new gospel that the world is looking for, but also believers, poets, heroes, who will re-create a soul in age-worn humanity.]

In a sense, then, Zola is taking up the cause where his hero, Pierre (in *Rome*), failed. He himself is playing the part of a latter-day Saint John the Baptist, the part of a prophet, while provisionally limiting his new hero, Mathieu, to the role of a patriarch. In a moment of frankness, however, the author comes out with the real truth: "Il faut bien permettre," he writes to Gustave Mirbeau (29 November 1899), "à mes vieux jours de rêver un peu"[11] [You really must allow me to dream a little in my old age].

In *Lourdes*, already, Zola had slated Catholic exaltation of virginity and what he saw as a "religion de la mort" (religion of death). Now he wishes to reassert his faith in the life-force, in a story that rewards those who reproduce freely and punishes those who restrict the birthrate for selfish, hedonistic, or materialistic reasons. The hero, Mathieu Froment, passes the test early in the novel, when he sets aside his misgivings about the four children he has already and allows the languorous spring evening to persuade him to make love to his wife Marianne, unconditionally, without reservations as to the consequences.

Zola's overdrawn picture of the lustful redhead, Séraphine, a promiscuous widow who would not mind seducing Mathieu back into her bed, suggests that he has not yet mastered the obsession with decadent eroticism that inspired the novel *Nana* and related figures in subsequent novels. At the same time, his constant linking of wholesome sexuality with procreation suggests that even Jeanne Rozerot has not delivered him completely from the puritanical stance we detected in *L'Argent*.¹²

Zola's first description of Mathieu's wife, Marianne, is more than a little reminiscent of Jahan's *Fécondité* statue in the author's preceding novel (*Paris*):

> Et ce fut ainsi que (Mathieu) la trouva, debout sous les étoiles, riante, saine, robuste, dans sa taille superbe sur ses hanches fortes, avec sa gorge nourricière, menue et ferme. (O.C. 8, p. 80)

> [And this is how (Mathieu) found her, standing in the starlight, smiling, healthy, strong, with her splendid waist above her broad hips, her small, firm, nursing mother's breasts.]

This is appropiate enough, as she is to be the hero's fellow-servant in the temple of the divinity: both of them together will represent the life-force on earth, but Marianne, in particular, will incarnate it in human form, more or less the way a statue in a Greek temple made the divinity present to his devotees. A moment later, the author refers to the heroine's "calme sacré de bonne déesse féconde" (O.C. 8, p. 80) (holy calm of a benevolent fertility goddess), and, by the end of the chapter, he has her husband, metaphorically, worship her as a divine earth-mother: "Une vénération l'envahit, il l'adora, comme un dévot mis en présence de son Dieu, au seuil du mystère" (O.C. 8, p. 96) [He was filled with veneration, like a devotee brought into the presence of his God, on the threshold of mystery.] In the same context, her abdomen (she is by now over seven months' pregnant) is said to be "soulevé comme un dôme sacré, d'où allait sortir un monde" (O.C. 8, p. 96) [raised like a sacred dome from which a world would issue forth]. The end of the scene in question shows us a Mathieu still lost in contemplation of his modern-day Cybele (he has been waiting on his heavily pregnant spouse with great devotion:)

C'était plus haut et plus vrai que le culte de la vierge, le culte de la mère, la mère aimée et glorifiée. . . . (O.C. 8, p. 108)

[This was a loftier and more genuine cult than the cult of the virgin, this cult of the mother, the beloved and glorified mother.]

In overobvious contrast, Séraphine's ovariotomy in Dr. Mainfroyd's clinic and Valérie Morange's ill-advised recourse to abortion in a filthy, back-street establishment are utterly condemned: through his hero, or should we say, high priest, Zola indicts "l'immonde avortement qui supprime la vie à sa source" (vile abortion that cuts short life at its source), for to him the operation is a form of sacrilege, an unforgivable sin against the life-principle of the earth: "Il n'y avait pas de profanation plus criminelle, d'injure plus ignoble à l'éternelle fécondité de la terre" (O.C. 8, p. 180) [There was no profanation more criminal, no insult more ignoble to the eternal fertility of the earth]. In the case of the second offender, the penalty is imposed on the spot: Valérie pays for her "crime" with her life.

In fact, Zola is increasingly inclined to resort to poetic justice—a habit that does little for his literary reputation. While Marianne produces another son, for instance, prompting Zola to entone "le poëme de l'éternelle vie par l'éternel amour" (O.C. 8, p. 167) [the poem of eternal life, springing from eternal love], the unworthy mother, Valentine Séguin, who has continued her foolish, socialite life-style during most of her pregnancy, nearly expires giving birth to a daughter. Zola's new religion of the life-force seems to involve more or less the same system of punishment and reward one associates with the Jehovah of the Old Testament!

These quasi-religious dispositions will prevail to the end of the novel. They become so systematic and predictable, in fact, that the reader, no longer able or willing to maintain that "suspension of disbelief" called for in all literary fiction, stops caring what happens to the characters. Mathieu's employer, the promiscuous Alexandre Beauchêne, may eventually lose his only son; Alexandre's jealous wife, Constance may die of heart failure after engineering the death of Mathieu's pride and joy; an artist's wife, Mme Angelin, who waits too long to have her first child may die of strangulation; corrupted young Reine Morange may repeat her mother's fate of bleeding to death in an abortionist's clinic; lascivious Séraphine may shrivel up and lose the ability to reach orgasm—but the reader knows full well that such a concatenation of events does not occur in the real world and soon refuses to take it seriously.

Nor is the reader overinterested to learn that the mechanic's daughter, Norine Moineaud, is saved from depravity when she is persuaded first to nurse and then to keep her latest illegitimate baby—"Vous l'avez sauvé et il vous sauve" [You saved him and now he is saving you] pontificates Mathieu (O.C. 8, p. 307). Even the most wide-awake reader loses track of the Froment children and grandchildren. By the time we are halfway through the novel, we have long since foreseen that Mathieu, who has turned farmer and extends his crops each time he has a new mouth to feed, will eventually take over his unworthy employer's home and factory.

The never-ending story of his growing domain—in pure capitalist style!—is interrupted by a few trials, some of them quite tragic, so that Zola may bring on his hero's time of self-doubt and crisis, but the return of prosperity and joy is as inevitable as the sermons we are offered regularly on subjects dear to the author's heart. The following summary, heavily curtailed though it be, offers an overview of Zola's preoccupations while he is enduring his exile in England and cannot always enjoy the comforts of home and the "pleasures" of his home away from home: "la divine maternité" (p. 145) (divine maternity), the symbolic implications of breast-feeding, especially when carried out in the open air (p. 171); universal salvation through reverence for the mother—the eternal flow of life-giving milk (p. 240); the divinity of making love—and the all-conquering sovereignty of fertility.

The apotheosis chapter at the end of the novel, when 158 descendants (not counting the great-grandchildren) acclaim our patriarch and his still beautiful spouse, is particularly rich in uplifting paragraphs. In the midst of proceedings, who should arrive from the Sudan but Dominique, one of Mathieu's grandsons, the founder of a dynasty of Fromentins in virgin-Africa that is about to be transformed into paradise by an irrigation system involving the Niger River! The reader, whose appetite has been whetted by these details and who lacks the time or inclination to plough through over five hundred pages of small print, may like to meditate on the following dithyrambic ode to the divine, creative force of desire: (Zola is describing the happy couple at their diamond wedding):

> Et, dans leur grandeur de héros, il y avait aussi tout le désir dont ils avaient brûlé, le divin désir, fabricateur et régulateur du monde, qui

les avaient visités en coups de flamme, à chacun de leurs enfantements nouveaux. Ils étaient comme le temple sacré que le dieu avait habité constamment, ils s'étaient aimés du feu inextinguible dont l'univers brûle, pour la continuelle création. (O.C. 8, pp. 499–500)

[And in their heroic greatness there was all the desire with which they had burned, divine desire, maker, and regulator of the world, which had visited them in waves of flame, every time another child of theirs was born. They were like the holy temple where the god was in permanent residence; they had loved each other with the unquenchable fire with which the universe burns, for continual creation.]

It would appear that Zola's reverence for the life-force has taken him right back into the arms of Dionysus. Mathieu and Marianne could not be described as a messianic couple, in the Judeo-Christian sense but, from the author's point of view, they have been so filled with divinity, that their exemplary life-style is enough to save the world. The novel ends—consistently enough—on a rhetorical flight into what Zola calls the heavens, but that in reality is no more than the realm of make-believe:

Et le divin rêve, l'utopie généreuse, vole à plein ciel, la famille fondue dans la nation, la nation fondue dans l'humanité, un seul peuple fraternel faisant du monde un cité unique de paix, de vérité et de justice. (O.C. 8, p. 502)

[And the divine dream, the generous Utopia soars in the open sky, the family merging into the nation, the nation merging with the whole of humanity—one fraternal people making the world into a single city of peace, truth, and justice.]

The same letter in which Zola craves indulgence for an old man's dreams, contains a confession that shows he is not unaware of some of *Fécondité* 's many shortcomings:

Je connais bien les défauts de mon livre, les invraisemblances, les symétries trop volontaires, les vérités banales de morale en action....[13]

[I am quite familiar with the flaws in my book—the improbabilities, the overarbitrary symmetries, the clichés of morality in action.]

However, the author has made his choice: in his next two gospels he may try consciously to lay foundations of solid reality, but the temptation to dream will often prevail—with unfortunate results.

We have noted Zola's personal messianic aspirations as they reemerge, for instance, in his letters of 1898. More evidence of revived messianism is to be found in another such letter, addressed to Jean Jaurès, the future leader of French socialism (already elected into parliament at the time) who had just visited him in London: "Je veux donner tout mon effort à la libération des hommes"[14] [I want to devote all my endeavors to the liberation of man]. Not long after his return from exile (June 1899), he sets to work on gathering material for his next novel, *Travail* [Work] (1901). He has been fascinated by Tolstoy's egalitarian ideas and has been doing research on the economic theorist and reformer, Charles Fourier. This utopian philosopher advocates the voluntary association of working-class, bourgeoisie, capital, and talent into cooperative cells or communities—the so-called "phalanstères"—whose success is supposed to result in the rapid fading away of existing oppressive and exploitative structures.

Readers familiar with Zola's *Travail* will have no difficulty in recognizing the Fourierist scenario in the novel, but the work owes just as much to the author's own past and present aspirations. *Travail* could be seen, for example, as a variation on the early tales "Aventures du grand Sidoine et du petit Médéric" and "Le Forgeron" [The Black Smith] or even an alternative approach to the subject treated in *Germinal*, the main innovation being that, this time around, the hero is entirely successful. In his Dossier préparatoire, Zola refers to his new savior as "messie" [messiah], as "l'homme attendu pour que la nouvelle société soit" [the man everyone was waiting for so that the new society might come into being]. Preferring to dismiss from his mind the long list of ineffectual dreamers that feature in his earlier novels, he specifies that his latest hero is to be

... un apôtre avec tous les dons voulus, mais un apôtre agissant et très pratique, réalisant les vérités qu'il apporte.[15]

[... an apostle with all the requisite gifts, but an active, very down-to-earth apostle, putting into practice the truths he brings.]

We have seen elsewhere that, as early as 1884, when Zola was working on *Germinal*, he had misgivings about a violent revolution or a nihilist holocaust and favored salvation through a gentle messiah, even if, at the time, he had grave doubts about Utopia eventuating. The author has not changed his mind about violence in 1900: his hero, Luc, will pursue a purely peaceful route to reform.

Just after publishing *Le Docteur Pascal*, Zola spoke publicly on the role of work as (1) the regulator that guides the world toward its hidden purpose and (2) the best remedy for man's perennial hankering after the infinite: any task faithfully fulfilled, he assured the assembled students, "Vous délivrera du tourment de l'infini"[16] (will deliver you from the torment of the infinite). Significantly, that speech is virtually summarized in the very first fiche of Zola's dossier for *Travail*, for there he refers to "Le travail qui organise et réglemente la vie (il fait de la vie, lui aussi)"[17] [Work that organizes and regulates life (it also creates life)]. Those interested in the hidden, subjective origins of a literary work will find food for thought in Jean Borie's declaration that *Travail* celebrates Zola's victory over his oedipal obsessions and reflects his belated assumption of a father's role: "Dans *Travail*, Luc sauve la mère humiliée, remplace le père et s'érige en messie"[18] [In *Travail*, Luc saves the humiliated mother, replaces the father, and sets himself up as a messiah]. (The present writer holds that Zola's discovery of fatherhood led him toward a patriarchal, rather than a messianic, perspective, and that his return to messianism is due primarily to his need for hope or, perhaps to the unspoken conviction that his fertile love for Jeanne has finally canceled out his disastrous experience with Berthe, the young prostitute who refused to be redeemed and tarnished her would-be savior's halo for decades to come.)

And so a number of factors contribute to the spirit of the work he is about to attempt: his exposure to Tolstoy and Fourier, his adolescent dreams, the meditations of his maturity and, no doubt, the new lease of life afforded him by his young mistress and the birth of his children. As he had done for novels like *Germinal*, *La Bête humaine* and, more recently, *Lourdes* and *Rome*, the author documents himself by some on the spot observation. He will model l'Abîme, the mill that features in the early part of his novel, on the usines d'Unieux [the Unieux works] in the Loire, founded by the Alsatian Jacob Holtzner. Zola, who was acquainted with the wider family of the proprietor, was invited to stay and had ample opportunity to visit the steelworks.

Viewed from a different angle, *Travail* becomes another work that incarnates Zola's ideal self—a modern-day messiah who, in the author's opinion, succeeds where Christ failed. That is the conclusion arrived at by Philip D. Walker, when he claims that "Luc, the saviour of mankind, reigning over his grateful, happy followers, like Christ among his disciples, embodies Zola's most glorious dream of what he himself wanted to be."[19] *Travail* opens with a glimpse of Josine, the thin, abused, poorly dressed young woman Luc is to save before long from the brutal, alcoholic Ragu. Zola's factual "entrée en matière" gains in significance when interpreted in the light of various notes included in his Dossier préparatoire: "C'est cette fille que (Luc) veut sauver et en la sauvant il crée la cité." [This is the girl [Luc] wants to save and in saving her he creates the city.] and again: "C'est par la femme et pour la femme que Luc crée la cité"[20] [It is for the woman and through the woman that Luc creates the city]. When the author returns to the subject a third time, he possibly conveys a good deal more than intended: "Et cette femme qu'il veut sauver, c'est le point de départ de tout son apostolat"[21] [And this woman whom he wants to save is the point of departure of his whole apostolate]. Is Zola by any chance ascribing to Luc the desire that, more than any other, explains his own lifelong obsession with messiahs and antichrists? Is the hastily written note just quoted not only a key to *Travail*, but also an unconscious revelation of how the Berthe trauma involved the author in a never-ending compulsion to pursue ideals of messiahship (by way of compensation or because the dream of being a savior was preexistent and needed to be rescued if Zola's life was to make sense)? If that is so, *Travail* is, perhaps, not just an inversion of the plot of *La Confession de Claude*, or an optimistic alternative scenario to that of *Germinal*, but a dramatization of the hidden myths that have powered most of Zola's life and work—including his recent intervention in the Dreyfus Affair. We shall see later that the figure of the Great Whore and the theme of Apocalypse have not been forgotten.

Luc has been summoned to La Crêcherie, a smelting-works, by Jordan, who needs some advice. As he awaits the return of his scientist-friend from an unexpected funeral, Luc is preoccupied with finding a solution to industrial evils. Immediately Zola sets the stage for his hero's future role by having him wonder:

> Etait-ce donc en Messie qu'une force inconnue le faisait tomber en ce coin de pays douloureux pour la mission rêvée de délivrance et de bonheur? (O.C. 8, p. 549)

> [Was it then in the role of Messiah that he had been caused, by some unknown power, to chance upon this sad country place, for the mission of deliverance and joy that he dreamed of?]

During an exploratory visit to the nearby township of Beauclair, the hero notices how well the children of workers, shopkeepers, and peasants relate to each other—a preview of the messianic younger generation that will repeatedly strengthen his sense of hope.

It is a pity that Zola does not disguise the children-interludes more skillfully when he sprinkles them throughout the novel. When, a little later, Luc places fragments of food in the mouth of starving Josine who had been thrown out into the street earlier that day, he strikes her as godlike: ". . . il lui apparaissait comme un dieu" (O.C. 8, p. 507) [He appeared like a god to her]. The author is still grooming his hero for his messianic calling.

Having been introduced to the collectivist Bonnaire, Luc's future ally, and the anarchist Lange, who is prophesying doom for the townsfolk, we meet beautiful Fernande, the hard, cruel, spiteful, and sexually perverse wife of the works-manager Delaveau. Luc, troubled by his contrasting glimpses of working-class wretchedness and bourgeois comfort, feels a hunger for creating justice take hold of him:

> Et c'était un cri de justice qui jaillissait de son être entier, et il n'y avait d'autre mission aujourd'hui, que d'aller au secours des misérables et de refaire un peu de justice sur la terre. (O.C. 8, p. 620)

> [And the cry that broke from his whole being was a cry for justice, and there was no other mission today than going to the help of the destitute and restoring a little justice on earth.]

After the arrival by train of frail Martial Jordan and his faithful, gentle younger sister Soeurette, who looks after him, Zola makes a point of juxtaposing Jordan's faith in the redeeming role of science and Luc's hopes for social and industrial reform. The hero's meditations, during the sleepless night that follows, may well cast light on the distant origins of both Luc and Zola's messianic aspirations:

> Et [Luc] sentit bien alors que ce rêve, en lui, venait de loin, qu'il l'avait toujours fait, depuis qu'il vivait à Paris, dans un quartier pauvre, parmi les héros obscurs et les dolentes victimes du travail. C'était comme l'inquiétude intérieure d'un avenir qu'il n'osait préciser, d'une mission dont il se sentait gros. (O.C. 8, p. 651)

> [And Luc felt with certainty then that this dream went back a long way, that he had always had it since he had been living in Paris, in a poor neighborhood, among the obscure heroes and the doleful victims of work. It was like an inner uneasiness about a future he dared not define, a mission with which he felt pregnant.]

Most providentially, the still wide-awake hero finds peace of mind after chancing upon the gospel according to Fourier, which is neatly summarized for the benefit of the reader.

Next day, after another brief exposure to Lange's "poésie noire" [dark poetry] (he has ideas of blowing up the whole administrative centre of Beauclair), Luc hears Jordan, his alter ego, intone his "hosanna au travail sauveur" (hosanna to work that saves) and proclaim his conviction that

> ... la découverte de la moindre des vérités scientifiques fait plus pour le progrès que cinquante ans de lutte sociale. (O.C. 8, p. 667)

> [... the discovery of the least scientific truth does more for progress than fifty years of social conflict.]

Jordan's vision of the cosmos at work is not without poetic appeal:

> L'univers n'est-il pas un immense atelier où l'on ne chôme jamais, où les infiniment petits font chaque jour un labeur géant, où la matière agit, fabrique, enfante sans relâche, depuis les simples ferments jusqu'aux créatures les plus parfaites? (O.C. 8, p. 669)

> [Isn't the universe an immense workshop where there is never any unemployment, where, everyday, infinitely small [agents] perform gigantic labors, where matter acts, fabricates, and gives birth unceasingly, from the simplest moulds to the most perfect creatures?]

but already Zola's oversystematic survey of past and contemporary visions and dreams is steering him perilously close to the cliffs of didacticism: and we have only just reached the end of the first of three books!

When Book Two opens, three years have passed. Thanks to funds provided by his friend Jordan, Luc has built a bright, clean, and spacious factory, including attractive workers' cottages, in competition with the Abîme [literally "abyss"] works (nomen est omen) [the name itself is an omen] at Beauclair. He has instituted educational reforms for the young and has encouraged a struggling village to adopt cooperative farming—all this more or less for the sake of Josine, a symbol to Luc of suffering, exploited woman.

There is growing resistance to his innovations, not only from diabolic Fernande, who feels her luxurious, sensuous life-style is threatened (in fact, it is she who is secretly ruining her husband and undermining the factory's viability), but also from the shopkeepers of Beauclair who are losing custom. They cannot compete with the cheaper cooperative set up by the workers. Taken to court on some pretext, Luc defends himself eloquently, but then has to face a hostile crowd calling for his death. Thereupon, Zola has Luc rewalk Jesus' via dolorosa—the road that Zola now knows, from personal experience, to be the fate of any upright person:

> ... Il s'était fait l'apôtre de demain. ... Mais quelle amertume, quelle souffrance, dans cette aventure commune de calvaire que tout juste doit gravir sous les coups de ceux mêmes dont il veut le rachat! (O.C. 8, p. 724)
>
> [... He had made himself the apostle of the future. ... But what bitterness, what suffering there was in this common experience of the Calvary that every just person has to climb, beneath the blows of the very people he wants to redeem!]

Luc forgives his persecutors, as Christ did. He is wounded twice by stones and spat upon. That evening, the lonely hero grieves, like Christ weeping over Jerusalem, "sur ce cher et triste peuple qui ne veut pas être sauvé" (O.C. 8, p. 729) [over these dear, sad folk who don't want to be saved]: "... il buvait sa souffrance jusqu'à la lie" (O.C. 8, p. 730) [... he drained his cup of suffering to the dregs]. David Baguley's comment, that Zola has recourse to biblical parallels for reasons of persuasion and prestige,[22] does not ring true: the overobvious adoption of the Calvary scenario is more likely to produce the opposite effect. We will probably be closer to the truth, if we assume that Zola's own treatment by hostile crowds, after his court appearance of 1898, reminded him of the Passion story and that, subsequently, it naturally came to mind when he imagined a hero in a similar predicament. In addition, there must have been some moral comfort for the homeless and humiliated writer in being able to insert his own troubles into a messianic perspective.

The scene that follows Luc's draining of the cup of suffering is highly significant: Zola abruptly abandons his biblical scenario in order to incorporate his own experiences with Jeanne Rozerot. It looks suspiciously as though he is trying to justify these in his own eyes, especially when he condones Luc and Josine's lovemaking. (The young woman, who has been assaulted again by Ragu, calls on discouraged Luc and impulsively falls into his arms):

> Aucun remords n'était possible, ils s'aimaient comme ils existaient, afin d'être sains, d'être forts et d'être féconds . . . l'apôtre en lui ne pouvait rester infécond, il avait besoin d'une femme pour racheter l'humanité . . . le jour où il aurait sauvé la femme, le monde serait sauvé. (O.C. 8, p. 731)

> [There was no room for remorse: they (simply) loved each other in the same way that they existed, so as to be healthy, strong, and fertile; . . . the apostle in him could not remain infertile; he needed a woman in order to redeem humanity; . . . the day that he saved the woman, the world would be saved.]

And so the act that proved a stumbling block to Claude (in *La Confession*) that constituted l'abbé Mouret's "faute" (sin), which robbed Hélène Grandjean of her peace of mind (*Une Page d'amour*), has at last been turned into an indispensable ingredient of messiahship. Zola has cut the Gordian knot—or has he?

After that, Luc still has to cope with his disciples' lack of love for each other, while Jordan has to come to terms with his provisional failure to invent an economical form of energy transmission. Depression nearly gets the better of the hero (as it had of Zola in the 1880s):

> C'était l'heure mauvaise, l'heure noire que connaissent bien tous les héros, tous les apôtres, l'heure où la grâce s'en va, où la mission s'obscurcit, où l'oeuvre paraît impossible. (O.C. 8, p. 754)

> [It was the evil hour, the dark hour that every hero and every apostle know, the hour when grace disappears, when one's mission becomes unclear, when the task [ahead] seems impossible.]

He is saved, however, by Jordan's courageous profession of faith in work: "Ah! travail sacré, travail créateur et sauveur, qui est ma vie, mon unique raison de vivre!" (O.C. 8, p. 756) [Ah! sacred work, creative, saving work, my life, my one reason for living!]. It takes no great psychological expertise to observe that Zola has just acted out, through Luc and Jordan, the story of his own crisis and the way in which he overcame it through a combination of work and the experience of romantic love.

From that moment onward, the hero's faith in the future is strengthened, although he is yet to consummate his messianic sacrifice. When Luc learns that he is going to be a father, Zola uses his hero's reaction in order to jettison his old impregnation theory (as featured originally in the novel, *Madeleine Férat*):

> Le seul époux était le père, le plaisir qu'on volait à une femme ne laissait rien, ne comptait pas, un seul lien nouait le couple, solide, éternel, l'enfant, la vie propagée, un être nouveau, né de l'indissoluble union de deux êtres. (O.C. 8, p. 771)
>
> [The only husband was the father [of the child]; the pleasure one had from a woman left behind nothing and did not count; a single bond tied the couple together, a secure, eternal bond: the child, the life they had propagated, a new being born out of the indissoluble union between two living beings.]

Not only does this ploy give the author the satisfaction of believing that Jeanne, not Alexandrine, is his "real" spouse, but it enables him to write off his episode with Berthe, in retrospect, as a matter of no consequence: it is not only in his novels that Zola plays games with reality!

Fernande, who informs Ragu of Luc's union with Josine, is rewarded by being raped on the spot—an experience that turns out to be her most intense sexual thrill up to that point. She prompts the enraged Ragu to murder Luc, but his stab in the back inflicts only a minor flesh wound. Soeurette, who had betrayed her tacit love for Luc when she thought him doomed, now pledges her sisterly devotion to him. As a result our wounded hero is pampered by two women simultaneously. Luc looks tenderly at "ses deux anges, l'un à gauche, l'autre à droite de son lit" [his two angels, one to the left, the other to the right of his bed]—a most satisfactory arrangement that Zola would no doubt have liked to reproduce in his private life. This quotation continues as follows:

> Il y eut un long silence. Le sang de l'apôtre eut coulé, et c'était le calvaire, la passion d'où allait sortir le triomphe. (O.C. 8, p. 785)
>
> [There was a long silence. The apostle's blood had flowed, and this was the Calvary, the passion out of which the triumph would come.]

In Zola's *Au Bonheur des dames*, already, Mme Hédouin had lost her life on the excavated foundations of Octave Mouret's new emporium, but this time it is the messianic hero himself who offers the blood sacrifice.

Luc soon recovers. Nevertheless, public mockery, Crucifixion, and resurrection are not enough to bring in the kingdom, Zola remembers. And so, in the very next chapter, it is time for Apocalypse and the doom of the Great Whore, the scarlet woman of the Book of Revelation. Fernande flaunts her unfaithfulness in front of her husband. When she drives him too far and dares him to kill her, he at last recognizes the true identity of the destroyer and perverter who slept so seductively by his side. He kicks some burning logs from the fireplace and prevents his screaming wife from fleeing the mounting flames. The inferno of the Delaveau home, the Abîme administrative center, and the the whole furnace block is a dramatization of the myth of debased, infernal lust that makes delusive promises of access to some infinite experience, but actually results in a consumption, a burning up of the self.

The author resorts to his stock apocalyptic allusion (about no stone remaining upon another): "Une demie-heure plus tard la maison s'écroulait, pas une pierre n'en restait debout" (O.C. 8, p. 818) [Half an hour later the house came tumbling down: not a stone of it remained standing]. For good measure, he adds the comment that the decadent bourgeoisie has lit its own funeral pyre, whereupon he adopts a frankly anarchist scenario:

> Le feu vengeur, le feu purificateur venait de tomber là en coup de foudre, et il rasait le champ entier, et il le déblayait des décombres, dont la chute du vieux monde l'avait obstrué. Maintenant la besogne était faite, l'horizon était libre, à l'infini, et la Cité naissante de justice et de paix pouvait...." (O.C. 8, p. 819)

> [The fire of vengeance, the fire of purification had just fallen there like a thunderbolt, clearing the whole field, sweeping away the rubble with which the fall of the old world had cluttered it. Now the work was done, the horizon was clear as far as the eye could see, and the newly born City of justice and peace could....]

As though two women were not enough—even for a messiah—Luc is given a further helper in Book 3, Suzanne, an old flame, the wife of empoverished mill-owner, Boisgelin, who will conveniently hang himself. She now becomes his soul-sister and will assist him in his endeavors to bring about heaven on earth.

Practically the whole of Book 3, starting with Luc's dream of converting the vacant Boisgelin estate into a resort for mothers and young children, can be placed under the heading of Utopia:

> ... et le parc toujours fleuri appartenait maintenant aux petits de ce monde, jardin immense, paradis de rêve où jouaient les enfants, où les mères retrouvaient de la santé, où tout le peuple venait se recréer comme en un palais de la nature.... (O.C. 8, pp. 844–45)

[. . . and the park that was always full of flowers now belonged to the humble people of this world—an immense garden, a dream paradise where the children played and the mothers regained their health, where the whole populace took some recreation, as though in a palace (built by) nature.]

Poor old abbé Marle, who has been covering the sins of the bourgeoisie under the mantle of religion, very much like l'abbé Mauduit in *Pot-Bouille*, comes to an appropriate end, when his neglected church collapses on him, as he is saying mass, and buries him beneath the rubble. Having disposed of the Great Whore at the end of Book 2, Zola has thus settled accounts with the apostate church as well.

For the sake of protecting Zola's reputation, limited use should perhaps be made of the many scenes featuring industrial Utopia. The following sample may suffice:

> Et ces hommes qui chantaient, autour de ces machines si douces et si fortes en leur silence, dans l'éclat de leurs aciers et de leurs cuivres, disaient la joie du juste travail, glorieux et sauveur. (O.C. 8, p. 894)

> [And the men, singing around those machines that were so gentle and strong, with their silence and their gleaming steel and copper parts, spoke of the joys of fair, glorious, redeeming labor.]

On a given festival day, the same machines are garlanded with roses, which are also strewn on the streets and pavements of the workers' village. The very birds have lost their fear of man, to symbolize the universal peace that prevails among "les hommes, les bêtes et les choses" (O.C. 8, p. 938) (men and beasts and things). The setting sun places a halo around the head of Luc, who is now described as "le Fondateur, le Créateur" and "le Père" (O.C. 8, p. 938) [Founder, Creator, and Father]. That evening our quasi-divine hero offers his people a solemn communion feast, as they have joined tables, out in the streets of the village:

> ... la Pâque de ce peuple fraternel allait s'achever sous les étoiles, en une immense communion, coude à coude, sur la même nappe, parmi les mêmes roses effeuillées. (O.C. 8, p. 941)

> [. . . the paschal feast of this fraternal people was going to be completed under the stars—a great communion, side by side, on the one tablecloth, among the same rose-petals.]

In the final chapter of the novel, Suzanne moves in with the Fromentin household to look after the now chair-bound hero.

Jordan visits his friend for the last time, before dying in peace: "Allons, dit-il avec un sourire, c'est fini et c'est très bien; je puis m'en aller à présent" (O.C. 8, p. 947) [Come now, he said with a smile, it is finished and all is well. I can go now]. (We are back to aged Simeon's sentiments in the Nunc Dimittis). Luc, the aging patriarch, has time to review his life and work and to indulge in diverse uplifting meditations, before he too passes away: "Et Luc expira, entra dans le torrent d'universel amour, d'éternelle vie" (O.C. 8, p. 969) [And Luc breathed his last, entering into the great river of universal love and eternal life]. (In Zola's Utopia, people do not die, they pass onto another dimension.)

We have deliberately cut short our analysis of Book 3, where the faults of the utopian genre manifest themselves in full. *Travail* was celebrated by workers' associations and unions that do not seem to have noticed Zola's facile messianism or his incorporation of outdated socialistic theories, Luc's incorrigible paternalism, and the novel's eventual stagnation in tedious celebrations. The worst feature of the novel is probably the suspicion it raises that the author is whitewashing his past and that, in the apotheosis of his hero, Zola is vicariously satisfying his own vanity. Perhaps it would be more charitable to suggest that the aging author is merely indulging in some harmless wishful thinking.

To end on a more positive note, one can pay tribute to Zola's prophetic insight, once he looks away from the overidyllic scenes of his Utopia, on the last page of the novel. Suzanne, prophetically but in the perfect tense, relates the last terrible wars to visit humanity—wars initiated by periods of tremendous social upheaval. At first dividing Europe against itself, they gradually involved the whole world. The definitive battle was fought out over a month in the plains of central Europe with unspeakable carnage:

> La science avait inventé des explosifs, des engins capables de porter la mort à des distances prodigieuses, d'engloutir brusquement tout un peuple, comme en un tremblement de terre. (O.C. 8, p. 969)

> [Science had invented explosives, [war]machines capable of carrying death over prodigious distances, of suddenly engulfing a whole population, as though in an earthquake.]

Western Europe may have escaped most of the class-conflict that haunted Zola's imagination, but the Armageddon scenario is one that the modern reader has little trouble in accepting as highly plausible. Zola may have chosen to escape into his private millennium, but has not altogether lost contact with reality.

For the purposes of this study, we should note first of all that, while *Travail* utilizes the full panoply of messianic myth—the noble outsider who passes through suffering and a resurrection in order to bring salvation to a community—it does so in a clumsy, self-conscious manner that does not allow for the organic integration of myth and plot.

Secondly, it should be stressed that there is a growing inconsistency between the agnostic, humanist, or vaguely mystical position of the author and the Christian scenarios, allusions, and imagery he insists on using. It is still acceptable that a martyr to social reform, like Luc, should be presented in terms of the Passion story, but an author who believes only in material causation should not make the church fall in on an unfaithful priest or commit his great harlot to the lake of fire.

In order to explain this strange anomaly, it is pointless to suggest that religious allusions lend the novel greater authenticity or prestige. One can only speculate that, in spite of Zola's rationalist emancipation, there remains a part of him that, metaphorically speaking, ever wants to be a priest, which is inescapably caught up in the patterns, values, and moral systems of Christianity. *Vérité*, [Truth] the last "gospel" to be completed by Zola, will not escape from the same basic incongruity between mind and spirit, science and myth that seems to be an inherent part of his being.

Critics and reading public realized from the start that *Vérité* (1903) was a transposition of the Dreyfus Affair. One Joseph Reinach, for instance, defined the novel as follows in *La Petite république* (24 February 1903): ". . . la transposition de l'affaire Dreyfus dans le monde des instituteurs et des ignorantins" [. . . the transposition of the Dreyfus Affair into the world of primary-schoolteachers and ignoramuses]. Just how closely Zola based his story on the chief events of the historical saga has been demonstrated by Alain Pagès in his recent edition of the novel.[23]

Zola, starting from his own conviction that most of France had failed to rally to the defense of the wrongly convicted Jew through ignorance and lack of instruction in rational thinking, was led to muse about the value of knowledge. In his Dossier préparatoire, he claims—like the serpent of old in the Garden of Eden, but in somewhat more naive and simplistic terms:

... savoir, et savoir surtout la vérité, permettrait la réalisation rapide de tous les progrès, assurerait le bonheur universel.²⁴

[... knowledge and, above all, knowledge of the truth, would quickly facilitate progress in every direction, and would ensure universal happiness.]

adding a little later: "Il faut . . . que tout le monde sache, si l'on veut que tout le peuple soit bon et heureux"²⁵ [Everyone has to know, if you want the whole population to be good and happy]. This, in turn, inspired him to dedicate his next novel to exalting the humble "instituteur" or primary-schoolteacher, whose unique role it was, Zola decided, to enlighten the younger generation:

Enfin, ne pas oublier que je fais le poème de l'instituteur primaire. L'exalter, le mettre à son rang, le premier, le semeur d'hommes.²⁶

[Finally, don't forget that I am writing the poem of the primary-schoolteacher. [I must] extol him, assign him to his rank—the front rank—that of sower of men.]

If there is to be any kind of messiah in Vérité, then, he will be a lowly, purely human one.

A number of factors explain the strong anticlerical tone of Vérité. In the early 1880s, Zola had lived through the republican campaign that resulted in the provision of free, compulsory, and nonreligious instruction for all. More recently, he had taken part in the political and ideological struggle between prochurch and antichurch groups, stimulated, no doubt, by his perception of the Catholic Church's role in the Dreyfus Affair—its one-sided support, often in officially backed publications, of army and establishment, at the expense of an upright fellow-citizen, who was as devoted to family and country as he was to the honor of his regiment. Zola's notes show too that he fully intended to strike another blow against racial prejudice; he refers to ". . . tout l'anti-sémitisme que je traquerai avec véhémence"²⁷ [all the anti-Semitism that I will track down ruthlessly]. While his personal brush with religious factions during the Dreyfus Affair is, no doubt, chiefly responsible for his more scathing tone, there are indications, in the text of the novel, that the author also resented the church's continuing hold over women. This was a fairly common grievance held by anticlerical groups: some confessors, it was reported, were not beyond recommending blackmail in the bedroom, if this could move the unbelieving heart of recalcitrant husbands. In the case of Zola, however, it could be suggested that he may have been a little peeved that priests should have had first access to his mother (and later to his mistress), before ever he (Zola) entered the scene. Or does the truth lie a little deeper? Is the author, perhaps, resentful about the hold religion gained over his own soul, in his tender years—the spell from which his reason freed him in late adolescence, but that left him marked for life? Is he bitter with God, Christ, and the church for so "impregnating" his being that indiscreet critics will forever be whispering: "Il y a du prêtre dans cet homme" [There is something of the priest in this man]?

In the same way, the present author has long suspected that when Zola regretfully renounced Jesus as messiah, because of his alleged failure to save the world, this was at least in part because religion had failed to save young Emile from unchastity. To be more specific, it could be argued that, at the time of his Berthe trauma, Zola blamed the church for the sense of death that came over him after his sexual lapse. The real stumbling block was not the sexual impurity—which could have been easily coped with through confession—but the fact that engaging in any sexuality at all involved Zola in an irreconcilable clash with his mother fixation.

Whatever the reasons for Zola's anticlericalism, *Vérité* suffers from fanatic hostility to organized religion. In *La Conquête de Plassans*, the author exposes a sinister priest who manipulates women like Marthe Mouret; in *La Faute*, he features a neurotic priest who cannot reconcile life and religion; in *Rome*, he draws a most unflattering picture of the church hierarchy. In *Vérité*, however, priests and religious at large will be the victims of his scorn and abhorrence. Out of some vestige of respect for fairness and moderation, he allows for one or two ineffectual weaklings, who are, basically, men of goodwill, but all the rest are reduced to a gang of con-men, cheats and liars, perverts and seducers, murderers and women-bashers. The reader is faced incessantly with a body of men more interested in raising funds or wielding power than in serving the cause of Christ. Mitterand is not mistaken, when he says of *Vérité*: ". . . ce roman, . . . plus que tous les autres, est un roman à thèse"[28] [. . . this novel, more than any other, is a novel with an ax to grind]. The plot of the novel is structured around the schoolmaster, Marc Froment's struggle to establish the innocence of his Jewish colleague, Simon, banished to Cayenne [French Guyana] for allegedly raping and murdering his young Catholic nephew. From the opening chapter, another colleague of Marc's, bitter, financially struggling Férou, prophesies that the murder story will be exploited by church interests for propaganda purposes (Marc, Simon, and Férou are all part of the nonreligious, state-system of education):

> En voilà une histoire qui va permettre à cette sale prêtraille de taper sur nous, les pervertisseurs, les empoisonneurs de la laïque. O.C. 8, p. 1026)

> [There is a tale for you that will give that filthy band of priests the opportunity to strike out at us, the corrupters, the poisoners of the laity.]

Marc, clearly another incarnation of the author's ideal self, is said to have an "absolue passion de la vérité" (1033) (absolute passion for truth) and to be good at expressing truth clearly and simply, once has has found it. In contrast, the local Capuchin brothers are said to be spreading superstition and to be making money out of their miracle-working saint, St. Anthony of Padua.

Following a poisoned article in the provincial paper, *Le Petit Beaumontais*, about to become a tool of indoctrination, Simon is abused in the street: "A mort, à mort! l'assassin, le sacrilège, ... A mort, à mort le juif!" (O.C. 8, p. 1063) [Down with the assassin, down with the profaner, down with the Jew!]. He is duly arrested, condemned on false evidence, and dispatched to French Guyana for life. The author immediately slips in a conversation between the hero and Simon's brother, David, to air his views on anti-Semitism:

> Il n'y avait pas de question juive, il n'y avait que la question de l'argent amassé, empoisonneur et pourrisseur. (O.C. 8, p. 1071)

> [There was no such thing as a Jewish question; there was only the question of accumulated money—money that poisons and corrupts (society).]

After drawing attention to the plight of Simon's wife, Rachel, her parents (the Lehmanns) and children—all of whom are being discriminated against by the locals—the author turns his attention to his gospel of truth and its humble apostles, the underpaid schoolmasters who are becoming hard to recruit. (Marc is having a discussion with Salvan, the director of the Ecole Normale

[Teachers' Training College], who first encouraged him to take up his profession):

> Ah! où était-il, le bataillon sacré des instituteurs primaires qui devaient instruire tout le peuple de France, à la seule clarté des certitudes scientifiques établies, pour le délivrer des ténèbres séculaires et le rendre enfin capable de vérité, de liberté et de justice! (O.C. 8, p. 1115)

> [And where was the sacred battalion of primary-schoolteachers who were to instruct the entire population of France by the light of scientific certainty alone, in order to deliver (the people) from centuries of darkness!]

It is high time, Zola demonstrates through his plot, for locally, bishop and priest have yielded to the irresistible tide of superstition and miracle-mongering, promoted by Father Théodose and his Capuchin monks. If France as a whole is not to share "la misère et le néant dont le catholicisme a frappé toutes les terres où il a régné" (p. 1128) [the misery and nothingness that Catholicism has inflicted on all the lands it has ruled] (!!), if the country is to escape the slavery and exploitation that have resulted from Christ's words "Blessed are the poor in spirit," a new gospel is called for.

It is sitting on a bench, waiting for his wife's train to arrive—and not on the road to Damascus—that Marc has a revelation of the truth and formulates his new gospel:

> Heureux ceux qui savent, heureux les intelligents, les hommes de volonté et d'action, parce que le royaume de la terre leur appartiendra. (O.C. 8, p. 1131)

> [Blessed are those who have knowledge, blessed are the intelligent, the men of will and action, because the kingdom of the earth will belong to them.]

The hero has seen the light: he will accept Salvan's request that he take up a post in the benighted village of Maillebois and he will seek to redeem it: "C'était sa mission qui tout d'un coup se précisait, son apostolat de la vérité" (O.C. 8, p. 1132) [All of a sudden, his mission became clear: his apostolate of truth]. Marc's wife, Geneviève, brought up a Catholic, but no longer practicing since her marriage to Marc, is not enthusiastic about the new posting, for her hard, tyrannical, dogmatic grandmother lives in Maillebois (together with Geneviève's widowed mother) and the old lady might well look on Marc as an incarnation of evil: "... elle va croire que tu viens faire ici la besogne de l'Antéchrist" (O.C. 8, p. 1133) [... she is going to think that you have come here to do the work of the Antichrist]. Initially Marc has a difficult time in his new school, but he wins over the pupils, thanks to his justice, his patience, the clarity of his explanations, and his practical approach. In the end he manages to teach them cleanliness, honesty, and a sense of fair play. Unfortunately the latter virtue is not immediately evident in the thoughts that cross Marc's mind, when he visits his former village of Jonville and notices its loss of cleanliness:

> La saleté et la vermine se sont mises dans tous les pays où le catholicisme a triomphé, partout il a passé comme un souffle de mort, frappant de stérilité la terre, jetant les hommes à la paresse et à l'imbécilité morne, car il est la négation même de la vie, il tue les nations modernes, ainsi qu'un poison lent et sûr. (O.C. 8, p. 1157)

> [Dirt and vermin have installed themselves in all the countries where Catholicism has triumphed; everywhere it has passed through like a wind of death, striking the earth with sterility, casting men into laziness and dismal imbecility, for it is the very negation of life; it kills modern nations like some slow, sure poison.]

It is ironic that Zola, a tireless campaigner against anti-Semitism, should forestall, in these anti-Catholic sentiments, the kind of Nazi propaganda of the thirties that branded Jews as noxious vermin.

True to his belief that every apostle or messiah, every just person, in fact, will be subjected to trials and tribulations, the author now pulls the persecution-lever—as he did in *Travail* for Marc's brother, Luc. As the hero's influence in the township grows and he becomes engrossed in saving his Jewish colleague, it is his turn to be maligned in *Le Petit Beaumontais*. At the same time, Marc begins to sense that the college director, Crabot, is working on Geneviève in order to destroy him emotionally. The Jesuit's smooth, insinuating ways—in the best Faujas tradition (*La Conquête de Plassans*)—slowly estrange her from her husband. Marc realizes that it is Crabot, too, who engineers Geneviève's change of confessor from the mild local priest, Quandieu to the handsome, fiery-eyed Théodose, who entangles her in some sensuously mystical substitute for conjugal relations. The situation culminates in pregnant Geneviéve's leaving home and husband. She moves in with her grandmother, implacable Mme Duparque, who has already brought suffering, darkness, and misery to her daughter (Geneviève's mother). Zola has revived the world of *Madeleine Férat*, the harsh, loveless religion championed by the old Huguenot housekeeper (Geneviève), who kept on assuring the heroine that God the father does not forgive.

Nevertheless, our lonely, persecuted hero is providentially granted some succor: he finds a platonic soul mate in Mlle Mazeline, another idealistic schoolteacher, who becomes his confidante, helper, and comforter. Marc's isolation intensifies as his sensible daughter, Louise, who had at first decided to stay with her father, resolves to move in with wicked Great-grandmama, so that she may counter the old lady's evil promptings and quietly confront her mother with sane reality.

Meanwhile Marc and his allies, notably Simon's brother, David, and energetic lawyer Delbos, have uncovered fresh evidence and have obtained a retrial for the banished Jew: the latter will be repatriated from Guyana as soon as he recovers from a serious illness. While Théodose makes indecent overtures to Marc's wife, an underground clerical campaign is organized to intimidate and brainwash the jury at Simon's trial. The poor wretch is found guilty a second time and condemned to another ten years, to add to the fifteen he has managed to survive so far.

At that point, Zola disengages his persecution-lever and, immediately, Marc's situation begins to improve. Father Théodose may launch a lucrative trade in shares in paradise—"des obligations hypothécaires sur le paradis" (O.C. 8, p. 1355)—but Geneviève has read through a copy of courtroom proceedings and now believes in Simon's innocence. As a result, she has frequent scenes with her "terrible aïeule" [dreadful grandmother]. When Geneviève's mother prevails on her to leave "cette maison de mensonge et de mort" (O.C. 8, p. 1363) [that house of lies and death], the old dragon abandons her descendants to their damnation. Marc, who has just learned of his transfer back to Jonville, is delighted to have his wife and children return home, but note the exact nature of his triumph:

> N'était-ce pas sa grande oeuvre? reprendre la femme à l'Eglise, lui donner près de l'homme sa vraie place de mère et de compagne.... (O.C. 8, p. 1373)

> [Wasn't this his great task—to take back woman from the church and give her her rightful place next to the man, as mother and companion?]

For Marc, as for Zola, ideology is becoming more important than figures of flesh and blood, who speak and react like human beings.

The hero serenely continues his "modeste apostolat moderne" [modest modern apostleship], (O.C. 8, p. 1377), while Théodose dreams up new money-making schemes (reserving expensive garden-plots in paradise). Mme Duparque is discovered dead, sitting up rigidly against her pillow and clutching a large crucifix. (Zola has just pulled the poetic justice lever.) Marc wins another victory when he succeeds in freeing the Jonville parish from its dedication to the Sacred Heart—a form of devotion that has been branded repeatedly by the hero, alias Zola, as a revival of slaughterhouse-religion and as a ploy to seduce France back into the bosom of the church.

When uncouth Brother Gorgias, the real murderer, confesses that he was pressured by his superiors into giving false evidence at the trial, and a surviving jury-man submits a written statement on irregularities and a fraudulent document in the jury-room, Simon's sentence is quashed by the Court of Appeal and no retrial is ordered.

While we await Simon's glorious return from Cayenne, Zola settles accounts with the church. St. Anthony having fallen out of favor, the new priest of Jonville turns his church into a veritable abattoir [slaughterhouse] of bleeding hearts, but to no avail, we are told, as part of a sermonette:

> Mais cette seconde incarnation de Jésus, si grossière, ne touchait plus les foules qui avaient compris qu'un peuple, frappé de désastres, se relève par le travail, par la raison, et non par la pénitence, aux pieds de monstrueuses idoles. (O.C. 8, p. 1435)

> [But this second incarnation of Jesus—how vulgar it was!—no longer moved the crowds who had understood that a nation struck by disasters raises itself through work and reason, and not through penitence at the feet of monstrous idols.]

In any case, the Catholic Church as a whole is dying a well-deserved death, for having chosen the side of falsehood. In the words of the expiring emeritus priest of Jonville: "Ils ont recondamné et crucifié une seconde fois Jésus, l'Eglise en mourra" (O.C. 8, p. 1435) [They have condemned Jesus again and crucified him a second time; the church will die of it]. The village of Maillebois intends to make reparation to Simon for his long martyrdom by building him a home bearing a dedication-stone signed "Les petits-fils de ses bourreaux" (O.C. 8, p. 1441) [the grandsons of his torturers].

And so Marc (who has suddenly turned into an old man) can look back over a long teaching career that has not been in vain:

> Et il avait voulu cela, c'était son oeuvre qui s'accomplissait, la délivrance d'un peuple par l'école primaire, tous les citoyens tirés de l'iniquité où ils croupissaient, en stupide troupeau, devenus enfin capables de vérité et de justice. (O.C. 8, p. 1449)
>
> [And that is what he had wanted; his work was being accomplished—the deliverance of a people through primary school: all the citizens, rescued from the iniquity in which they had been crouching like a flock of stupid (sheep), (had) at last become capable of truth and justice.]

The crazy Gorgias publicly confesses to his crime, from which he has been duly absolved by Father Théodose, he claims, so that no one can lay a finger on him! (He will be found murdered soon after, in spite of official absolution.) Simon arrives, in apotheosis, cheered by a flower-throwing crowd. A few days later, the ringleader of the plot against the Jewish teacher, Jesuit Crabot, is crushed by a collapsing statue of St. Anthony (Zola is developing a sense of humor in his old age!). During the same thunderstorm, idolatrous Théodose is struck by lightning: "Le père Théodose, incendié à l'autel, flamba ainsi qu'une torche" (O.C. 8, p. 1466) [Father Théodose, set on fire at the altar, flamed like a torch]. Just as the reader is about to throw the novel aside, in disgust over so much melodrama, Zola has a change of heart: in a final chapter that reads like a postscript, he gives the by now eighty-year-old Marc a grandson, François, who betrays his wife with Théodose's illegitimate daughter, Colette. On top of that, Rose, François' twelve-year-old daughter, is assaulted by a stranger whom, in her confusion, she takes for her own father. The false accusation is quickly dealt with, thanks to the now sensible, honest townsfolk (who have profited from Marc's teaching), but Zola is wise enough to let the broken relationship of François and his wife stand. Marc is made to realize something that momentarily eluded Zola in his Dossier préparatoire: that knowledge by itself is not enough to ensure happiness, if passions cannot be controlled (the author is still leaving chance and the violence of nature out of his reckoning).

Thérèse, the wronged wife, is unable to take back her husband, but, she too, accepts the mysterious need for suffering that seems to be part of the scheme of things:

> Ah! la souffrance, avouons qu'elle sera éternelle. Elle est en nous, sans doute, pour une des besognes ignorées de la vie. . . ." (O.C. 8, p. 1487)

> [Ah! suffering: let us admit that it will always be there. It is in us, no doubt, for one of life's unknown tasks. . . .]

(the sermonette continues for another five lines).

The novel ends with a renewed attack on Christ's Sermon on the Mount:

> Une parole exécrable avait osé dire 'Heureux les pauvres d'esprit!' et la misère de deux mille ans était née de cette mortelle erreur. (O.C. 8, p. 1487)

> [An execrable utterance had dared to announce: "Blessed are the poor in spirit" and two thousand years of misery had been born from that fatal error.]

and with a résumé of Zola's *Evangiles:*

> Et, après la Famille enfantée, après la Cité fondée, la Nation se trouvait constituée, du jour où, par l'instruction intégrale de tous les citoyens, elle était devenue capable de vérité et de justice. (O.C. 8, p. 1488)

> [And after the birthing of the Family, the founding of the City, the Nation was constituted, from the day when—thanks to the complete education of all citizens—it had become capable of truth and justice.]

There is no need to dwell on the faults of *Vérité*, which are legion, but a few remarks are called for to spell out what has become of Zola's messianic myth and related themes. First of all, the author has given up the idea of an exalted, superhuman messiah. Throughout the novel, he has made a point of referring to the "humble instituteur" (humble primary-schoolteacher) as the nation's savior. On the second last page of the novel he puts these words into the mouth of his hero:

> Mes enfants, mes enfants, il ne faut pas faire de moi un dieu. . . . Je ne suis qu'un ouvrier laborieux qui a fait sa journée. (O.C. 8, p. 1487)

[Children, children, you must not make a god of me. I am simply a diligent worker who has done his day's stint.]

That, at least, is a great improvement on the overdone apotheosis-scene of *Travail*.

Secondly, it is worth noting that, in the last novel he was to complete, Zola has merged into one body his figures of false prophet, Great Whore, and Antichrist, for the church he evokes combines the qualities of all three: it falsifies the message of its Founder, it fornicates—both literally and metaphorically—and, as the dying priest of Jonville declares, it has crucified Christ all over again.

Thirdly, Geneviève's casual remark (that her harsh grandmother, Mme Duparque, may see Marc's endeavors in Maillebois as those of Anrichrist) offers us a clue that may be of capital importance: it hints at the genesis of Zola's preoccupation, throughout his literary career, with false messiahs and antichrists.

We have met implacable old women before, notably Pâquerette in *La Confession*; the Huguenot maidservant, in *Madeleine Férat*; and the mother of Thérèse Raquin, all of whom feature in Zola's early novels as incarnations of fate or death. It was suggested, in chapter 3 of this study, that such figures are caricatures of the mother figure Zola sensed, irrationally, he had betrayed by unchastity and his loss of faith. However, the destructive mother figure persists in Zola's fictional world, emerging, for instance, in wicked Félicité who survives Pascal and who destroys his life's work. When a similar symbol makes a final appearance in *Vérité*, just as the hero is about to take up a messianic mission at Maillebois, and when that representation of a loveless and dying faith is expected to accuse him of being Antichrist, we may draw the following conclusion: it is precisely the continuing presence in the author's psyche of the strong, religious mother figure that gives birth to irrational anxiety: Zola may fear subconsciously that, in upholding values contrary to those of that figure, he is acting as a false messiah or Antichrist (hence the long list of corresponding villains in *Les Rougon-Macquart*). Exposing Mother-Church as the Great Harlot would only compound the felony and result in more repressed anxiety (projecting his personal Antichrist-complex onto the church is a form of symbolic problem solving that does not really help to exorcise his demons). Zola may emancipate himself from what he considers outdated beliefs, but he has no control over the archetypes that inhabit the depth of his psyche. In any case, most rebels against a traditional system of belief, who proclaim a new gospel, will almost inevitably have moments of weakness, moments of doubt when they are haunted by the specter of being a false prophet.

The most disturbing aspect of the novel is that, by making such immoderate attacks on the church, by describing the first Beatitude as a "parole exécrable" (execrable utterance), and by presuming to hold Jesus responsible for two thousand years of misery, Zola himself risks being regarded, by some readers at least, as a false prophet. The author is entitled to his opinion, but excessive caricature is counterproductive, even for propaganda purposes: it tends to reflect on its author, rather than on what is under attack.

Conclusion

IN CHAPTER 1 AN ATTEMPT WAS MADE TO GIVE AN OUTLINE OF THE Judeo-Christian messianic myth and associated motifs such as Antichrist, the Great Whore, and Apocalypse.

Starting from the observation that messianic hopes and aspirations are triggered off in the human psyche by crisis situations that threaten with insecurity, fear, or despair, we speculated on young Emile Zola's being led to assume the role of family savior. Adolescent Zola, we noted, developed a social conscience that was no doubt reinforced by his own sense of deprivation. Following the drift of his youthful stories, we saw him turn from idealistic messianic dreams to a rejection of violent saviors and to an eventual repudiation of the Christian messianic tradition in general.

After the Berthe fiasco of 1861, we witnessed Zola's provisional disillusionment with the messianic myth (*La Confession de Claude*) yield to a more hopeful perspective. Maybe by way of compensation for his sexual lapse, we suggested, Zola turned the fairly common messianic aspirations of adolescence into a fully fledged "messiah-complex." This hypothesis seemed corroborated by the author's creation of heroes such as Daniel in *Le Voeu d'une morte* and Marius, in *Les Mystères de Marseille*, both of whom incarnate orthodox Christian ideals of self-sacrifice and redemption. The subsequent emergence of ineffectual, flawed, or false messiahs was ascribed to Zola's suppressed, but persistent sense of failure—the vague sense of not having been able to live up to his original vision of his role and calling. In the pivotal work, *Les Mystères*, already, we watched the themes of redemption and atonement change into a scenario of expiation through death. In *Thérèse Raquin* and *Madeleine Férat*, especially, we noted that Laurent and Jacques ultimately brought death to those who first saw them as saviors and deliverers.

Turning to the early volumes of the *Rougon-Macquart*, we were faced with an author who seemed confirmed in his skepticism. On the one hand, we traced the fate of innocent or ineffectual dreamers like Silvère (*La Fortune des Rougon*) and Florent (*Le*

Ventre de Paris). On the other hand we encountered villains who consciously set out to deceive and defraud. After watching the machinations of phony messiahs such as Pierre Rougon and his son, Aristide (=Saccard), we saw Zola devote a whole novel to a false shepherd, Faujas, in *La Conquête de Plassans*, who turned out to be nothing short of a devil in disguise.

In a second quartet of novels, we found the author reiterating his reasons for discarding the traditional messiah. He did this through little Jeanne, in *Une Page d'amour*, for instance, who saves her mother from life rather than from death, or through the young priest in *La Faute* whose identification with the crucified Christ amounted to a rejection of instinct, beauty, and nature. Coming upon another helpless messiah in Gervaise's neighbor, Goujet, and another false messiah in the unscrupulous statesman, Eugène Rougon, we began to formulate a suspicion that had vaguely come to mind earlier: could it be that, through his recurring weak idealists, the author was trying to confess the futile messianic dreams of his youth? And could he be featuring forceful, self-seeking figures such as Saccard and Eugène to reflect his later attraction to power and ambition—temptations that might assume the outward garb of messiahship, but that actually aligned him (Zola) with the myth of Lucifer or Antichrist?

The author takes a preliminary step toward self-knowledge and exorcising his demons when, in *Nana*, he dramatizes the destructive power of rampant sexuality or when, in *Pot-Bouille*, he exposes the sordid promiscuity of the bourgeoisie and the hypocrisy of a clergy that covers this scandal with the mantle of religion. To pillory the Great Whore, literally in Nana or figuratively in an apostate church, is one thing, but the author does not realize as yet, that he cannot fullfil his calling to be a savior, a prophet of the life-force, until he himself deals with the repressed sexuality that tends to run amok in his novels, until he stops using his own messianic aspirations as a mask or cover. At this stage, Nana serves merely to show up the evilness of evil, to prefigure its demise, and to usher in Apocalypse for the pleasure-seeking Paris of the Second Empire. There is no indication at all that Zola realizes his need for a personal holocaust to bring expiation and cleansing, to clear the stage for a fresh beginning.

We find evidence of progress in the right direction in *Au Bonheur des dames*, which shows how the caring, serving, redemptive spirit of Denise prevails in the end over the entrepreneurial, empire-building drive of Octave Mouret. There is no doubt that Zola is still fascinated with modern commercialism, the golden calf of money and power, but he has detected the false messiahship inherent in the system and pays tribute to the better choice made by Denise. That same spirit of selflessness and compassion, at work in the Pauline of *La Joie de vivre*, may not cure Lazare's obsession with death and futility, but does offer hope for the future: the heroine ensures the survival of Lazare's frail child. Having wrested it from death, in true messianic style, she holds it out to the ocean—the life-force that can be destructive, but whose sovereign design transcends all our petty human goals.

The battle between the dream of messianic glory and the call to humble service of the life-force continues in *Germinal* and *L'Oeuvre*. Etienne fails as a self-appointed messiah. After slaying Chaval, an incarnation of the author's darker, purely instinctual side, however, he experiences a type of resurrection and walks out into a future where he may yet serve the life-force. The painter Claude has a revelation of the same life-force through meeting Christine, but goes astray because of overweening pride: in trying to rival the God of creation, he oversteps his role as prophet, destroying both his art and his life. Yet his shocked realization that he has turned his portrait of the living Christine into a monstrous, obscene idol shows that Zola has become aware of his own sexual obsession (manifested, e.g., in *Nana*) as something that interferes with his hold on reality.

Jean, the well-meaning outsider in *La Terre*, has messianic qualities, but fails through his imperfect "incarnation": insufficiently integrated into his adopted milieu, he cannot retain either wife or property. Himself in tune with the life-force, he is unable to redeem the locals from their one-sided physicality and attachment to the land. *Le Rêve* is, for Zola, simply a moment of respite, a chance to reassert the more spiritual side of his personality, an opportunity to remind himself of his most idealistic dreams that he still believes unattainable, but cannot renounce altogether.

The final volumes of the *Rougon-Macquart* cycle reflect some momentous changes in Zola's attitude to the world and to himself—changes that will culminate in a serene renunciation of messiahship on the part of a hero, Dr. Pascal, who is patently close to the author's heart.

Setting out to write a work on the survival in modern man of the primitive brute, Zola ended up projecting his own obsession with sadism. We have seen how the charitable comments of a critic like Lemaître helped the author to clear a psychological hurdle at which he had been baulking for years.

The author's approach to the Lucifer myth (the absolute inversion of his messianic ideals) becomes even more ambiguous. In *Son Excellence Eugène Rougon*, already, he portrayed the rise and fall of an impressive rogue who is allowed a second and then a third chance. Contemplating a similar scenario for *L'Argent*, the author at first intends to annihilate his incarnation of Satan after his vain challenge of Gundermann, alias Jehovah. In the finished novel, however, the plot is given a different denouement altogether. It transpires that even compassionate, noble-minded Caroline is in two minds about her lover. Zola himself ultimately permits his beloved villain to escape to Holland where he is likely to pursue more grandiose schemes. In contrast, the frail idealist, Sigismund Busch, is shown to expire pathetically, with none of his messianic ideals realized, sustained only by his vision of the Golden City.

In keeping with his greater lenience toward sinners, Zola relents in his hitherto very negative attitude to Napoleon III. The author must have realized that the emperor was not the only self-styled messiah to misbehave sexually or fall short of his ideals! In the novel in question, *La Débâcle*, the hero, Jean, rejects as defeatist and destructive, his friend Maurice's despairing call for doom and destruction. Yet Jean comes to believe that the apocalyptic events of the Franco-Prussian War and the holocaust of the Commune that followed amount to a national Calvary, a salutary experience of expiation opening up the way for future restoration. It appears to have dawned on Zola that even a satanic figure like Saccard and the consuming fire of judgment may play a part in bringing in the kingdom.

Another surprising development occurs when Dr. Pascal, after his intoxicating initiation to love, resolves to give up his personal dream of messiahship—even messiahship of a purely earthly and humanist sort. Surrendering to the flow of the life-force, the hero is content to be a patriarch, a simple link in the chain of life, and to place his hopes for the future in the progress of science and in a messiah outside of himself.

In *Lourdes*, Zola makes a gesture toward retrieving the religious certainties of his youth. Bernadette incarnates, for Pierre, (and the author he represents) the divine illusion he craves but cannot believe in, the perennial messianic dream nurtured by the suffering and oppressed. In *Rome* , Pierre's hopes in a revived church and a messianic pope prove unfounded: the hero has to come to terms with moribund conservatives or an apostate, power-hungry hierarchy that has betrayed its Founder. Finally convinced that Christian charity is futile and that the Gospel of

Jesus has failed to redeem the world, Pierre lays aside his priestly robes (*Paris*) along with his messianic quest. As far as he is concerned, the future must be built, not on messianism, but on the civilizing effect of reason and science, on the achievements of creative or constructive effort. The anarchist gospel that nearly destroys his scientist-brother is once again rejected.

Zola's *Evangiles* are little more than pathetic documents on the author's escape into Utopia. *Fécondité* features a husband and wife who virtually become high priest and high priestess of the life-force. Their dedication to "fruitfulness" constitutes an exemplary blueprint deemed capable of bringing back the golden age.

The need for hope tempts our aging writer to revert to the messianic myth in *Travail*. This time, Zola is intent on portraying a peaceable, practical messiah who succeeds where Jesus failed. We have noted that the author's policy of forcing his profane cast to conform to a biblical scenario, does not make for a convincing plot. The problems that Zola himself found daunting in the past are now simply dissolved in the mists of Utopia. Even Fernande, the author's last incarnation of the Great Whore, is made to serve, indirectly, the messianic cause. And Zola's original stumbling block, unchastity, is conveniently transformed into an essential ingredient of messiahship: Luc cannot save the world without his mistress! A token blood-sacrifice on the part of the hero is enough to ensure his triumph and to gradually create what Scripture calls "the days of heaven on earth."

Having somewhat overdone the apotheosis scenes at the end of *Travail*, Zola settles for a humbler messiah in *Justice*: Marc and his fellow schoolmasters are shown to bring enlightenment and a sense of fair play to the young generation. Suffering persecution at the hands of a perverted and mendacious church, the hero prevails in the end, even if he has to learn, to his sorrow, that knowledge alone is not enough to bring in perfect happiness.

Gathering in the threads of this rapid survey, we arrive at a fairly complex pattern. Young Zola may be described simply as a romantic idealist in whom messianic aspirations mingle with other forms of inspiration. After the Berthe experience of 1861, the author develops a full-scale "messiah-complex," by way of compensation, but this is soon inverted as he loses his religious faith and begins to do battle in his psyche with very unmessianic qualities such as lust, ambition, materialism, not to mention the love of money and the fleshpots.

Accordingly, we see the emergence of a long list of ineffectual, flawed, failing, and often false messiahs, who may even reach the status of Great Whore, Devil, or Antichrist. As the maturing Zola has a progressive revelation of the grandiose and mysterious designs of the life-force, he modifies his early negative messianic pattern. This larger vision, the author comes to believe, can accommodate promiscuity, the entrepreneurial spirit and even warfare; Apocalypse, too, can be pressed into its service. The life-force is self-propagating, which obviates the need for personal messiahs.

Living with Jeanne Rozerot, a traditonal believer, prompts Zola to attempt reviving the religious dreams of his youth, but this proves impossible. In the end, he is content to remain a prophet of the life-force, work, and the clarity of reason. Wandering along utopian paths, he at first raises mere mortals to the status of messianic demigods, but his ultimate preference is for modest, practical saviors who are able to grow through personal trials, who trust in the beneficence of the life-force and patiently share their vision of a fruitful, constructive, creative, and enlightened society.

Notes

Chapter 1. The Judeo-Christian Messianic Tradition

1. See *Réalité et mythe chez Zola*, vol. 1, Université de Lille III (1981), pp. 1–5.
2. Pierre Aubéry, "Imitations de Jésus chez Zola: *Germinal*," in *Les Cahiers naturalistes*, no. 53 (1979), pp. 31–45.
3. All quotations from the Bible are taken from the Authorized (King James) Version.

Chapter 2. The Genesis of the Messianic Myth

1. Page numbers involving Zola's *Contes à Ninon* refer to Roger Ripoll's Pléïade edition of Zola's *Contes et nouvelles* [Tales and Novellas], Gallimard, Paris (1976).
2. *Le Docteur Pascal* (1893).
3. *Les Quatre evangiles*.
4. See especially the story "La mort d'Olivier Bécaille," in *Contes et nouvelles* (1884).
5. See *Réalité et mythe chez Zola*, vol. 1, p. 102.
6. See the poem "Le Vallon," in *Les Méditations* (1820).

Chapter 3. From Messianic Dreams to Messiah Complex

1. In *Zola Before the Rougon-Macquart*, University of Toronto Press (1964), p. 49.
2. Zola's *Correspondance*, eds. B. H. Bakker et al., Montréal University Press (1978), vol 1, p. 259.
3. See my earlier article "Mythic Prefigurations of Zola's World-view in *La Confession de Claude*, AUMLA, no. 77 (May 1992), pp. 20–31.
4. In "Fascination et fatalité," *Les Cahiers Naturalistes*, Paris (1966), no. 32.
5. Page numbers refer to H. Mitterand's edition of Zola's *Oeuvres complètes*, Cercle du Livre Précieux, Paris (1966).
6. Quoted by Henri Guillemin in *Zola légende et vérité*, René Julliard (1960), p. 13.
7. See my article "Zola's Conversion to Science," in *Nineteeenth Century French Studies* (May 1995), pp. 469–78.
8. Zola's *Correspondance*, vol. 1, p. 509.
9. See H. Mitterand's edition of Zola's *Oeuvres complètes*.
10. Quoted by H. Troyat, *Zola*, Flammarion, Paris (1992), p. 31.
11. P. Ouvrard, *Zola et le prêtre*, Beauchesne, Paris (1986), p. 13.

12. "Can One Bury the Past? A Psychoanalytical Study of Confinement, Guilt and Death in Zola's *Thérèse Raquin*", *Excavatio*©, International Review for Multidisciplinary Approaches and Comparative Studies related to Emile Zola and his Time, Naturalism, Naturalist Writers and Artists around the World. Vol. IX, 1997. pp. 73–81. © Monique Fol, ed. Association International for Multidisciplinary Approaches and Comparative Studies related to Emile Zola and his Time, Naturalism, Naturalist Writers and Artists, Naturalism and the Cinema Around the World (AIZEN©), 101 Rainbow Drive, #8072, Livingston, TX 77351, USA.

13. Some material in the following section on *Madeleine Férat* was first printed in "Zola and the Unpardonable Sin: A Psychoanalytical Study of *Madeleine Férat*," *Excavatio*©, International Review for Multidisciplinary Approaches and Comparative Studies related to Emile Zola and his Time, Naturalism, Naturalist Writers and Artists around the World. Vol. IX, 1997. In production. © Monique Fol, ed. Association International for Multidisciplinary Approaches and Comparative Studies related to Emile Zola and his Time, Naturalism, Naturalist Writers and Artists, Naturalism and the Cinema Around the World (AIZEN©), 101 Rainbow Drive, #8072, Livingston, TX 77351, USA.

14. In *Les Cahiers Naturalistes*, no. 32 (1966).

CHAPTER 4. FALSE AND FLAWED MESSIAHS

1. All subsequent quotes from the Pléiade edition of the *Rougon-Macquart* will be referred to by volume and page number only.
2. Op. cit, p. 445.
3. "Die Strukturelle Bedeutung des Fremden-Motifs in den *Rougon-Macquart* von Zola," *Germanisch-Romanisch Monatsschrift*, no. 21 (1971), p. 30.
4. Op.cit, p. 40.
5. Reproduced by F. Bernouard in his notes on *Le Ventre de Paris* (1928), vol. 6, p. 343 (B.N. Ms 10338, n. folio).
6. *Zola*, Flammarion, Paris (1992), p. 110.
7. See *Zola et le prêtre*, Beauchesne, Paris (1986), p. 33.
8. *Réalité et mythe chez Zola*, Université de Lille III (1981).
9. Op. cit., p. 33.
10. Preface to the Folio edition of *La Conquête de Plassans*, Paris (1992), p. 15.

CHAPTER 5. THE MESSIANIC MERRY-GO-ROUND

1. Bibl. Nat., Ms 10294 Fo 3.
2. *Emile Zola* (1882), p. 149.
3. Ibid.
4. Ibid.
5. See *Zola et le prêtre*, p. 75.
6. *Zola*, Routledge and Kegan Paul, London (1985), p. 130.

7. Quoted by Mitterand in his edition of *Les Rougon-Macquart*, 2, p. 1610.
8. Notes on Zola's *Une Page d'amour*, L. de P., Fasquelle, Paris (1985), p. 369.
9. Ibid.

Chapter 6. The Great Apostasy

1. See B.N. Ms 10313 Fo 208.
2. Introduction to Zola's *Nana*, Flammarion, Paris (1968), p. 23.
3. *Correspondance*, Fasquelle, Paris (1928), vol. 4, pp. 365–66.
4. Article in *Le Voltaire*, 28 October 1880, quoted by Mitterand, 2, pp. 1689–90.
5. In "Les trois visages de Nana," *The French Review* 44 (1971), p. 117.
6. *Réalité et mythe chez Zola*, vol. 1, p. 17.
7. *Les trois visages de Nana*, p. 128.
8. *Réalité et mythe chez Zola*, vol. 1, p. 23.
9. *Zola*, Flammarion, Paris (1992), p. 146.
10. *Emile Zola*, Charpentier, Paris (1882), p. 113.
11. In *Zola*, Routledge and Kegan Paul, London (1985), p. 146.
12. See B.N. Ms 10313 Fo 208.
13. *Les trois visages de Nana*, p. 125.
14. Quoted by Roger Ripoll, op. cit., p. 18.
15. In *Zola vivant*, included in Mitterand's edition of Zola's *Oeuvres complètes*, Cercle du livre précieux, Paris (1966), vol. 1, p. 155.
16. B.N. Ms 10313 Fo 208.
17. *Les trois visages de Nana*, p. 122.
18. Quoted by Mitterand, 3, p. 1634.
19. Preface to Zola's *Pot-Bouille*, Flammarion, Paris (1969), p. 20.
20. B.N. Ms 1032 Fo 1 (quoted by Mitterand, 3, p. 1619).
21. In "Le personnage de l'abbé Mauduit dans *Pot-Bouille*," *Les Cahiers Naturalistes*, no. 44 (1972), p. 207.
22. Preface to Zola's *Pot-Bouille*, p. 20.
23. Quoted by Mitterand, 3, p. 1680.
24. Op. cit., Hatier, Paris (1982), p. 45.
25. Ibid.
26. Quoted by Mitterand, 3, pp. 1682, 1684.
27. Ibid., p. 1699.
28. *Profile of Au bonheur des dames*, p. 41.
29. Op. cit., p. 135.
30. Cf. *Zola et les mythes* (1971), p. 29.
31. *Présentation des Rougon-Macquart*, Gallimard, Paris (1964), p. 24.
32. Quoted by Mitterand, 3, p. 1742.
33. See ibid., pp. 1742–45.
34. See introduction to Zola's *La Joie de vivre*, Flammarion, Paris (1974), pp. 16–18.
35. "In the Days of My Youth," quoted by Mitterand, 3, p. 1743.
36. Quoted by Mitterand, 3, p. 1782.

37. Quoted by Colette Becker in her notes on Zola's *La Joie de vivre*, Flammabrion, Paris (1974), p. 363.
38. In *Europe*, nos. 468–69 (April–May 1968), p. 124.

Chapter 7. Messianic Myth in Crisis

1. B.N. Ms 10307 Fo 402.
2. *Correspondance* 2, p. 651, quoted by Mitterand, 3, p. 1822.
3. "The Infertile Rabbit," in *Nineteenth Century French Studies*, 10, nos. 3–4, pp. 340–53.
4. "La Côte-Verte et le Tartaret," in *Poétique*, no. 4 (1979), p. 482.
5. B.N. Ms 10307 Fos 232, 233.
6. *"La Côte-Verte et le Tartare,"* p. 482 ff.
7. Preface to Zola's *Germinal*, Folio, Gallimard, Paris (1978).
8. In *Les Cahiers Naturalistes*, no. 53 (1979), pp. 31–46.
9. *Germinal, un roman anti-peuple*, p. 163.
10. Letter dated 14 March 1885, quoted by Mitterand, 3, p. 1867.
11. Article in *La Justice*, 14 July 1885, quoted by Mitterand, 3, p. 1865.
12. *Emile Zola*, Les Belles Lettres, Paris (1951), p. 99.
13. Ibid, p. 101.
14. "L'Assommoir et la pensée religieuse de Zola," in *Les Cahiers Naturalistes* no. 52 (1978), p. 68.
15. See "The Slaying of the Dragon," *Symposium* (winter 1972), pp. 349–61.
16. *Réalité et mythe chez Zola*, Atelier des Reproductions des Thèses, Université de Lille III (1981), vol. 1, p. 196.
17. "Zola et la lutte avec l'Ange," in *Les Cahiers Naturalistes*, no. 42 (1972), p. 81.
18. B.N. Ms 10316 Fo 262.
19. Mitterand 4, p. 1379.
20. Ibid, p. 1384.
21. Article in *La Justice*, 12 May 1886, quoted by Mitterand, 4, p. 1391.
22. Introduction to Zola's *L'Oeuvre*, Garnier, Flammarion, Paris (1974), p. 11.
23. B.N. Ms 10316 Fos 317–18.
24. Cf *Les Cahiers Naturalistes*, no. 42 (1972), pp. 79–92.
25. *La Terre d'Emile Zola*, Les Belles Lettres, Paris (1952), p. 379.
26. *Réalité et mythe chez Zola* vol. 1, pp. 361–90.
27. Op. cit. Gallimard, Paris (1980), p. 18.
28. Letter to van Santen Kolff 27 May 1886, quoted by Mitterand, 4, p. 1502.
29. Op. cit. p. 387.
30. B.N. Ms 10345 Fo 13, quoted by Guy Robert, op. cit. p. 388.
31. B.N. Ms 10329 Fo 260, quoted by Mitterand, 4, p. 1600.
32. B.N. Ms 10328 Fo 422, quoted by Mitterand, 4, p. 1511.
33. Op. cit p. 219.
34. Quoted by Colette Becker in her introduction to Zola's *Le Rêve*, Garnier, Flammarion, Paris (1975), p. 14.
35. B.N. Ms 10323 Fo 222.
36. Letter to van Santen Kolff 5 March 1888, quoted by Mitterand, 4, p. 1647.
37. Mitterand, 4, p. 1622.

38. Op. cit., in *Travaux de linguistique et de littérature*, Strasbourg (1968), vol. 6, no. 2, p. 178.
39. Introduction to Zola's *Le Rêve*, p. 17.
40. B.N. Ms 10323 Fo 227.
41. *Présentation des Rougon-Macquart*, p. 320.
42. *Légende et vérité*, p. 80.
43. Mitterand, 4, p. 1623.
44. B.N. Ms 10323 Fo 222.
45. "Hérédité ou mimétisme familial: Pour une nouvelle lecture du *Rêve*," in *Les Cahiers Naturalistes*, no. 57 (1983), p. 101.
46. B.N. Ms 10323 Fo 199.
47. Ibid Fo 200.
48. Ibid Fo 231.
49. Ibid Fo 240.
50. Dossier préparatoire, B.N. Ms 10294, quoted by Colette Becker in her introduction to Zola's *Le Rêve*, p. 27 (cf34).

Chapter 8. From Death and Disaster to Messianic Hope

1. Article dated 13 December 1868, quoted by Mitterand, 4, pp. 1710–11.
2. Cf A. Feldman: "Zola and the Riddle of Sadism," in *American Imago* 13 (1956) pp. 415–25.
3. In *Le Figaro*, 8 March 1890, quoted by Mitterand, 4, p. 1748.
4. Op. cit., Folio, Gallimard, Paris (1977), p. 13.
5. Ibid., p. 23.
6. Ibid.
7. B.N. Ms 10268 Fo 428.
8. Ms 10269 Fo 17.
9. Letter dated 20 January 1892, quoted by Mitterand, 5, p. 1369.
10. See *Travaux de linguistique et de littérature*, Strasbourg (1968), vol 6, no. 2, pp. 177–83.
11. See his article "Le Personnage de Napoléon III dans les Rougon-Macquart," in *Archives des lettres modernes*, no. 114 (1970), quoted by Colette Becker in *Les Critiques de notre temps et Zola*, Garnier, Paris (1972), pp. 62–65.
12. Preface to Zola's *La Débâcle*, folio, Gallimard, Paris (1987), p. 10.
13. See *Revue politique et littéraire*, 25 June 1892, quoted by Mitterand, 5, p. 1433.
14. Quoted by Mitterand, 5, p. 1413.
15. Article "Retour de voyage," in *Le Figaro*, 10 October 1892, quoted by Mitterand, 5, p. 1455.
16. Quoted by Armand Lanoux in his *Zola vivant*, p. 104.
17. In *La Revue politique et littéraire*, 7 April 1886, quoted by Mitterand, 4, p. 1395).
18. Emile Zola, *Principes et caractères généraux de son oeuvre*, quoted by Colette Becker in her *Les Critiques de notre temps et Zola*, p. 169.
19. Sylvie Thorel-Cailleteau: "A propos de *La Débâcle*," in *Les Cahiers Naturalistes*, no. 67 (1993), p. 62.
20. See *Réalité et mythe chez Zola*, vol 1, pp. 102–6.
21. See Girardet, Preface to Zola's *La Débacle* Folio, p. 12.

22. Article in *Le Figaro*, dated 10 October 1892, quoted by Mitterand, 5, p. 1458.
23. Quoted by Mitterand, 5, p. 1570.
24. Ibid.
25. Bodmer Ms 10290 Fos 60–70, summarized by Mitterand, 5, p. 1594.
26. "Cercle familial et cycle romanesque," in *Les Cahiers Naturalistes*, no. 67 (1993), p. 129.
27. Op. cit., p. 20.
28. "Du Naturalisme au mythe," in *Les Cahiers Naturalistes*, no. 48 (1974), p. 158.
29. Bodmer Ms 10290, Fos 60–70, quoted by Mitterand, 5, p. 1594.
30. *Réalité et mythe chez Zola*, vol 1, p. 220.
31. Cf "Du Naturalisme au mythe," p. 163.
32. "Zola et la lutte avec l'Ange," in *Les Cahiers Naturalistes*, no. 42 (1971), p. 92.
33. "Cercle familial et cycle romanesque," p. 127.
34. "Discours aux étudiants," 18 March 1893, quoted by Mitterand, 5, p. 1611.
35. See letter dated 22 February 1893, quoted by Mitterand, 5, p. 1608.
36. Ibid.

Chapter 9. The Impossible Quest

1. Letter to Henri Céard, quoted by Colette Becker in her *Dictionnaire d'Emile Zola*, Robert Laffont, Paris (1993), p. 230.
2. O.C. refers to H. Mitterand's edition of Zola's *Oeuvres complètes*, Cercle du livre précieux, Paris (1968–69).
3. Introduction to Zola's *Lourdes*, in O.C. 7, p. 14.
4. Bibl. Méjanes, MS 1455 Fo 33.
5. Ibid. Ms 1456 Fo 208.
6. *Zola et le prêtre*, Beauchesne, Paris (1986).
7. Bibl. Méjanes, Ms 1455 Fo 72.
8. Ibid. Ms 1456 Fo 208.
9. O.C. vol. 1, p. 209.
10. In *Les Romans d'Emile Zola*, Lausanne, n.d., vol 22, p. 141.
11. Bibl. Méjanes, Ms 1455 Fo 15.
12. Op. cit., Les Belles Lettres, Paris (1952), p. 144.
13. Bibl. Méjanes, Ms 1455 Fo 33.
14. "De la catastrophe à l'apaisement," in *Les Cahiers Naturalistes*, no. 67 (1993), pp. 151–52.
15. Article 11 October 1892, quoted by Mitterand, Notice to *Rome* O.C. 7, p. 1129.
16. Op. cit., p. 44.
17. Bibl. Méjanes, Ms 1462 Fo 8 and passim.
18. Préface to *Rome*, in *Les Romans d'Emile Zola*, n.d., vol. 23, p. 9.
19. See Bibl. Méjanes, Ms. 1455 Fo 72.
20. Op. cit., p. 243.
21. Bibl. Méjanes, Ms 1465 Fo 460.
22. Op. cit., Bernigaud et Privat, Dijon (1961), p. 625.
23. Bibl. Méjanes Ms 1471 Fo 41.

24. "De la catastrophe à l'apaisement," in Les Cahiers Naturalistes," no. 67, p. 152.
25. Introduction to Zola's *Paris*, O.C. 7, p. 1167.

Chapter 10. Toward a Humanist Messiah

1. *Zola et son temps*, pp. 677–78.
2. In *Les Cahiers Naturalistes*, no. 42 (1971), p. 92.
3. "Du récit polémique au discours utopique," in *Les Cahiers Naturalistes*, no. 54 (1980), p. 118.
4. Ibid, see pp. 116–18.
5. Quoted by Colette Becker in her *Dictionnaire d'Emile Zola*, p. 145.
6. Quoted by Guy Robert in *Emile Zola*, pp. 158–59.
7. Quoted by Dorothy Speirs in her "Etat présent des études sur *Les Quatre Evangiles*, in *Les Cahiers Naturalistes*, no. 48 (1974), p. 218.
8. "De la catastrophe à l'apaisement," in *Les Cahiers Naturalistes*," no. 67, p. 151.
9. Quoted by Pierre Cogny in his introduction to Zola's *Fécondité*, O.C. 8, p. 13.
10. Letter to Saint-Georges de Bouhélier, 7 November 1899, quoted by Pierre Cogny, op. cit., p. 14.
11. Idem.
12. See Jacques Pelletier's article "Zola évangéliste," in *Les Cahiers Naturalistes*, no. 48 (1974), p. 211.
13. See Letter to Saint-Georges de Bouhélier. 7 November 1899.
14. Quoted by Mitterand in his Notice to *Travail*, O.C. 8, p. 977.
15. B.N. Ms 10344 Fos 4–5.
16. "Discours aux étudiants," 16 March 1893, quoted by Mitterand, (Pléiade), 5, p. 1608.
17. B.N. Ms 10301 Fo 1.
18. *Zola et les mythes* (1971), p. 190.
19. *Zola*, (1985), p. 243.
20. Quoted by Mitterand, O.C. 8, p. 978.
21. B.N. Ms 10333 Fo 360.
22. "Du récit polémique au discours utopique," in *Les Cahiers Naturalistes* no. 54 p. 115.
23. See *Vérité*, Christian Pirot, Paris (1993), vol. 2, pp. 333–38.
24. B.N. Ms 10343 Fo 303.
25. Ibid, Fo 310.
26. Ibid, Fo 384.
27. Ibid, Fo 320.
28. O.C. 8, p. 1499.

Bibliography

Quotations from Zola's *Contes* are taken from Roger Ripoll's Pléïade edition of *Contes et nouvelles*, Gallimard, Paris (1976).

Quotations from Zola's novels before and after *Les Rougon-Macquart* are taken from H. Mitterand's edition of Zola's *Oeuvres complètes*, Cercle du Livre Précieux, Paris (1966).

Quotations from Zola's *Rougon-Macquart* are taken from H. Mitterand's Pléïade edition of *Les Rougon-Macquart*, Gallimard, Paris (1960–67).

Wherever possible, quotations from Zola's letters are taken from Zola's *Correspondance*, eds. B. H. Bakker et al. vol 1 (1858–67); ed. Colette Becker, Paris and Montreal, Les P. U. de Montréal/Paris, Editions du CNRS 1978–96 (10 vols.).

STUDIES DEVOTED TO ZOLA'S LIFE AND WORK OR TO PARTICULAR THEMES

Alexis. Paul, *Emile Zola*, Charpentier, Paris (1882).

Becker. Colette, (1) *Les Critiques de notre temps et Zola*, Garnier, Paris (1972); (2) *Emile Zola: Germinal*, Paris University Press (1984); (3) *Zola*, Garnier, Paris (1972).

Bernard. Marc, *Zola par lui-même*, Editions du Seuil, Paris (1952).

Borie. Jean, *Zola et les mythes*, Editions du Seuil, Paris (1971).

Butler. R, *La Terre*, Grant and Cutler, London (1984).

Grant, E. M., (1) *Emile Zola*, Twayne, New York (1966); (2) *Zola's Germinal*, Leicester University Press (1962).

Guillemin. Henri, (1) *Présentation des Rougon-Macquart*, Gallimard, Paris (1964); (2) *Zola, légende et vérité*, René Juliard, Paris (1960).

Hemmings. F. W. J. (1)*The Life and Times of Emile Zola*, Scribner, New York (1977); (2) *Emile Zola*, Clarendon Press, Oxford (1953).

Lanoux. Armand, *Zola vivant*, in vol. 1 of Mitterand's edition of Zola's *Oeuvres complètes*, Cercle du livre Précieux, Paris (1966).

Lapp. John, *Zola before the Rougon-Macquart*, Toronto University Press (1964).

Le Blond-Zola. Denise, *Vie d'Emile Zola*, in F. Bernouard's edition of Zola's *Oeuvres complètes*, Paris (1928).

Lejeune. Philippe, *Germinal, un roman anti-peuple*, Nizet, Paris (1978).

Ouvrard. Pierre, *Zola et le prêtre*, Beauchesne, Paris (1986).

Pelletier. Jacques, *Zola evangéliste*. Ph.D. diss., University of Aix-en-Provence (1972).

Proulx. Alfred C., *Aspects épiques des Rougon-Macquart*, Monton, The Hague (1966).

Ripoll. Roger, *Réalité et mythe chez Zola*, 2 vols., University de Lille III (1981)/ Honoré Champion, Paris (1981).

Robert. Guy, (1) *Emile Zola (Principes et caractères généraux de son oeuvre)*, Les Belles Lettres, Paris (1951); (2) *La Terre d'Emile Zola*, Les Belles Lettres, Paris (1952).

Ternois. René, *Zola et son temps: Lourdes, Rome, Paris*, Les Belles Lettres, Paris (1961).

Troyat. Henri, *Zola*, Flammarion, Paris (1992).

Walker. Philip D., (1) *Profiles in Literature: Emile Zola*, Routledge and Kegan Paul, London (1968); (2) *Zola*, Routledge and Kegan Paul, London (1985).

Wilson. Angus, *Emile Zola*, Secker, London (1964).

ARTICLES ON ZOLA AND CRITICAL INTRODUCTIONS TO PARTICULAR NOVELS

Albérès. R. M., Introduction to Zola's *Travail*, in Zola's *Oeuvres complètes*, Edition Mitterand, Cercle du Livre Précieux, Paris, (1966), vol. 8.

Aubéry. Pierre, "Imitations de Jésus chez Zola: *Germinal*," in *Les Cahiers Naturalistes*, no. 53 (1979), pp. 31–45.

Baguley. David, "De la mer ténébreuse à l'eau maternelle," in *Travaux de linguistique et de littérature* 12, no. 2, Strasbourg (1974), pp. 79–91.

———. "Du naturalisme au mythe: l'alchimie du Docteur Pascal," in *Les Cahiers Naturalistes*, no. 48 (1974), pp. 141–63

———. "Du récit polémique au discours utopique," in *Les Cahiers Naturalistes*, no. 54 (1980), pp. 106–21

———. "*Fécondité* d'Emile Zola: Roman à thèse, évangile, mythe," Toronto University Press (1973)

———. "The Function of Zola's Souvarine," in *Modern Language Review*, (October 1971), pp. 786–97.

Becker. Colette, Introduction to Zola's *La Bête humaine*, Robert Laffaut, Paris (1993)

———. Introduction to Zola's *La Débâcle*, Robert Laffaut, Paris (1993)

———. Introduction to Zola's *La joie de vivre*, Garnier, Flammarion, Paris (1974)

———. Introduction to Zola's *La Joie de vivre*, Robert Laffaut, Paris (1992).

———. Introduction to Zola's *L'Argent*, Robert Laffaut, Paris (1993).

———. Introduction to Zola's *Le Rêve*, Garnier, Flammarion, Paris (1975).

———. Introduction to Zola's *Pot-Bouille*, Garnier, Flammarion, Paris (1969).

——— (together with Jeanne Gaillard). Profile of Zola's *Au Bonheur des Dames*, Hatier, Paris (1982).

Bernard. Claudie, "Cercle familial et cercle romanesque dans *Le Docteur Pascal*," in *Les Cahiers Naturalistes*, no. 67 (1993), pp. 127–40.

Bonnefis. Philippe, "Le Bestiaire d'Emile Zola," in *Europe* (April–May 1968).

Borie. Jean, Introduction to Zola's *Le Docteur Pascal*, Garnier, Paris (1976).

———. Introduction to Zola's *Vérité*, in Zola's *Oeuvres complètes*, ed. Mitterand, Cercle du Livre précieux, Paris (1966), vol 8.

Boulier. Jean, "Les Tros villes: Lourdes, Rome, Paris," in Europe, nos. 468–69, (April–May 1968).

Buvik. P., "Nana et les hommes," in Les Cahiers Naturalistes, no. 49 (1975), pp. 105–24.

Cogny. Pierre, Introduction to Zola's Fécondité, in Zola's Oeuvres complètes, ed. Mitterand, Cercle du Livre Précieux, Paris (1966),vol. 8.

Compagnon. Antoine, "Zola dans la décadence," in Les Cahiers Naturalistes, no. 67 (1993), pp. 211–32.

Conray. P. V., "The Metaphorical Web in Zola's Nana," in University of Toronto Quarterly 47 (1978), pp. 239–58.

Cosset. Evelyne, "L'espace de l'utopie," in Les Cahiers Naturalistes, no. 63 (1989), pp. 138–47.

Launay. Marc de, Preface to Zola's La Conquête de Plassans, Folio, Gallimard, Paris (1992).

Deleuze. Gilles, Preface to Zola's La Bête humaine, Folio, Gallimard, Paris (1977).

Ladurie. D'Emmanuel Le Roy, Preface to Zola's La Terre, Gallimard, Paris (1980).

Descotes. Maurice, "Le Personnage de Napoléon III dans Les Rougon-Macquart," in Archives des Lettres Modernes, no. 114 (1970) (79 pp).

Dezalay. Auguste, "La 'Nouvelle Phèdre' de Zola," in Travaux de linguistique et de littérature 9, no. 2, Strasbourg (1971), pp. 121–24.

———. "Le fil d'Ariane: de l'image à la structure du labyrinthe," in Les Cahiers Naturalistes, no. 40 (1970), pp. 121–34.

———. "Le Thème du souterrain chez Zola," in Europe, (1968) pp. 110–21.

———. "Zola et Le Rêve," in Travaux de linguistique et de littérature, 6, no. 2, Strasbourg (1968), pp. 177–83.

Durand. Gilbert, "Les mythes et symboles de l'intimité et le XIXe siècle: contribution à la mythocritique," in Intime, intimité, intimisme, University de Lille III, Editions Universitaires (1976), pp. 81–98.

Ehrard. Antoinette Introduction to Zola's L'Oeuvre, Flammarion, Paris (1974).

Evenhuis. Anthony, "Can One Bury the Past?" in Excavatio (1993), pp. 73–81.

———. "Mythic Prefigurations of Zola's Worldview in La Confession de Claude," in AUMLA, no. 77 (May 1992), pp. 20–31.

———. "Zola's Conversion to Science," in Nineteenth Century French Studies (May 1995), pp. 469–78.

Feldman. A. B., "Zola and the Riddle of Sadism," in American Imago, vol. 13, (1956), pp. 415–25.

Fernandez-Zoila. Adolfo, "Discontinuités et paroxysmes dans L'Argent," in Les Cahiers Naturalistes, no. 67 (1993), pp. 107–21.

Fuller. Coral, "The Infertile Rabbit," in Nineteenth Century French Studies 10, nos. 3–4, pp. 346–53.

Georgin. Robert, "Le Thème du labyrinthe," in La Structure et le style, L'Age de l'homme, Lausanne (1975), pp. 33–39.

Gingell. E., "The theme of fertility in Zola's Rougon-Macquart," in Forum of Modern Language Studies 13, no. 4 (October 1977), pp. 350–58.

Girard. Marcel, "L'Univers de *Germinal*," in *Revue des sciences humaines* (January–March 1953), pp. 59–76.

Girardet. Raoul, Preface to Zola's *La Débâcle*, Folio, Gallimard, Paris (1987).

Got. Olivier, "L'idylle de Miette et de Silvère dans *La Fortune des Rougon*: Structure d'un mythe," in *Les Cahiers Naturalistes*, no. 46 (1973), pp. 146–64.

Greaves. A. A., "Religion et réalité dans l'oeuvre de Zola," in *Europe*, nos. 468–69, (April–May 1968).

Grenier. Jean, "La structure de la mer dans *La Joie de vivre*," in *Les Cahiers Naturalistes*, no. 58 (1980), pp. 63–69.

Guillemin. Henri, Introductions to his edition of Zola's novels, *Les Romans d'Emile Zola* (24 vols.), Neuchatel, n.d.

Hamon. Philippe, "Le personnage de l'abbé Mauduit dans *Pot-Bouille*," in *Les Cahiers Naturalistes*, no. 44 (1972), pp. 201–24.

Harvey. Lawrence, "The Cycle Myth in *La Terre* of Zola," in*Philological Quarterly* 38 (January 1959), pp. 89–95.

Hemmings. F. W. J., "Emile Zola et la religion," in *Europe*, (1968), pp. 468–69.

Bertrand-Jennings. Chantal, "Le Conquérant zolien: de l'arriviste au héros mythique," in *Romantisme*, no. 23 (1979), pp. 45–53.

———. "Les trois visages de Nana," in *French Revue*, Special Issue no. 2 (winter 1971), pp. 117–28.

———. "Zola féministe," in *Les Cahiers Naturalistes*, no. 44 (1972), pp. 172–87.

Marel. Henri, "A propos de *Germinal* et des *Rougon-Macquart*," in *Les Cahiers Naturalistes*, no. 45 (1973).

Marotte. Pierre, Notes on Zola's *Une Page d'amour*, L. de P., Fasquelle, Paris (1985).

Maurin. Mario, "Zola's Labyrinths," in *Yale French Studies*, no 42 (1969), pp. 89–104.

Minogue. Valerie, "Zola's Mythology: That Forbidden Tree," in *Forum for Modern Language Studies*, 14 (1978), pp. 217–30.

Nelson. Brian, "*Pot-Bouille*, étude sociale et roman comique," in *Les Cahiers Naturalistes*, no. 55 (1981), pp. 74–92.

Noiray. Jacques, "De la catastrophe à l'apaisement: l'image du fleuve de lait dans les *Villes* et les *Evangiles*," in *Les Cahiers Naturalistes*, no. 67 (1993).

Nucera. Louis, Preface to Zola's *Une Page d'amour*, L. de P., Fasquelle, Paris (1985).

Pagès. Alain, Introduction to Zola's *Vérité*, Christian Pirot, Paris (1993), 2 vols.

Pelckmans. Paul, "Hérédité ou mimétisme familial? pour une nouvelle lecture du *Rêve*," in *Les Cahiers Naturalistes*, no. 57 (1983), pp. 95–107.

Pelletier. Jacques, "Zola évangéliste," in *Les Cahiers Naturalistes*, no. 48 (1974), pp. 205–14.

Rannaud. Gerald, "Notes sur la structure d'un refuge: la mine dans *Germinal*," in *Circé* (Cahiers de recherche sur l'imaginaire), 3 (1972), pp. 301–13.

Ripoll. Roger, "Fascination et réalité: le regard dans l'oeuvre de Zola," in *Les Cahiers Naturalistes*, no. 32 (1966), pp. 104–16.

———. Introduction to Zola's *Nana*, Flammarion, Paris (1968).

———. "Le Symbolisme végétal dans La Faute de l'abbé Mouret," in French Studies, (July 1959), pp. 226–39.
Rachel, Rosenberg. "The Slaying of the Dragon," in Symposium 26 (1972), pp. 344–61.
Rita, Schober. "Le Docteur Pascal ou le sens de la vie," in Les Cahiers Naturalistes, no. 53 (1979), pp. 53–74.
Dorothy Speirs. "Etat présent des études sur les quatre Evangiles," in Les Cahiers Naturalistes, no. 48 (1974), pp. 215–35.
René, Ternois. Introduction to Zola's Lourdes and Paris, in Zola's Oeuvres complètes, édition Mitterand, Cercle du Livre Précieux, Paris (1966), vol. 7.
Sylvie, Thorel-Cailleteau. "A propos deLa Débâcle," in Les Cahiers Naturalistes, no. 67 (1993), pp. 57–62.
Toubin, Catherine, and Malinas. Yves "Les clés et les portes," in Les Cahiers Naturalistes, no. 41 (1971).
Sara, Via. "Une Phèdre décadente chez les Naturalistes," in Revue des Sciences humaines, no. 153 (1974), pp. 29–38.
Philip, Walker. "Germinal et la la pensée religieuse de Zola," in Les Cahiers Naturalistes, no. 50 (1976), pp. 134–44.
———. "L'Assommoir et la pensée religieuse de Zola," in Les Cahiers Naturalistes, no. 52 (1978), pp. 68–79.
———. "Prophetic Myths in Zola," in PMLA (Journal of Modern Language Association of America), 74 (1959), pp. 444–52.
———. "Zola et la lutte avec l'Ange," in Les Cahiers Naturalistes, no. 42 (1971), pp. 79–92.
———. "Zola, Myth and the Birth of the Modern World," in Symposium 25 (1971).
Friedrich, Wolfzettel. "Die strukturelle Bedeutung des Fremden-Motivs in den Rougon-Macquart von Zola," in Germanisch-romanische Monatsschrift, Heidelberg, new series 21 (1971), pp. 28–42.
Wurmser. André, Introduction to Zola's Germinal, Folio, Gallimard, Paris (1978).

Index

abortion, 235, 238
Antichrist, 9, 11, 16, 18, 19, 23, 30, 39, 59, 62, 63, 65, 88, 112, 113, 129, 207, 257, 262
anticlericalism, 61, 133, 253–54, 256–57, 258–59
apocalypse, 16, 24, 26, 80–81, 83, 99, 125, 126–27, 141, 145, 147, 153–56, 172, 173, 179, 182, 186, 187, 188, 192–94, 196–97, 207, 220, 221, 222, 224, 225, 244
apostasy, 84, 100, 212, 229, 250
archetype, 19, 20, 187
Argent, 'L, 172–86
Armagaddon, 16, 18, 25
Assommoir, 'L, 73–78
Au Bonheur des dames, 101–13
Aventures du grand Sidoine et du petit Médéric, 21–23, 26

Berthe affair, 29, 39, 45, 49, 242, 243, 248
Bête humaine, La, 166–72

Christ figures, 35, 36, 42, 54, 76, 78, 79, 81–82, 104
Confession de Claude, La, 28–33
Conquête de Plassans, La, 59–65
Contes à Ninon, 21–26
Curée, La, 50–53

Débâcle, La, 186–97
demonic figures, 61–65, 69, 71, 87, 172, 173, 177, 180, 182, 185, 215, 245
Devil (Satan), 17–18
Docteur Pascal, Le, 169–208
Dreyfus Case, 231, 252–254

false prophets, 18, 106, 126, 176
fatherhood (paternity myth), 169, 206, 232, 233, 235, 242

Faute de l'abbé Mouret, La, 66–68
fear of death, 23, 31, 34, 114, 115, 131–32, 145, 165
Fécondité, 231–40
fertility, 138, 227, 232
Fortune des Rougon, La, 47–50
Fourier, Charles, 241, 242, 245
Freud, Siegmund, 19, 25, 37, 159, 163, 168, 169, 170, 181, 204, 242

Germinal, 10, 124–38
God of wrath (Jehovah), 44, 45, 68, 70, 71, 83, 92, 134, 162, 163, 172–73, 175, 180, 185, 186
Great Whore, 18, 85, 89, 91, 95, 248, 249, 262

hell, 130, 131

ideal self, 37, 198, 199, 200, 201, 211, 225, 242, 255
idolatry, 18, 52, 71, 90, 91, 102, 112, 124, 133, 134, 146, 148
incest, 44, 45, 50

Jesus Christ: New Testament portrayal of Christ, 14–16; Old Testament prophecies applied to Christ, 11–14; Zola's attitude to Christ, 23–26, 28, 41, 67, 78, 82, 100–1, 152, 211–12, 215, 227, 254, 256, 261, 263
Joie de vivre, La, 115–21
Jung, Karl Gustav, 9, 10, 19, 95, 111, 121, 158, 189

life-force, 67, 78, 86, 93, 94, 121, 122, 123, 124, 125, 126, 132, 138, 141, 142, 144, 146, 148, 151, 156, 164–65, 174, 185, 186, 198, 200, 202, 206, 207, 215, 236, 237, 238
Lourdes, 209–16

Madeleine Férat, 28, 42–45
Mammon, 52, 113
messiah complex, 28, 30
Mystères de Marseille, Les, 28, 36–41

Nana, 85–96
nihilism, 1, 22, 23, 26, 83, 124, 128–29, 196, 218, 222, 226, 228–29

Oedipus complex, 163, 168, 169, 206, 242
Oeuvre, 'L, 139–48

Page d'amour, Une 78–83
pantheism, 123, 137, 142
paradise, 22, 23, 24, 26, 32, 49, 50, 53, 61, 67, 73, 131, 142, 152, 227
Paris, 223–30
Pot-Bouille, 96–101

Quatre évangiles, Les, 231–63

rejection complex, 28
resurrection, 15, 26, 42, 44, 55, 68, 136
Rêve, Le, 156–64
roman à thèse, 217
romantic idealism, 33, 35, 213
Rome, 216–23
Rozerot, Jeanne, 111, 167, 180, 199, 222, 246, 248

sadism, 69, 152, 167, 168–70
Sang, Le, 23–26
Schopenhauer, Arthur, 116, 124
Second Coming (The), 13, 15, 43
Second Empire, 54, 80, 86, 88, 95, 177, 179, 186, 188, 189
Sermon on the Mount, 15
sexuality, 30, 31, 37, 42, 43, 45, 49, 53, 57, 62, 63, 67, 81, 86, 89, 91, 92, 95, 98, 106, 118, 129, 132, 143, 147, 148, 149, 151, 164, 165, 203, 237, 239, 240, 244, 254
Soeur-des-Pauvres, 21, 26
Son Excellence Eugène Rougon, 68–73
stranger myth, 30, 59, 148, 149, 150

Terre, La, 148–56
Thérèse Raquin, 28, 41–42
Travail, 241–52
Trois villes, Les, 209–30

unpardonable sin, 42, 63
Utopia, 9, 10, 32, 55, 99, 127–28, 131, 199, 224, 229, 230, 233–34, 236, 240, 241, 249–51

Ventre de Paris, Le, 54–59
Vérité, 252–63
Voeu d'une morte, Le, 28, 33–36

OHIO UNIVERSITY LIBRARY

Please return this book when finished with it. The latest date stamped below is the date by which the book must be returned. All books are subject to recall after two weeks or immediately if needed for reserve.

CF